The difficulties and collateral consequences confronting family members, and especially romantic partners, of registered sexual offenders are well documented. In this important work, Zilney delves below the surface into what it really means to face the world as a woman who chooses to remain or to be in an intimate relationship with a man convicted of a sexual crime. Often shunned by family, friends, and society, these women live with the same restrictions and ostracism as the men with whom they have chosen to love and offer support. This examination of why and how they do what they do is a must-read for students of America's sexual offense laws and what they mean for our society.

NARSOL – National Association for Rational Sexual Offense Laws

A sex offense conviction affects many facets of life. Sex crime scholarship thus far has prioritized the registrant experience, examining for instance, the adaption to the label of "sex offender." In her new book, *Impacts of Sex Crime Laws on the Female Partners of Convicted Offenders: Never Free of Collateral Consequences,* Zilney digs much deeper, studying a largely omitted population, the families of registrants, and their experience dealing and coping with arguably the most unwanted and feared label affecting a loved one. As the population of registered individuals continues to climb in the U.S., there comes a crucial need to identify the collateral consequences of registry and notification laws from a much broader framework. Zilney makes it her mission to fill this glaring gap by conducting in-depth and intensely revealing interviews to investigate her research questions concerning collateral consequences experienced by loved ones. Importantly, she is careful to situate findings into the current literature and policy landscape. Who needs to read this book? Everyone. As we reach the 1 million registered sex offender mark, the odds are most people—practitioners, academics, students, and those in the general population—will, in some way, be affected by the registry. Having a knowledge base by which to assess any potential effects of registry systems is critical for all of us, whether directly or indirectly affected.

Christina Mancini, Ph.D., Virginia Commonwealth University

This book is a valuable resource for both students studying the complex issues of the criminal justice system and those touched by the far-reaching consequences of sexual offense registration and notification policies. Interviews with the female partners of convicted sexual offenders shed light on the often overlooked challenges experienced by those who maintain relationships with the men required to register. Their raw feedback will allow readers of all opinions and backgrounds to consider opposing perspectives.

Kristen M. Zgoba, Ph.D., Florida International University

Often lost in the simplistic outrage that sexual crimes elicits, is an understanding of the complexity of an offenders' future and those they call family. Offenders are also brothers, children, wives, fathers and significant others. When these offenders return to the community after their criminal sentence, they will begin to restructure their lives to try and become productive citizens. Their families and support systems also face a set of challenges. Dr. Zilney's thoughtful and well-organized work documents the many unintended consequences of our prolonged, entrenched sex offender laws and its impact on not only the offenders, but their support systems. Humanizing and contextualizing people who have committed real harm is an important social goal. Dr. Zilney's research not only accomplishes this but equally importantly requires us to rethink how we help support these people and their families in developing healthy and safe relationships.

Richard G. Wright, Ph.D., Bridgewater State University

So rarely does a book on sex crime laws delve into the substantial effect that such laws have on family members and intimate partners. By combining academic analysis with transcribed interviews, Zilney offers a unique look at life behind the legislation, portrayed from the perspective of the women who are inadvertently caught up in the collateral consequences of a partner's sex crime conviction.

Heather Ellis Cucolo, J.D., New York Law School

Zilney's book, *Impacts of Sex Crime Laws on the Female Partners of Convicted Offenders,* offers much needed insight into the complex emotional and social challenges faced by those in relationships with sex offenders. It uniquely focuses on the varied dynamics between couples, reinforcing the importance of family on reintegration. Policies that stigmatize offenders stigmatize those who love them, and this in-depth study provides a much-needed analysis of the nuances of intimacy and support that are understood to be key to successful reintegration.

Diana Rickard, PhD, Borough of Manhattan Community College, CUNY

IMPACTS OF SEX CRIME LAWS ON THE FEMALE PARTNERS OF CONVICTED OFFENDERS

This work is an exploratory examination of the experiences, motivations, and coping mechanisms of women who are involved in intimate relationships with registered sexual offenders. The study focuses both on women who were involved with an offender prior to the commission of his offense and who stayed with him post-conviction, and on women who became involved with a registered offender after his sex offense conviction. Like the offender himself, these women face a variety of challenges in responding to treatment of them by friends, family, the community, and the criminal justice system.

Utilizing the results of intensive interviews, this work provides a unique look at the women who are one of the few sources of support for registered sexual offenders and assesses the effectiveness and wide-ranging implications of community notification and registration laws on public safety, policy, and practice. This work offers alternative approaches based on evidence and case studies and considers the significance of familial contact in buffering sexual recidivism. These women are the heretofore unstudied victims of sexual offending legislation.

This book is essential reading for those in sociology, criminology, psychology, and social work. For undergraduate or graduate students, practitioners, researchers, or policymakers, this thought-provoking book will shed light on how to optimize the reintegration of sex offenders. It assesses the effectiveness and wide-ranging implications of sex offender legislation on public safety, policy, and practice and considers alternative approaches to reduce sexual violence.

Lisa Anne Zilney is an Associate Professor of Justice Studies at Montclair State University in New Jersey. She earned her Ph.D. in Sociology from the University of Tennessee, an MS in Criminal Justice from Eastern Kentucky University, and a BA in Psychology from the University of Windsor. Her primary research interests are in the area of sexual offending legislation and its collateral impacts on the partners and families of sexual offenders. She has published widely in journals and has authored or co-authored four previous books. She is a member of the Academy of Criminal Justice Sciences (ACJS), the National Organisation for the Treatment of Sexual Abusers (NOTA), and the American Society of Criminology (ASC).

IMPACTS OF SEX CRIME LAWS ON THE FEMALE PARTNERS OF CONVICTED OFFENDERS

Never Free of Collateral Consequences

Lisa Anne Zilney

NEW YORK AND LONDON

First published 2021
by Routledge
52 Vanderbilt Avenue, New York, NY 10017

and by Routledge
2 Park Square, Milton Park, Abingdon, Oxon, OX14 4RN

Routledge is an imprint of the Taylor & Francis Group, an informa business

© 2021 Taylor & Francis

The right of Lisa Anne Zilney to be identified as author of this work
has been asserted by her in accordance with sections 77 and 78 of the
Copyright, Designs and Patents Act 1988.

All rights reserved. No part of this book may be reprinted or reproduced or
utilized in any form or by any electronic, mechanical, or other means, now
known or hereafter invented, including photocopying and recording, or in
any information storage or retrieval system, without permission in writing
from the publishers.

Trademark notice: Product or corporate names may be trademarks or
registered trademarks, and are used only for identification and explanation
without intent to infringe.

Library of Congress Cataloging-in-Publication Data
Names: Zilney, Lisa Anne, author.
Title: Impacts of sex crime laws on the female partners of convicted
offenders : never free of collateral consequences / Lisa Anne Zilney.
Description: New York, NY : Routledge, 2020. | Includes bibliographical
references and index.
Identifiers: LCCN 2020004799 (print) | LCCN 2020004800 (ebook) |
ISBN 9780367490461 (hbk) | ISBN 9780367490454 (pbk) |
ISBN 9781003044185 (ebk)
Subjects: LCSH: Sex crimes. | Sex offenders' spouses. | Man-woman
relationships. | Stigma (Social psychology) | Sex crimes–Law and
legislation.
Classification: LCC HV6556 .Z55 2020 (print) | LCC HV6556 (ebook) |
DDC 362.83/952–dc23
LC record available at https://lccn.loc.gov/2020004799
LC ebook record available at https://lccn.loc.gov/2020004800

ISBN: 978-0-367-49046-1 (hbk)
ISBN: 978-0-367-49045-4 (pbk)
ISBN: 978-1-003-04418-5 (ebk)

Typeset in Bembo
by Wearset Ltd, Boldon, Tyne and Wear

Who is wise in love, love most, say least.
~ Alfred Lord Tennyson

To my dearest husband, Jimmy,
You have shown me the meaning of true love.
I see it every time you look at me,
Feel it every time your hand touches mine.
I love you for always;
More than yesterday,
Less than tomorrow!

CONTENTS

Preface	*xi*
Acknowledgments	*xix*

PART I
Legislation and Sexual Offenders   1

1	Politics, the Media, and Laws	3
2	Time for a Reality Check	32

PART II
Life With a Registered Sex Offender   57

3	Relationship and Revelation	59
4	Understanding and Consequences	94

PART III
Collateral Consequences for Partners of Registered Sex Offenders   125

5	Registration and Community Notification	127

x Contents

6 Employment, Housing, and Parenting Challenges 167

PART IV
Moving Forward 207

7 Coping Strategies and (Re)Integration 209

Appendix *245*
Index *252*

PREFACE

Purpose of the Work

In today's society, sex offenders are perhaps the most hated and feared of all offenders. We describe sex offenders as "sick," "monsters," "perverts," and care little about the circumstances that led to their offending or the factors that may reduce future offending. Each law that is suggested to further control sex offenders is passed, with little regard for the impact on the offender, or whether said law will actually improve public safety. Each successive law increases public safety and boosts the ratings of get-tough-on-crime politicians. As a result, there are residency restrictions, community notification laws, a sex offense registry, laws that restrict social media access, laws that restrict associating with fellow sex offenders, laws that restrict access to minors (even one's own children), and GPS monitoring, to name a few. There are thousands of laws targeting and labeling sex offenders for the American public in the name of safety.

The labeling extends far beyond the offender, to his family members and significant partner. Loved ones are subject to the shame and embarrassment of being tied to a "monster" and may need to comply with the restrictions placed on sex offenders as part of legal community management. A sex offender's partner is implicated in the criminal justice system response should they choose to remain with the offender, abiding by restrictions implemented by a fear-based public designed to pacify the appearance of vengeance, rather than the creation of sound legislation designed to reduce sexual violence. The wives and girlfriends of sex offenders have not, up to this point, been the participants of serious criminological study.

The sociological/criminological theory of social reaction, commonly known as labeling theory, asserts that some behaviors, and therefore the individuals that engage in these behaviors, are labeled negatively by society and by the criminal justice system. This act of labeling results in stigmatization of the individual by conventional society, resulting in a negative societal response. In the case of sexual offenses, labeling theory is useful in exploring the ramifications of an individual being labeled publicly as a sexual offender and the impact of labeling on the ability of an individual and his partner to (re)integrate successfully into a community. Because an overwhelming percentage of those labeled as sexual offenders by the system are male, this study focuses strictly on male offenders and their female significant partners. According to social reaction theorists, once an offense has been widely revealed and is labeled by others as deviant or criminal, the individual may continue the deviant behavior because they have internalized the personality characteristics that other people expect. Following this logic then, the likelihood of subsequent sexual offenses may be decreased if society, and the criminal justice system, did not publicly label individuals through the myriad of sexual offender legislation. This is not to suggest that sexual offenders should not be punished, but that overt community notification and registration policies may do more harm than good in reintegrating a sexual offender into a community and may additionally serve to target the offender's family.

What is of greatest interest for this work is the labeling that extends beyond the sexual offender, to the offender's significant partner. These family members are the unstudied victims of sexual offending legislation. This book explores the legislation that currently exists to label sexual offenders and their families. There are a litany of sex offender laws and almost all of them were created as knee-jerk responses to a very high-profile case. As such, these laws served to abate the public's fear, but in the long run have done very little to protect the public from sexual offenses or to reduce recidivism. The law commonly used to label sex offenders and their family members is community notification and registration. These laws exist nationwide and require sex offenders to register with the police at various time intervals depending upon their tier level and in many states require law enforcement officials to notify communities when an offender moves into the neighborhood. The notification of community members and the notion of who has the right to be notified is the most controversial aspect of this law and is the aspect of the law that most negatively impacts family members of offenders. There are no national standards, so depending on the state, and on the offender's tier status, varying degrees of information about the offender are available to the public. In order to notify the community, letters may be delivered by police to various community organizations or to neighbors, website notification may be involved, or billboard notification is possible.

Research remains speculative about the positive impacts of community notification laws in terms of decreased recidivism. Research shows that these policies increase feelings of public safety, but what are the effects of these laws on the lives of the offenders and their family members? Such laws decrease the possibility of community reintegration, making it difficult to secure housing, employment, and

Preface **xiii**

other opportunities, as well as undermining rehabilitative efforts. Years of criminological literature reveals that the factors that encourage continued desistance
from offending include integration or reintegration into the community, management of individual stress, and establishment of a stable lifestyle. This means the
offender must find a community with supportive friends and/or family, a stable
place of employment and residence, and develop appropriate social relationships.
Obviously broad-based community notification policies can hinder all aspects of
reintegration. Offenders and their families may also experience harassment by
community members who may not know all the facts. Though the U.S. Supreme
Court in *Doe v. Poritz* suggested this would not be a problem and that the public
would act responsibly with the information obtained from such laws, a smattering
of vigilante cases have occurred across the country.

In addition to community notification and registration laws, sex offenders
and their families are also impacted by the continually expanded and refined
laws that restrict where they may live, work, or visit. Distance requirements
can be as severe as 3,000-feet from facilities where children congregate, to the
least restrictive laws which involve a 500-foot distance requirement (Levenson &
Cotter, 2005). These laws were passed in great numbers in many states despite no
empirical research to demonstrate that residency restrictions lower recidivism or
make communities safer. In many jurisdictions all tiers of sex offenders are subject
to residency restrictions, and these laws may have no time limit and therefore
theoretically extend past the time an offender is required to register as a sexual
offender.

As they exist, residency restrictions have the unintended consequence of overwhelming a select group of communities with sexual offenders and their families
because there are so few areas in which offenders are permitted to reside. Such
laws may force sexual offenders to live under bridges or in the woods. These
laws, combined with the unwillingness of landlords to rent to sex offenders,
makes locating housing difficult and increases the likelihood of homelessness,
which is extremely problematic as sex offenders are required by law to register an
address with law enforcement or face imprisonment. Residency restrictions have
a significant impact on the family of the offender – many areas where offenders
are permitted to live would not be areas where his family would want to relocate. This has the potential to interfere with community reintegration and may
prevent an offender from living with supportive family members.

This book is an exploratory examination of the experiences, perceptions,
motivations, and coping mechanisms of the women who are involved in intimate relationships with registered sexual offenders (RSOs). Like the offender
himself, these women face a variety of challenges in responding to how the
criminal justice system and society treats the sexual offender and those who
associate closely with him post-conviction. The study focuses on both women
who were involved with the offender prior to the commission of his offense
and who remain involved with him after criminal justice sanctioning, and on

women who became involved with men who have been sanctioned by the criminal justice system for sexual offenses. These women are unique in that they provide one of the few sources of support for sexual offender reintegration into the community, but they are also subject to much of the same labeling, and if they reside with the offender are subject to criminal justice sanctions (such as residency restrictions) as well. Familial contact, as has been well established by sociological and criminological research, is a significant buffer against recidivism, yet this notion has not been explored regarding the sex offender population – a population perhaps in greatest need of a support system to prevent further sexual recidivism.

Methodological Outline

This work examined the motivating factors for a woman to remain in, or start, a relationship with a registered sex offender (RSO). It also examined the coping strategies by women who were in a relationship with an RSO to deal with the negative consequences of these laws and other labeling impacts. This study used 94 in-depth, qualitative interviews with women who were dating or married to RSOs across the United States (regardless of tier level) to explore the following research questions:

- What were the motivating factors for a woman to remain in, or start, a relationship with a registered sexual offender?
- How were the women impacted by community notification and registration laws?
- How were the women impacted by residency restriction laws?
- What were the coping strategies implemented to deal with the negative consequences of community notification and registration laws, residency restrictions, and other labeling impacts?

Participants were recruited via an email announcement looking for adult women who were "dating or married to a registered sex offender." Participation was sought through all state RSOL (Reform Sex Offender Laws) groups, the dailystrength.org support group, National Association for Rational Sex Offense Laws (NARSOL), Women Against Registry (WAR), Sex Abuse Treatment Alliance, and the Association for the Treatment of Sexual Abusers. The National Association for Rational Sex Offense Laws and 27 state RSOL groups replied indicating they would distribute my call for participants to the members of their groups. Individuals willing to participate contacted the principal investigator to set up a mutually agreeable time for a phone interview. All adult women dating or married to a registered sex offender who were willing to participate were welcome in the study. Partners of registered sex offenders of all tier levels were included to cover a range of experiences. Women were welcome in the study irrespective of whether their partner claimed he had been falsely accused of the sexual offense, as long as he was still subject to the registry.

Consenting participants were interviewed by myself (the primary investigator), over a two-year period via telephone. The interview inquired as to the initial reaction to, and perception of, the sexual offense, the participant's responses and experiences with the offender's conviction (for women who were with the offender prior to the offense – and incarceration, if applicable), the motivations for her intimate involvement with a registered sexual offender, the societal reactions to the participant for her involvement with the offender, and obstacles she has faced on a structural and personal level as a result, as well as the mechanisms she used to cope with these obstacles.

Interviews with the partners of sex offenders were conducted, transcribed, and analyzed using the techniques elaborated by Atkinson's life story interview (2001) and Braun and Clarke's (2006) thematic analysis approach. Each transcript was read in its entirety twice prior to coding. Transcripts were read a third time in sections and words, sentences, and phrases were highlighted that were relevant to each of the research questions. Data analyses focused on exploring the motivations of participants to remain with a sex offender, the impacts on the participants of sex offender legislation, and the descriptions of their experiences. When several interviews included overlapping experiences and/or feelings, themes were identified and patterns coded. Additionally, I was open to the formation of themes unrecognized in the research questions, as this study was charting new theoretical ground. Accordingly, the study utilized both inductive and deductive analysis. Themes were coded and organized into significant groups for analysis. Drawing on grounded theory, social reaction theory and techniques of neutralization, emergent themes that participants expressed were identified and categorized over repeated readings using color-coding to permit categorization of concepts and data organization. Throughout the book, quotes are selected that best encapsulate themes the participants discussed.

All interviews were transcribed verbatim in order to preserve actual speech of the participants. So, for example, "y'know" was left in the transcribed interview instead of changing to "you know." As principal investigator and transcriber, I checked each interview against the original recording for accuracy a minimum of twice. Because of the average age of participants, when anonymizing names for this publication, I used the Social Security Administration's Top Names of the 1970s (n.d.) and assigned names based on the participant's numerical code in the study. This random assignment was used to protect the participant's confidentiality.

Organization of the Work

This is the first study of its kind to explore women's involvement with registered sexual offenders and how they are impacted collaterally by the criminal

xvi Preface

justice system. Part I of the book examines Legislation and Sexual Offenders. Chapter 1: Politics, the Media, and Laws explores the moral panic created in the media around sexual offenders which has resulted in various sex offender laws. The discussion begins in the 1930s and examines how as social, moral, and political aspects of society change, so do the definitions of a sexual offense. The chapter explores how high-profile, atypical sex offenses led to the passage of the most serious sex offense laws the United States has currently. This legislation includes the Jacob Wetterling Act, Megan's Law, the Adam Walsh Child Protection and Safety Act, social media regulations, residency restrictions, GPS monitoring, and civil commitment. The public's view on sex offenders is discussed, as are the views of the 94 women involved with sex offenders who participated in this study. Chapter 2: Time for a Reality Check examines the statistics with regard to sexual offenders and offenses. The public has a misperception regarding how many sex offenders there are in society and this chapter provides the facts using Uniform Crime Report (UCR) and National Crime Victimization Survey (NCVS) data. The chapter examines the prevalence of sexual offending in the areas of child sexual abuse, adult sexual abuse, college victimization, and internet sexual offenses. It also provides offender profiles for juvenile offenders, female offenders, as well as data on incarceration and recidivism.

Part II explores Life With a Sex Offender. Chapter 3: Relationship and Revelation explores the motivations for a relationship with a registered sexual offender. The chapter examines the motivations for starting a relationship with someone who has committed a sex offense prior to dating or marriage, and the motivations for staying in a relationship or marriage with someone who commits an offense during the partnership. It also explores the hesitations that women experience in starting such a relationship and the changes women experience when an offense occurs within the context of a relationship. This chapter examines the circumstances surrounding the discovery of the offense, whether their partners kept the offense hidden or was voluntarily forthcoming with offense-related information and explores the women's reactions to learning about the offense. Chapter 4: Understanding and Consequences explores how the offense is understood by the female partners and how life changes when family and friends find out about the woman's involvement with a registered sex offender. Understanding the offense involves an examination of the theoretical principals of techniques of neutralization, including the four types of techniques of neutralization used by women to justify their partner's behavior. Also, the chapter explores responses to the female partner by family members and friends when it is discovered that she is associated with a registered sexual offender.

Part III is a discussion of Collateral Consequences for Partners of Registered Sex Offenders. Chapter 5: Registration and Community Notification discusses a brief legal history of registration and community notification laws. Attitudes of the public, law enforcement, and treatment professionals toward SORN (Sex Offender Registration Notification) laws are examined, as are effects on recidivism and community integration of the offender. The chapter delves into the collateral consequences of SORN policies on the partners of sex offenders. These collateral consequences include reclassification of tiers which results in a longer time on the registry; stigma from the community; as well as fear and harassment in the community from neighbors and law enforcement. Also, the chapter elaborates on potential improvements to current SORN laws. Chapter 6: Employment, Housing, and Parenting Challenges explores challenges for sex offenders and their families in the areas of employment, housing, and at home. Employment challenges for the offender's family are examined, as are the consequences of underemployment and unemployment. A brief legal history of Sex Offender Residency Restrictions (SORRs) are provided, and legal challenges to these policies are discussed. This chapter includes a discussion of whether SORRs prevent sex offenses or sexual recidivism, and the collateral consequences of these policies on the partners of registered sex offenders. On the home front, this chapter details the prohibition from contact with minors faced by most sex offenders, and the negative impacts of this restriction on parenting, traveling, and church attendance.

Part IV explores women Moving Forward. Chapter 7: Coping Strategies and (Re)Integration details the emotional impacts that the formal and informal social controls on sex offenders have on their partners. The chapter also delves into the negative coping mechanisms and positive coping strategies used by women to deal with these emotional impacts. Positive coping strategies include self-help groups, counseling, physical fitness, spirituality, or involvement in groups that advocate change. This chapter elaborates on the integration or reintegration of offenders and their families into communities and provides suggestions from partners of sex offenders on how to more successfully reintegration offenders. The chapter ends with policy suggestions for sex offense legislation moving forward.

This work suggests that community management of sexual offenders needs to be about striking the delicate balance between protecting community safety from the high-risk offenders and permitting low-risk offenders to successfully reintegrate back into society and into a social and family life. The labeling of a sexual offender in American society extends far beyond that one individual to his family members. These individuals are subject to the shame and embarrassment of being tied to a "monster," and if they want to help their family member reintegrate into society successfully, they may need to comply with the many restrictions placed on sexual offenders as part of community management. This work clearly demonstrates that a partner experiences similar isolation and guilt as the offender. In our fear-based need to control sex offenders, a sex offender's partner has been implicated in the criminal justice system response, should they choose to remain with the offender after his conviction; having to abide by restrictions implemented by knee-jerk legislation designed to pacify the public. These women are collateral, hidden victims of the criminal justice system. We need to work

xviii Preface

toward sound legislation that works to diminish the likelihood of sexual violence in society, and the promotion of reintegration.

References

Atkinson, Robert. (2001). The life story interview. In Jaber F. Gubrium & James A. Holstein (Eds.), *Handbook of interview research: Context and method* (pp. 121–140). Thousand Oaks, CA: Sage Publications.

Braun, V., & Clarke, V. (2006). Using thematic analysis in psychology. *Qualitative Research in Psychology, 3*, 77–101.

Levenson, Jill S., & Cotter, Leo P. (2005). The effect of Megan's Law on sex offender reintegration. *Journal of Contemporary Criminal Justice*, 21, 49-66.

Top Names of the 1970s. (n.d.). *Social Security Administration*. Retrieved from www.ssa. gov/oact/babynames/decades/names1970s.html

ACKNOWLEDGMENTS

I am extremely thankful to the 94 women who courageously shared their stories with me! Daily they are negotiating lives burdened by over-zealous laws and stereotypes regarding the men they love. Their lives and relationships are complicated in ways that most people do not experience, and they were brave enough to share their stories. I hope they feel this research has shed some light on their struggle for more reasonable laws and done justice to their stories. Thank you to the organizers of all state RSOL (Reform Sex Offender Laws) groups, the daily-strength.org support group, National Association for Rational Sex Offense Laws (NARSOL), Women Against Registry (WAR), Sex Abuse Treatment Alliance, the Association for the Treatment of Sexual Abusers, and other groups I may not be aware of, who shared my call for participation in this project. Thanks to all the individuals advocating and working tirelessly in these groups and other activist groups who lobby policymakers and fight to change legislation so that it is both reasonable for offenders and their families and aims to prevent sexual violence!

I am enormously grateful to my mother, Mary Zilney for reading, editing, and providing critical evaluation on every single chapter of this work. Her feedback was extraordinarily elucidating! Her routine "check-ins" kept me on track, and her positive comments were inspiring. Not many academics are fortunate enough to have a parent who is both interested and who can positively contribute to their work. This project definitely brought us closer, and for that I am very blessed!

I am grateful to Kate Taylor for seeing the manuscript smoothly through the production process. And much thanks to Ellen Boyne at Routledge Press for always being available to answer my questions. The process was uneventful thanks to her!

I am most thankful to colleague and friend Lawrence Walsh (Montclair State University) for his invaluable statistical work on this project. A love for statistics

xx Acknowledgments

like his, I cannot fathom! Without his SPSS genius, this work would not have been the same!

A project such as this one carries with it an emotional toll for the author. This project took longer than I wanted to reach its destination. I struggled with the stories I was handed and the responsibility to share them in a way that was meaningful, and in a way that could potentially shape policy. My emotional toll was lifted daily in my Pennsylvania retreat: thank you to my safe-haven husband and my two furry friends, Annie and Tennessen, who provided multiple daily reminders to break for sanity!

Despite all outside input, any errors in interpretation remain my own.

PART I

Legislation and Sexual Offenders

1

POLITICS, THE MEDIA, AND LAWS

The Sex Offender Moral Panic in the Media

Laws are the narratives that represent the values of a society. "As law is enforced through an elaborate system of rules and regulations, expectations and exhortations, what emerges is a moral universe, a system of checks and balances that maintains clear gradations between what constitutes acceptable versus anti-social behavior" (Schultz, 2011: 168). We define crimes, we label criminals, and throughout history the level of outrage associated with various types of criminals has changed, yet the moral disgust directed at sex offenses and sex offenders has remained relatively constant. The public is fearful of those portrayed in the media as "beasts," "devils," "perverts," "fiends," or "evil" (Kitzinger, 2004). "Sex offenders are construed as predators, in much the same way as the monsters that populated the medieval imagination were construed as a combination of human and animal in some manner associated with sinful sexual conduct" (Douard, 2007: 43). The media applies the term "sexual predator" indiscriminately to crimes ranging from minor sexual offenses such as voyeurism, to violent sexual assaults, to homicides with sexual components (Schultz, 2011). We pass laws dealing with sexual offenders based on the most high-profile and most serious cases, yet most offenders do not fit these categories. How did we get to this place?

Legal regulation of sexual behavior can be traced to the earliest civilizations. However, as social, moral, and political aspects of society change, so do the definitions of a sexual offense, a sexual offender, and the perceived socially appropriate responses to such offenders. The historical roots of American sex offender laws can be traced to the 1900s United Kingdom's dangerous offender legislation. In the American 1930s, the focus was on "perverts" with sexual urges and

4 Legislation and Sexual Offenders

increasingly violent behavior. Due in part to the merging of the medical and legal fields, the result was the medicalization of sexual offenses. The solution to sexual offenses was indefinite confinement in a psychiatric facility as it was believed mental or personality disorders predisposed one to commit sexual violence (Lucken & Latina, 2002).

Morality statutes prohibited offenses such as sodomy, adultery, bestiality, and homosexuality. Sodomy was a catch-all legal term that encompassed many consensual behaviors, most often between homosexuals. By way of example: in New York, consensual sodomy was punishable by a maximum of one-year imprisonment in the 1940s; however, in Georgia, the sentence was potentially life imprisonment. It was in this environment that sexual psychopath legislation was created. While official statistics demonstrate a rise in sex crimes beginning in the 1930s, most arrests during this period were for adult consensual encounters. As such, statistics reflected the morality of the time, rather than an increase in sex crimes (Lucken & Latina, 2002). So, this raises the question: how did the public become concerned about a perceived link between violence and sexual crimes? The answer has much to do with the media, which has a strong influence on how people perceive the world that surrounds them. Many scholars suggest that the American media has a preoccupation with crime, filling the news with the most gruesome and violent tales, despite that those are rare crime events (Moriearty, 2010).

In the early to mid-1930s, the media started highlighting articles on the murder and sexual assault of children. Beginning with the case of Albert Fish in New York state, there were a series of violent and sexually-involved offenses in a reasonably short timeframe that provoked public outrage and gave rise to new legislation (Lucken & Latina, 2002). Albert Fish was alleged to have violated hundreds of children and killed as many as 15 youths before he was apprehended in 1934 for the sexual assault, murder, and cannibalization of a 12-year-old boy. His case garnered much public fascination until his execution in 1936. During this same period, there was a serial rapist in Illinois. Gerald Thompson allegedly had a diary that listed more than 80 names of women he sought to violate. In 1935 he was found guilty and executed for rape and murder. Just a few years later, in Washington, DC, taxi driver Theodore Roosevelt Catoe admitted to raping and choking ten women. He was executed in 1943. These sexually related crimes, in addition to other high-profile crimes, struck fear into the public.[1]

Due primarily to the media's intense coverage of these cases, the public believed there was an epidemic of sexual offending and linked sexual offenses to serious violence. Parents feared predators like Albert Fish were lurking in the streets, and "sex offender" for many became synonymous with "child sex predator" (Lucken & Latina, 2002). It should come as no surprise that this fueled a conservative approach to crime reduction. In the 1930s social scientists had no conception of a "moral panic," however, in hindsight we can understand these events through this concept. Sociologist Stanley Cohen used the idea of a moral panic to refer to "a condition, episode, person or group of persons [that] emerges to become defined as a threat to societal values and interests" (Cohen, 1972: 9). The claim of the threat is disproportionate to the actual risk, and the issue becomes sensationalized through the media, to the point where hostility is engendered toward a targeted group, and a consensus toward action is formed. The consensus is often reactionary and punitive toward the targeted group, resulting in the criminalization of their behavior and resulting social injustices (Cohen, 1972). Using moral panic language to conceptualize legislative and societal responses to sexual offenses does not minimize the consequences of those victimized by sexual crimes. Instead, it is meant to highlight the exaggerated nature of fear over sexual crimes and the reactionary policies that do not serve to effectively prevent or reduce sexual violence.

> Citizens cannot understand a sex attack on a child, and this incomprehensibility fuels reactions of fear…. The attack and investigation become front-page news … describing the failure of the justice system to protect vulnerable persons, which fuels a strong public reaction…. Government officials then feel compelled to act.
>
> *(Lieb, Quinsey, & Berliner, 1998: 11)*

In a time of exaggerated fear, the public can see budding Albert Fish's in the most minor of sexual crime offenders. In this environment, police often crack down on petty offenses that normally would not have resulted in arrest or prosecution. For example: homosexuality-related offenses, exhibitionism, or prostitution. Minor crime arrests drive up the rate of official sex crime statistics. The local media is likely to report and contextualize local sex crimes (even minor ones) in the nationwide perspective of sexual offending, leading the public to the perception that on the local and national levels such offenses are increasing and potentially epidemic. The result is not an *actual* increase in the rate of serious sex crimes, but an increase in the public's *fear* due to increased media coverage. A natural reaction is a concern for the safety of children and personal safety, which is demanded by the public in get-tough legislation. In the 1930s, FBI leader J. Edgar Hoover declared a "war on sex crimes" to satiate the public's fear (Lucken & Latina, 2002). By the late 1930s "public indignation ha[d] reached almost a mass hysteria which ha[d] affected not only the public but also official authorities…. A sheriff in New York recommended shooting every child attacker on the spot" (Wertham, 1938: 847). What was lost in this panic, by both the public and lawmakers, was the reality that serious sexual violence and sexual homicides were rare incidents.

The panic over sexual offenders drew to a close with the end of the Lover's Lane murders in 1942. Though there were spikes in both media coverage and public fear again between 1947 to 1950 and 1953 to 1954 (Jenkins, 1998). *Time* magazine published a very short article in 1950 attempting to debunk stereotypes

6 Legislation and Sexual Offenders

perpetuated by the media. The article was misleadingly entitled "The Unknown Sex Fiend," and in its entirety read:

> Sex crimes, flamboyantly headlined in the press, are currently troubling both public and police. After seven months of poring over statistics and case histories, New Jersey's Commission on the Habitual Sex Offender last week issued a report. One of its main conclusions: the average citizen knows little about the scope and nature of sex crimes, but he is oversupplied with misinformation on the subject. Some of the popular convictions which the commissioners would like to correct: (1) That the sex offender progresses to more serious sex crimes. Statistics clearly show that "progression from minor to major sex crimes is exceptional." (2) That dangerous sex criminals are usually repeaters. Actually, of all serious crime categories, only homicide shows a lower record of repeaters. (3) That sex offenders are oversexed. Most of those treated have turned out to be physically undersexed. (4) That there are "tens of thousands" of homicidal sex fiends abroad in the land. Only an estimated 5% of convicted sex offenders have committed crimes of violence. The commission's cool, if not too reassuring, report: "Danger of murder by relative or other intimate associate is very much greater than the danger of murder by an unknown sex fiend."
>
> *("The Unknown Sex Fiend," 1950)*

These findings were a minuscule part of a report by the New Jersey Commission on the Habitual Sex Offender, and while it was noteworthy to have appeared at all in the national mainstream media, both the title and the note that the report was "not too reassuring" were undermining of the Commission's significant research endeavor.

The media is an important tool for informing public perception, especially as related to issues of crime. The media is one factor that can fuel social and legislative changes and is a mode of dissemination of information that may otherwise remain unavailable to the everyday citizen (Ducat, Thomas, & Blood, 2009). However, this relationship is not causal. While some states chose to respond to the public's fear and pressure for social changes with legislation that was tough on sexual offenders, at least 15 states responded with the establishment of a commission to study the social problem of sexual violence (Galliher & Tyree, 1985). In fact, the two major outcomes during this time period were either research from Commissions or academic communities, or the legislative passage of sexual psychopath laws. The public was fearful of sexual offenders, but the 1950s were a historical period wherein women and children held a different role than today. Physical collaboration of sexual assault was required by the courts, child sexual abuse was not deemed a social problem, and rape charges were frequently dismissed or resulted in plea bargains. The criminal justice system did not view sexual offenses seriously unless it was a stereotypical stranger offense that involved serious physical harm to the victim.

In the 1960s and 1970s, profound societal changes occurred as part of social movements for the rights of women, minorities, victims, and offenders. The legal landscape began to change and there were concerns regarding overcriminalization and the due process rights of criminals. There were relaxed restrictions on morality offenses, on the acceptance of pornography, and on consensual sexual behavior. As well, the public began to question if rehabilitation was possible within the prison setting. Women's groups challenged stereotypes regarding rapists as the "strangers lurking in the bushes" and suggested that sexual violence should be viewed as a broader structural problem. Women's groups also worked to strengthen rape laws and wanted society and the criminal justice system to understand that rape did not necessarily conform to existing rape myths that pervaded society (Corrigan, 2006). Victim's groups worked with law enforcement to increase knowledge regarding sexual violence, sought protection for the privacy of victims, encouraged reporting of victimizations, and created rape crisis centers (Bevacqua, 2000).

The laissez-faire moralism of the 1960s changed to a moral conservativism in the 1970s and 1980s. This period also brought increased concerns to issues surrounding child abuse by women's groups and social welfare groups. A major piece of legislation was passed in 1974, the Child Abuse Prevention and Treatment Act. This Act mandated reporting and subsequent investigation of all allegations of abuse, provided federal funds for child abuse investigation, established the Office on Child Abuse and Neglect for data collection, and created the National Center on Child Abuse and Neglect. This Act has been amended multiple times since 1974, most recently in 2016 as the Comprehensive Addiction and Recovery Act. In an increasingly conservative moral society, the media's investigations into the "epidemic of sexual violence" began anew. There were publications on "recovery literature," rape, incest, child sexual abuse, ritualized abuse, and the general message was that sexual violence was rampant.

One of the new fears covered in the media in the 1980s was child pornography and its presumable link to pedophilia. According to one researcher:

> The phenomenon of pornography rings became linked in the public mind with the idea of the pedophile as an organized career criminal, a violent predator who was potentially capable of abduction and serial homicide and who usually hunted in packs. The scandals of the early 1980s led law-enforcement agencies and the media to suggest that child pornography was often the work of organized pedophiles and that pedophiles, individually and in rings, molested large numbers of children, sometimes abducting their victims. Although a new departure in the stereotype of the molester, the sex ring idea developed immense

8 Legislation and Sexual Offenders

> force and retained a grasp on the public imagination long after the most extreme charges concerning these operations were discredited.
>
> *(Jenkins, 1998: 146)*

Once the public saw the link between pornography and sex crimes in the media "it [became] part of the public's image of the problem and may [have helped] justify new public policies" (Best, 1990: 46). Women's and victim's rights groups sought to extend this line of thinking to adult pornography and sought to pass legislation outlawing pornography in many jurisdictions. In the case of adult sexually explicit material, however, the courts have been clear that such printed and electronic matter is protected by the Constitution. That said, many moralists and feminists consider it offensive and obscene.

The 1980s saw an increase in the number of child sexual abuse cases prosecuted by the courts: cases of child pornography, child sex rings, and child sex abuse were recounted in courts and in the media. This time period saw widespread media discussion of sex trials and this served to reflect on and reinforce sexual norms, as well as challenge the shame and stigma attached to victims and translate those meanings into survivor stories (Serisier, 2017). As the 1990s began, there were high-profile cases involving children that were dramatic. Most notably the disappearance of Jacob Wetterling, the sexual assault and murder of Megan Kanka, the abduction and murder of Amber Hagerman, and the kidnapping and murder of Polly Klaas. These cases were presumed to involve children brutally harmed or murdered by previously convicted sexual offenders, and they launched a new wave of stranger-danger panic and a new call for get-tough legislation. The U.S. was at the forefront of the passage of innovative laws that were passed quickly in response to these high-profile cases that occurred in fairly rapid succession. These laws remain in effect today, despite having minimal, if any, impact on sex offender recidivism or community safety.

While stranger offenses are not the most common type of offenses, these themes remain the most popular in the mainstream media:

> Stranger-danger stories have great appeal to journalists. The random and public nature of such attacks makes every reader or viewer potentially at risk from the "pervert on the loose." Such cases often combine sex and murder. They also have ongoing narrative momentum (the appeal by parents for the missing child, the eventual tragic discovery) and they come with their own available images (the little girl in her school uniform, the security video footage of her last journey, the police searching wasteland).
>
> *(Kitzinger, 2004: 128)*

The problem with this media narrative is that it significantly skews the policies and laws that are supported by the public (Benedict, 1992; Carringella-MacDonald,

Politics, the Media, and Laws **9**

1998; Dowler, 2006). The discourse around sexual offenders has become integral to how people conceptualize sexual violence, and how we reflect on and expand legislation that targets sex offenders in the United States. "There is increasingly myopic focus on the 'predator' as personifying the danger to [communities] ... the predator template [has become] more and more central to how we think and talk about sexual violence" (Janus, 2006: 131). News media emphasizes sensationalized sexual offenses and this translates into a legislative and political "panic" (Greer, 2012; Kitzinger, 2004; Krinsky, 2016; Lancaster, 2011; Leon, 2011). In a content analysis of 323 *Los Angeles Times* articles spanning 25 years (1990 to 2015), research continued to find misrepresentations of sexual offenders. Mainstream media coverage of sexual offenders most likely focused on repeat offenders, multiple victims, crimes against children under the age of 12, and stranger kidnappings and murders (DiBennardo, 2018). While the media focuses on violent sex crimes, our laws continue to expand and encompass crimes as minor as sexting and public urination. As the laws expand, so too does society's definition of a sexual offender. Samantha had some insight into one of the survey questions that accompanied our interview:

> One of the questions on there was something like, "Do you feel that your spouse fits into society's definition of a sex offender?" And I thought about that a lot. I really think that society's definition, if you just pulled somebody off the street, I really think that society's definition of a sex offender is whoever the government tells me is a sex offender, that's a sex offender. It doesn't matter if you took a 13-year-old kid sexting on his phone or a 32-year-old guy who is a child molester; they are both looked at as a sex offender. Whatever they've been told, that is a sex offender. So, I had to say yes to the question. I mean, by society's definition, my husband is a sex offender because someone decided that he is. So, that's been kind of one of those things that's hard to think through, because how do you combat that? I mean, once you've been given that label by the government, people are going to believe it.

Before Samantha married her husband, he pled guilty to what he said was a false allegation of sexual contact with a minor. He was sentenced to 15 years on probation and later served five years on a drug violation. The female family member later recanted, acknowledging that she lied. This media environment continues today; a continuation of a hostile public toward sex offenders, and a criminal justice system that trends toward more punitive legislative measures and increased sentences (Thakker & Durrant, 2006; Zgoba, 2004).

What has changed is greater empowerment of victims, at least as represented in the media. The #MeToo Movement was launched in 2006 as a non-profit, dedicated to providing a space for survivors of sexual assault, a space for healing. It went viral in 2017 in the midst of the Harvey Weinstein scandal.

> This was the great unleashing that turned the #MeToo hashtag into a rallying cry. The phrase was first used more than a decade ago by social activist Tarana Burke as part of her work building solidarity among young survivors of harassment and assault. A friend of the actor Alyssa Milano sent her a screenshot of the phrase, and Milano, almost on a whim, tweeted it out on Oct. 15. "If you've been sexually harassed or assaulted write 'me too' as a reply to this tweet," she wrote, and then went to sleep. She woke up the next day to find that more than 30,000 people had used #MeToo. Milano burst into tears.
>
> *("The Silence Breakers," 2017)*

Initially, responders were in the entertainment industry, but the hashtag very quickly went viral and global. Within a month, there were #MeToo protests in the streets. In fact, the *Time* Person of the Year for 2017 was "The Silence Breakers." These were 61 women and men who reported sexual assault and harassment. Could this represent the cusp of change in American society in challenging sexual abuse? It may, but it also represents even greater media focus on sexual offenses, as men and women use social media to speak out about their experiences of sexual assault. What will this mean for new sex offender legislation? As of now, new legislation has not been passed directly on the heels of the MeToo movement. The consequences have been scores of accused individuals stepping down from their employment positions; even individuals associated with accused individuals have stepped down from prominent positions.[2] How can we balance the safety and protection of victims with the reasonableness of legislation? How can we maintain a community in which one is innocent until proven guilty while safeguarding the protection of women and children? Only time will be able to address these concerns as consciousness–raising is balanced with legal constraints (Gash & Harding, 2018).

A Brief Guide to Sex Offender Laws

The public's fear of sex offenders and the responsiveness of the government in legislation has resulted in increasingly punitive sex offender regulation in the United States over the past 30 years. This has included the Jacob Wetterling Act, Megan's Law, the Adam Walsh Child Protection and Safety Act, chemical castration laws, residency restrictions, augmented mandatory minimum sentencing, expanded requirements of probation, GPS monitoring, social media regulations, civil commitment legislation, and mandatory public registration in all 50 states for convicted adult sex offenders and in 37 states for juvenile sex offenders. The laws "exhibit[s] the classic signs of panic legislation, namely, poor conception and drafting, overly broad scope, and inadequate consideration of the likely side effects" (Jenkins, 1998: 6). Many of these pieces of legislation were designed in a state of panic, almost immediately following a high-profile crime. The laws are conciliatory and provide the public with a sense of security but are largely misdirected and underdeveloped (Zgoba, 2004).

Jacob Wetterling Act

Minnesota 1989: 11-year-old Jacob Wetterling, his brother and a friend, were riding their bicycles when confronted by a masked man with a gun. Jacob was abducted and the other two boys were told to run. Because a halfway house was located nearby, it was suspected that a previously convicted sex offender abducted Jacob, but no suspects were readily found. In 1993 the Jacob Wetterling Crimes Against Children and Sexually Violent Offender Registration Act came into effect. Twenty-seven years later, Danny Heinrich led law enforcement to Jacob's remains and admitted to his sexual assault and murder in 2016. The confession was part of a plea on a federal child pornography charge, for which Heinrich was sentenced to 20 years.

The Wetterling Act was amended in 1996 and evolved into a community notification law which mandated that all states have registration protocols for sex offenders or risk losing federal funds for crime measures. Every state has a mandatory registration law requiring sex offenders to register their home address with law enforcement every 90 days for Sexually Violent Predators and annually for other offenders. This registration is to last for life for Sexually Violent Predators and for a period of ten years for other offenders. Who has access to this information varies by state and by the offender's tier assessment. In most states, this information is publicly accessible via a website. A main purpose of the Wetterling Act was to establish the class of offenders deemed Sexually Violent Predators (SVPs).

Megan's Law

By the mid-1990s, though many states had implemented community notification guidelines, as outlined in the Wetterling Act, in 1996 Congress proceeded to pass Megan's Law. The federal law mandated public disclosure of sex offender registry information whenever deemed necessary for public safety. The impetus for Megan's Law was the 1994 rape and murder of a young, middle-class girl in New Jersey named Megan Kanka. The perpetrator was a paroled sex offender who lived in the neighborhood with two other paroled sex offenders. Jesse Timmendequas had two prior sex offense convictions and had plea-bargained on the most recent charge to a term of ten years (Pallone, 2003). He lured Megan to his house under the pretense of seeing his puppy. He sexually assaulted and murdered Megan, disposing of her body in a nearby park. The case brought intense media attention and outrage to the community. Megan's mother reportedly said: "We knew nothing about him. If we had been aware of his record, my daughter would be alive today" (Human Rights Watch, 2007: 47).

12 Legislation and Sexual Offenders

Within a month of the murder, Megan's Law was passed in New Jersey. This law became the standard for other states, with 16 states following New Jersey's lead within one year of Megan's murder. The stated goal was to increase public safety.

Megan's Law requires sex offenders to register with law enforcement at varied time intervals, depending on their tier level. For the most part, the type of crime an offender commits determines tier assignment. General guidelines for tier assignment exist, though there is variation by state. A Tier 1 offender is deemed to be the lowest risk to the public and has committed a non-violent offense against a victim who is an adult. Examples of Tier 1 offenses include possession of child pornography; voyeurism offenses; public indecency offenses; or non-penetrative sexual contact offenses without consent with an adult victim. A Tier 2 offender is deemed to be a higher risk to the public and is an individual who commits a second Tier 1 offense or a non-violent sexual offense against a minor. Examples of Tier 2 offenses include sexual contact with a minor aged 12 to 15; a sexual crime against an individual in the offender's custody (e.g., foster child); distribution or production of child pornography; sex trafficking of a minor; transporting a minor with the intent of sexual activity; or sexual coercion of a minor. A Tier 3 sexual offender is deemed to be at highest risk to the public and is an individual who is a repeat Tier 2 offender or an individual who commits a sexually penetrative act (as opposed to a crime involving sexual contact) or a sexual crime involving violence. Examples of Tier 3 offenses include sexual acts that involve threats, force, drugs, or intoxication, or the victim's mental or physical inability to consent; sexual acts or contact with a victim under the age of 12; and kidnapping or false imprisonment of a minor.

In many states, the most controversial aspect of Megan's Law is the requirement that authorities notify community members when a sex offender moves into the neighborhood. National standards do not exist regarding community notification guidelines, so it varies by state, depends on the offender's tier status, and there are varying amounts of information available to the public. A notification may be a letter to community organizations or neighbors, website notification, or it may mean a billboard with the sex offender's identifying information. Identification may also be placed on an offender's driver's license.

The rationale for community notification and registration laws was public safety, as echoed in President Bill Clinton's Presidential Radio Address:

> Nothing is more threatening to our families and communities and more destructive of our basic values than sex offenders who victimize children and families. Study after study tells us that they often repeat the same crimes. That's why we have to stop sex offenders before they commit their next crime, to make our children safe and give their parents peace of mind.
>
> *(Human Rights Watch, 2007: 47)*

It did not matter that claims of high recidivism were false, and it did not matter that a registry does not protect children from familial adults that were the most likely to harm them. Such legislation provides some sense of community empowerment, especially immediately after a high-profile offense.

Adam Walsh Child Protection and Safety Act

Florida 1982: Adam Walsh was a six-year-old boy who was abducted from a department store. Sixteen days later, fishermen found his severed head floating in a nearby canal. In 2006, on the 25th anniversary of Adam's abduction, the Adam Walsh Child Protection and Safety Act was signed into law. This Act completely rewrote the federal standards for registration and notification into SORNA (Sex Offender Registration and Notification Act), a national and comprehensive streamlined system wherein all states would have identical information posted about sex offenders online. Additionally, the legislation organizes offenders into tiers and requires Tier 1 offenders to register annually with law enforcement for 15 years, Tier 2 offenders to register semi-annually for 25 years, and Tier 3 offenders to register every three months for life. Failure to register with law enforcement or update personal information is a felony and can result in a fine of up to $250,000 and/or imprisonment of a maximum of ten years. Under SORNA, offenders as young as 14 years of age are required to register. The number of sexual offenses that require registration was expanded, and foreign convictions were included. The Office of Sex Offender Sentencing, Monitoring, Apprehending, Registering, and Tracking (SMART Office) was created within the Department of Justice. Additionally, the Department of Justice established the Dru Sjodin National Sex Offender Public Website[3] in order to maintain one access point for all sex offender registries. Though the constitutionality of the registration requirement has been legally challenged, it was upheld by the court in July 2008.[4]

The Act eliminated the statute of limitations for prosecution of felony child sexual offense cases and child abduction cases, established a federal DNA database, and funds electronic monitoring (GPS) of offenders. The Act also created mandatory minimum sentences for some offenses: 30 years for rape of a child, and 10 years for child sex trafficking or coerced child prostitution. Additionally, the minimum terms of imprisonment were lengthened for offenders traveling between states with minors. As well, the Act allowed victims of child abuse to civilly sue the offender for damages. All states were required to comply with the provisions of the Adam Walsh Child Protection and Safety Act and SORNA by July 2009 or risk a reduction in federal funds. The Adam Walsh Act is yet another example of how the government responds to fear-mongering instead of objective facts. This Act is a sweeping piece of federal legislation not based on any research regarding how to decrease sexual crimes.

14 Legislation and Sexual Offenders

KIDS Act and Social Media Regulations

As the internet became more widespread, it became an increasing concern that offenders would use social media to prey on minors. In 2008 the KIDS Act (Keeping the Internet Devoid of Predators) was passed, which added to SORNA the requirement that jurisdictions collect internet identifiers of sex offenders when they register. These identifiers were not, however, permitted to be posted on the public sex offender website. This same year, MySpace and Facebook increased safeguards to protect minors.

Legal restrictions on social media use and registration of internet identifiers are debated, however, as First Amendment issues. In a significant case in June 2017, a North Carolina law was struck down by the Supreme Court which barred sex offenders from utilizing social media sites such as Facebook, Twitter, Snapchat, LinkedIn, and YouTube. This case revolved around Lester Packingham whose initial sex offense occurred in 2002, and for which he was sentenced to 2 years of supervised probation. Fast forward 8 years to his arrest for a celebratory post on Facebook in response to a dismissal of a parking ticket (Wolf, 2017). The law Packingham violated stated that:

> It is unlawful for a sex offender who is registered ... to access a commercial social networking site where the sex offender knows that the site permits minor children to become members or to create or maintain personal Web pages on the commercial social networking site.
>
> *(de Vogue & Diaz, 2017: online)*

The court ruled unanimously that prohibitions such as these infringe on lawful speech and are therefore in violation of the First Amendment. In the decision, Justice Anthony Kennedy wrote:

> To foreclose access to social media altogether is to prevent the user from engaging in the legitimate exercise of First Amendment rights.... Even convicted criminals – and in some instances, especially convicted criminals – might receive legitimate benefits from these means for access to the world of ideas, in particular if they seek to reform and to pursue lawful and rewarding lives.
>
> *(Wolf, 2017: online)*

This ruling recognizes that much of community life today is structured through and/or around social media and sex offenders should have this right to free speech. There are some that disagree with the court's ruling. North Carolina's Senior Deputy Attorney General, Robert Montgomery claims that offenders use social media to gain information about minors for the purpose of sexual offending in more than 80 percent of cases. Thirteen states shared the Deputy

Attorney General's view and defended the North Carolina law (Wolf, 2017). In 2019, the Illinois Supreme Court further clarified that whether during or after supervision, a blanket ban on the use of social media is a violation of the First Amendment (*The People of The State of Illinois* v. *Conrad Allen Morger* 2019).

Even today, Facebook continues to have a section in their Help Center that permits users to "Report a Convicted Sex Offender" by providing the name of the offender, the URL of their registry profile, and the state in which they were convicted. Sometimes sexual offenders cannot use social media due to parole or probation restrictions, sometimes it is due to restrictions placed by the social media outlet itself (as in the case of Facebook and Instagram), and sometimes there are legal impediments to using social media. In 2018, an appeals court dismissed an indictment of a Tier 3 sex offender who failed to register his Facebook account with New York state. The law requires offenders to register their "internet identifiers," but the Justices suggested that:

> an internet identifier is not the social networking website or application itself.… Rather, it is how someone identifies himself or herself when accessing a social networking account, whether it be with an electronic mail address or some other name or title, such as a screen name or user name … [the] defendant's failure to disclose his use of Facebook is not a crime, rendering the indictment jurisdictionally defective.
>
> *(Russell, 2018: online)*

Additionally, legislation addressing sex offenders and social media currently makes no requirement that an offender disclose which social media they make use of in their life.

Other laws are more specific in targeting offenders who have a history of internet use as a part of their offense. For example, a 2007 New Jersey law prohibited offenders who used the internet in the commission of their crime from using the internet for personal use, allowing exceptions for employment purposes and to search for employment ("No Internet For Some Sex Offenders in New Jersey," 2007). In 2017, however, the New Jersey Supreme Court found this near-total internet ban to be an arbitrary infringement on an individual's rights (Sullivan, 2017). The Justices did not deem internet bans unconstitutional but did suggest that a formal hearing of the parole board was required to determine that a public safety reason necessitated an internet ban (Sullivan, 2017). There has been some ease of restriction on sex offenders' denial of social media in the past couple of years due to state Supreme Court cases that have questioned the due process and First Amendment concerns behind total internet bans for released offenders on the registry.[5] While the future will likely see an increase in such legislative challenges, it may also see more creative law-writing to limit access of offenders to various social media platforms.

Residency Restrictions

Sex offender residency restrictions (SORR) are laws that restrict where an offender may live, work, or visit. These laws are part of the panic surrounding sex crimes, the rationale being that sex offenders should be banished from places where minors are to increase the safety of children. The first SORR was passed in 1996 in Alabama and prohibited any offender convicted of a child sexual offense from residing within 1,000 feet of a school. Several other states followed this lead, as did some local governments which enacted their own residency restrictions. These laws were passed despite no empirical research that they lower recidivism or increase community safety. What these laws do is make the community feel safer. Roger Werholtz, secretary of the Kansas Department of Corrections and a member of the Kansas Sex Offender Policy Board was quoted in a hearing on the state's moratorium on SORRs as saying: "Yes, I hear all the data. Yes, I know what the research is saying. But you know what, this makes me feel safer" ("Kansas Rejects Buffer Zones," 2007: online). In some jurisdictions all tiers of sex offenders are subject to residency restrictions; in other jurisdictions only Tier 3 offenders are subject; and in other jurisdictions only child offenders are subject. There is significant variability in the laws. Additionally, the laws may last indefinitely, and therefore theoretically extend beyond an offender's length of required registration.

As created, SORRs have the unintended consequence of overwhelming select communities with sexual offenders and their families as there are few areas in which offenders are permitted to live. Some states have SORRs of 2,500 feet which severely limit options in housing for offenders, especially in a small town or a densely populated area (Wagner, 2009). When a town enacts a SORR, particularly with a strict restriction, neighboring towns fear offenders who are desperate for housing will encroach on their community.

> When Iowa restricted sex offenders from living within two thousand feet of schools, parks, and playgrounds, a border town in Nebraska had twenty-eight offenders move in from Iowa. Whether or not this migration of offenders is typical, the fear of such migration is a motivating factor for many politicians when considering the law. Legislatures feel they must move quickly to prevent this migration of sex offenders into their towns.
>
> *(Wagner, 2009: 189)*

Thus, lawmakers rush legislation in fear of migration from sex offenders from neighboring communities. Such legislation, in combination with the hesitation of landlords to rent to sex offenders, makes it a challenge for offenders and their families to find housing. A homeless sex offender is in a dilemma, as registration of an address with law enforcement is mandatory or imprisonment may result.

The neighborhoods that permit sex offenders are often not ideal, may be far from employment opportunities or high in crime, therefore potentially interfering with community reintegration, or preventing an offender from living with supportive family members. Currently, 27 states have SORRs, and a handful of states have banned SORRs as unconstitutional.

GPS Monitoring

Florida 2005: nine-year-old Jessica Lunsford was abducted from her home. Widespread media coverage followed and three weeks later a neighbor and registered sex offender admitted to her murder and sexual assault. John Couey had a borderline-retarded IQ, had failed to register his address with law enforcement, and skipped court-ordered counseling sessions. He was charged with first-degree murder, kidnapping, burglary, and sexual battery. Despite the prohibition on executing the mentally challenged, and Couey's very borderline intelligence, he was sentenced to be executed. Just a few weeks after Jessica Lunsford's murder, while the citizenry was still reeling, elsewhere in Florida, 13-year-old Sarah Lunde was abducted from her home. The public was incensed; the media was frenzied! A week later, Sarah's body was found in a nearby lake. A confession of sexual assault and murder came from a convicted rapist who had previously dated the girl's mother. Though David Onstott's confession was thrown out as he was denied access to an attorney, and there was no physical or forensic evidence in the case, Onstott was found guilty of second-degree murder and battery, and sentenced to life in prison.

The legislative change after these cases was the quick and unanimous passage of the Jessica Lunsford Act which allowed for a 25-year mandatory minimum sentence for an offender convicted of sexual assault of a person under the age of 12, and the Act requires lifetime electronic surveillance upon release. More than 30 states passed similar provisions for mandatory minimum sentences shortly thereafter, and approximately half of the states provide for GPS monitoring for offenders after imprisonment. Of note regarding GPS laws, is that they are often applied retroactively: the law can legally be applied to offenders who were convicted prior to the passage of the electronic monitoring law (Reyes, 2017). Additionally, in *Grady* v. *North Carolina* (2015), the U.S. Supreme Court ruled that while GPS monitoring is considered a "search" under the Fourth Amendment, the search is not necessarily unreasonable or unconstitutional, but that the circumstances must be considered in evaluating the reasonableness of privacy expectations on a case-by-case basis.

Monitoring of an offender may include more than an electronic ankle bracelet. It may also include polygraphs, random calling and voice verification by law enforcement, remote alcohol monitoring, and motion detection analysis (International Association of Chiefs of Police, 2008). These programs are costly to administer, and effectiveness remains questionable. For example, as of January 2018,

18 Legislation and Sexual Offenders

Wisconsin had 1,258 sex offenders under electronic monitoring and the cost was $9.7 million annually (Vetterkind, 2018). In many states the cost of monitoring is borne by the offender, ranging from $10–$15 per day. While some courts permit a sliding scale for offenders who have a compromised ability to pay, other states jail offenders for inability to pay (Karsten & West, 2017). Technological difficulties with GPS monitoring abound, including loss of signal; loss of power; equipment malfunction; inadequate broadband capacity (especially in rural areas); and battery failure (Vetterkind, 2018). Any of these problems can put an offender in jail or result in other serious consequences, such as loss of employment. The result is an increased workload for law enforcement and a false sense of security for the public. Advocates suggest that the benefits outweigh the drawbacks and the number of offenders electronically monitored continues to increase aggressively.

Civil Commitment

The historical view of sex offenders was that they were mentally ill persons that should therefore be given treatment and be preventively detained in a mental health facility versus confined in a prison. The sexual psychopath laws that started to be passed in the late 1930s allowed for the *involuntary* and *indefinite* commitment of an individual to a psychiatric facility once he was deemed a "sexual psychopath." He was to remain confined until his uncontrollable impulses were "cured." The "ever-flexible concept of the molester, the abuser, or the predator provides an invaluable gauge for the state of current social ideologies" (Jenkins, 1998: 13) as the language of the legislation reflected the moral views of the day.

Michigan was the first to pass a sexual psychopath law in 1937, though it was later deemed unconstitutional because it did not afford the protections provided by a jury trial and it violated the principle of double jeopardy. The law was revised and approved in 1939. Other states learned from Illinois' sexual psychopath law which permitted commitment without a criminal conviction, thus relying more on the procedural elements of an insanity hearing. For many states, conviction of a sexual offense was not required for commitment under sexual psychopath legislation! An individual merely needed to be at risk of sexual compulsivity! By the close of the 1950s, 26 states and the District of Columbia had sexual psychopath legislation.

Though there was some state-to-state variation, many sexual psychopath laws shared key language. The common elements in the statutes were:

- committing a crime of a sexual nature;
- a focus on the compulsive nature of the individual's pathology;
- an assumption that the offense, or a similar offense, would be committed again;

Politics, the Media, and Laws **19**

- an assumption that offenses would escalate;
- the potential risk to community safety; and
- the belief that treatment was possible.

If several of these elements were present in an offender, he was at risk of commitment under a standard sexual psychopath law (Group for the Advancement of Psychiatry, 1977). By way of specific example, the 1955 California Sexual Psychopath Act read:

> [S]exual psychopath means any person who is affected, in a form predisposing to the commission of sexual offenses, and in a degree constituting him a menace to the health or safety of others, with any of the following conditions:
>
> (a) Mental disease or disorder.
> (b) Psychopathic personality.
> (c) Marked departures from normal mentality.
> *(California Welfare and Institute Code of 1955 §5501)*

While these statutes were presumably created to prevent the community from repeat and dangerous sexual offenders, they were also used to examine individuals for sexual psychopathy who had committed minor and/or non-violent offenses. Not everyone who was examined for psychopathy was committed, but there was a substantial number of individuals who were committed for non-violent, morally offensive behaviors. For example, more than 50 percent of those committed in the state of Illinois under the sexual psychopath law were for passive offenses, such as exhibitionism (Burick, 1968). In New Jersey, commitment "was reserved for petty sex offenders who seemed likely to escalate their crimes…. Serious sex offenders were almost invariably returned to the criminal justice system for punishment" (Cole, 2000: 299). Although it may have been used improperly, sexual psychopath legislation was not used nearly to the extent that control strategies are used today for sex offenders. Most states during this time committed less than 20 persons on average per year (Jenkins, 1998).

The assumptions behind sexual psychopath legislation were that sex crime rates were increasing, and the criminal justice system could not effectively manage sex crime recidivism as continuous treatment was needed. The legislation was also based on the notion that sex offenders

> persist in their sexual crimes throughout life; that they always give warning that they are dangerous by first committing minor offenses; that any psychiatrist can diagnose them with a high degree of precision at an early age, before they have committed serious sex crimes; and that sexual psychopaths who are diagnosed and identified should be confined as

20 Legislation and Sexual Offenders

> irresponsible persons until they are pronounced by psychiatrists to be completely and permanently cured of their malady.
>
> *(Sutherland, 1950: 142)*

Sexual psychopath legislation, according to the Criminal Justice Mental Health Standards, rests on six assumptions:

> (1) there is a specific mental disability called sexual psychopathy ... (2) persons suffering from such a disability are more likely to commit serious crimes, especially dangerous sex offenses, than normal criminals; (3) such persons are easily identifiable by mental health professionals; (4) the dangerousness of these offenders can be predicted by mental health professionals; (5) treatment is available for the condition; and (6) large number of persons afflicted with the designated disabilities can be cured.
>
> *(La Fond, 2000: 157)*

But what if these assumptions were incorrect? What if these questions could not be answered? The bend toward treatment came to a halt when the public realized that individuals were being confined under these laws but not actually receiving any treatment at all. The U.S. Court of Appeals ruled that was not permissible: an individual could not be held in confinement under a sexual psychopath law without being provided treatment. Oregon responded in 1963 by constructing the first facility designed specifically for treating sexually dangerous offenders in the United States. Other states were suspected of providing no treatment, poor treatment, or abusive treatment (such as electroconvulsive therapy). And research revealed that less than one-quarter of offenders were ever deemed "cured" by treatment programs (LaFond, 2000).

Concerns began to increase about this legislation and the subjective determination of who was and who was not a sexual psychopath, both for the purposes of admittance and for the purposes of release. Psychiatrists became less comfortable with their close relationship with law enforcement and the speed at which they were expected to "diagnose" sexual psychopathy. The mental health community also began to question the confinement of those committing "minor" offenses under the auspices that they would escalate to "serious" sex offenders. Court decisions of the early 1970s made confinement of sexual offenders under sexual psychopath statutes very difficult unless the offender was an imminent risk to himself or others. Eventually these laws were repealed, resulting in the transfer of those held under these statutes to prisons.

This is not where the story of indefinite confinement of sexual offenders ends, however. Earl Shriner was the impetus for Special Commitment laws or Sexually Violent Predator (SVP) laws. In the 1960s he allegedly murdered a classmate and served a term of confinement in a mental facility. Following his release, there were multiple charges of molestation (1977, 1987, 1988). While imprisoned, Shriner expressed a desire to sexually assault minors, and there were failed attempts to involuntarily commit him to a mental health facility. After serving his full sentence Earl Shriner was released. In 1989, Shriner abducted, brutally sexually assaulted, and left a seven-year-old boy to die in Washington state. Following public outcry and a massive media campaign, within six months Washington state passed Sexually Violent Predator legislation. Many states followed Washington's lead, using almost verbatim language.

SVP laws confine offenders to a secure mental facility if they were deemed by "experts" to be "mentally abnormal and dangerous sex offenders" (Zonana, Bonnie, & Hoge, 2003: 132). Persons eligible for commitment under Washington state's SVP law included both adult and juvenile sexual violent offenders whose sentence was to end, and offenders charged with a sexually violent crime but who were found either incompetent to stand trial or not guilty at trial by reason of insanity.

SVP laws should resound with familiarity from the sexual psychopath legislation of the past, though they have important differences. SVP laws do not require the sexually offensive behavior to be recent and in many states a treatment program is not a requirement. Perhaps most different is that current SVP legislation requires an offender serve their prison sentence in its entirety *prior* to the state seeking civil commitment. This raises civil liberty arguments: "the primary goal of predator statutes is to provide a mechanism for continued confinement of sex offenders considered at risk of reoffending who can no longer be confined under the criminal justice system" (La Fond, 2000: 159). While this may sound like a clear-cut case of double jeopardy, the courts have ruled SVP statutes constitutional!

SVP laws were ruled constitutional in the 1997 landmark Supreme Court decision *Kansas* v. *Hendricks*. Leroy Hendricks had a long history of sexual offenses, including indecent exposure, and varied acts of sexual assault against children. He served numerous prison terms but was repeatedly released. In 1984 on two counts of child molestation, Hendricks was sentenced to a term of 5 to 20 years. During the 10th year of his sentence, the state sought to have Hendricks declared a SVP and committed indefinitely. His hearing determined he was "mentally abnormal" and a pedophile, and therefore a candidate for commitment. Hendricks challenged the ruling to the Supreme Court, asserting that his commitment was *ex post facto* punishment and a violation of double jeopardy. The court ruled:

> a state statute providing for the involuntary civil commitment of sexually violent predators…does not violate the double jeopardy clause of the Federal Constitution's Fifth Amendment where, because the state did not enact the statute with punitive intent, the statute does not establish criminal proceedings, and involuntary commitment pursuant to the statute is not punitive; thus, for purposes of analysis under the double jeopardy clause, (1) initiation of commitment proceedings under the statute

against a person upon his imminent release from prison after serving a sentence for the offenses which led to his being declared a violent sexual predator does not constitute a second prosecution, and (2) a person's involuntary detention under the statute does not violate the double jeopardy clause, even though that confinement follows a prison term.

(*Kansas v. Hendricks, 521 U.S. 346, 1997*)

The court established that the justification for commitment was the protection of society from a dangerous individual with a mental disorder. The court also determined that the commitment itself does not provide a constitutional right to treatment for the offender. As such, *Kansas* v. *Hendricks* (1997) clearly established the power of the state to protect the community over individual liberties. The court in this case also permitted statutes which provide for an offense that may have occurred 10 to 20 years prior to be continued justification for indefinite confinement. Some scholars and ethicists still believe this constitutes *ex post facto* punishment, under the guise of treatment (Cornwell, 2003).

Kansas v. *Hendricks* (1997) has been upheld since 1997, and the rationale is that these statutes are civil proceedings, rather than an additional criminal punishment (*Kansas* v. *Crane* 2002). As of 2019, the District of Columbia, the federal government, and 20 states have SVP statutes.[6] There is considerable language variation by state, and standards for commitment vary by state, but all involve a history of sexual offending, "serious difficulty controlling behavior," a "serious mental disorder," and some level of "dangerousness." For example, in Minnesota in order to be a candidate for commitment an individual must be "highly likely to reoffend," but in Wisconsin an offender must only be "most likely to reoffend" in order to be a candidate for commitment. By way of example, the procedure in New Jersey is outlined in the 1998 New Jersey Sexually Violent Predator Act:

> Effective August 1999, The New Jersey Sexually Violent Predator Act (SVPA) establishes an involuntary civil commitment procedure for a sexually violent predator, whom the bill defines as a person who: (1) has been convicted, adjudicated delinquent or found not guilty by reason of insanity for commission of a sexually violent offense, or has been charged with a sexually violent offense but found to be incompetent to stand trial; and (2) suffers from a mental abnormality or personality disorder that makes the person likely to engage in acts of sexual violence if not confined in a secure facility for control, care and treatment. The Attorney General may initiate a court proceeding for involuntary commitment under this bill by submitting to the court a clinical certificate for a sexually violent predator, completed by a psychiatrist on the person's treatment team.... Upon receipt of these documents, the court shall immediately review them to determine whether there is probable cause to believe that the person is a sexually violent predator in need

Politics, the Media, and Laws **23**

of involuntary commitment. If so, the court shall issue an order for a final hearing and temporarily authorize commitment to a secure facility designated for the custody, care and treatment of sexually violent predators.... The person's psychiatrist on the treatment team, who has examined the person no more than five calendar days prior to the court hearing, must testify to the clinical basis for the need for involuntary commitment as a sexually violent predator. Other treatment team members, relevant witnesses or next-of-kin are also permitted to testify.... At this hearing, and any subsequent review court hearing, the person has the following rights: The right to be represented by counsel or, if indigent, by appointed counsel; The right to be present at the court hearing unless the court determines that because of the person's conduct at the court hearing the proceeding cannot reasonably continue while the person is present; The right to present evidence; The right to cross-examine witnesses; and The right to a hearing in camera. The bill provides that if the court finds by clear and convincing evidence that the person is in need of involuntary commitment, it shall issue an order authorizing the involuntary commitment of the person to a facility designated for custody, care and treatment of sexually violent predators. Also, the court may order that the person be conditionally discharged in accordance with a plan to facilitate the person's adjustment and reintegration into the community, if the court finds that the person will not be likely to engage in acts of sexual violence because the person is amenable to and highly likely to comply with the plan. Additionally, the bill provides for annual court review hearings of the need for involuntary commitment as a sexually violent predator. The first hearing shall be conducted 12 months from the date of the first hearing, and subsequent hearings annually thereafter. In addition, at any time during involuntary commitment, if the person's treatment team determines that the person's mental condition has so changed that the person is not likely to engage in acts of sexual violence if released, the treatment team shall recommend that the Department of Human Services authorize the person to petition the court for discharge. Also, a person may petition the court for discharge without authorization from the department. In this case, the court shall review the petition to determine whether it is based on facts upon which a court could find that the person's condition had changed, or whether the petition is supported by a professional expert evaluation or report. If the petition fails to satisfy either of these requirements, the court shall deny the petition without a hearing.

(P.L. 1998, c.71 (S895 SCS))

In a commitment hearing, the standard of proof is "beyond a reasonable doubt," the same standard as in a criminal trial. Should an offender be deemed a Sexually

24 Legislation and Sexual Offenders

Violent Predator, he is then committed for an indeterminate period in order to treat the mental disorder believed to underlie his sexual violence. Some statutes provide for mandated re-evaluation at set intervals; other states do not. In order to be released into the community, the offender must be ruled no longer a risk of sexual violence (Lacoursiere, 2003; Washington State Institute for Public Policy (WSIPP), 2007). Deeming an offender no longer a risk of sexual violence, however, happens very, very infrequently.

Regarding the Kansas SVP program: "In the program's nearly 20-year history, it's been more likely that a resident will leave in a hearse than walk out to rejoin society. So far, only three have earned their freedom. Twenty-two have died" (Cooper & Rizzo, 2013: online). Research reveals that there are more than 5,000 offenders committed under SVP statutes across the country, at a cost of more than $500 million per year. In *Kansas* v. *Hendricks*, Justice Anthony Kennedy wrote, "If the civil system is used simply to impose punishment after the state makes an improvident plea bargain on the criminal side, then it is not performing its proper function." With states releasing so few offenders civilly committed, it raises constitutional questions, not to mention fiscal questions given the enormity of the costs of SVP programs.

The Public's View of Sex Offenders

New laws are suggested regularly to pacify the public's fear of sex offenders. For example, a 2018 bill is being considered in Oklahoma that would add it to a list of seven other states[7] that have laws permitting courts to order chemical castration for sexual offenders. This is probably the most invasive strategy that has been used by the law to control sexual offenders. Involuntary sterilization, of both habitual offenders and sex offenders, was allowed in the early 1900s in many states. That changed in 1942 with U.S. Supreme Court case *Skinner* v. *Oklahoma*. Since then, the use of hormones to reduce testosterone and sexual libido has been used sporadically as a form of treatment. Until 1996, when California passed the first chemical castration law in many years. While these laws are rarely enforced, they do raise serious Eighth Amendment concerns.

Many states have Halloween-specific laws that target sexual offenders: either offenders that are on the registry, or offenders who are on parole or on conditional release. This is based on the belief that children are less safe on Halloween than at other times of the year.

> In some New York counties, for example, sex offenders on probation are required to attend a 4-hour education program on Halloween night. In New Jersey, New York, Virginia, Wisconsin, California, South Carolina, and North Carolina, curfew policies prohibit registered sex offenders from going out or opening their doors on Halloween. New Jersey sex offenders caught giving out candy are considered in violation of

probation and face up to 3 years in jail. In Tennessee, sex offenders on probation are banned from Halloween costume parties and cannot put up decorations, and in Ohio, Illinois, Virginia, and North Carolina, offenders are ordered to attend meetings with law enforcement or probation officials during the evening hours of Halloween. In Idaho, Maryland, Florida, and Texas, sex offenders on probation are warned not to decorate their homes and are told to keep their houses dark on Halloween night. In Kentucky, sex offenders receive a letter from police telling them not to give out candy or have unauthorized contact with children. Michigan police told a Lansing television station that there are no laws in the state prohibiting a sex offender from handing out candy but recommended that parents check the sex offender registry before trick-or-treating.

(Chaffin, Levenson, Letourneau, & Stern, 2009: 364)

Curfews, and nighttime checks, and no costumes or candy laws … are these necessary? Do the numbers show greater harm to children from sex offenders on Halloween? In a study examining data from 1997 through 2005, researchers found that the answer was a resounding no (Chaffin et al., 2009). Yet, year after year, states continue to increase law enforcement attention to sex offenders on Halloween … the imaginary problem of increased risk to children on this night of fear.

Most of the laws discussed in this chapter were passed quickly and not in response to empirical evidence regarding sexual offenses and offenders. Instead, the laws were passed to pacify the public's fear and moral outrage surrounding sex offenders. It should come as no surprise then, that overwhelmingly, these laws have failed to serve the protective functions they were auspiciously designed for. Not surprisingly, the public has been found to have overwhelmingly negative attitudes toward sex offenders. Many studies examining views on sex offenders use the Attitudes to Sexual Offenders (ATS) scale, which is what this study implemented. It is a 36-item self-report measure that uses broad attitudinal statements to gauge an individual's level of agreement or disagreement (Hogue, 1993). Since 1993, the ATS-21 has been developed which loads items from the scale into the categories of Trust (affect-based judgments), Intent (cognitive or stereotype-based evaluations), and Social Distance (behavior-related views) (Hogue & Harper, 2019).

What do we know about attitudes toward sex offenders? Demographically, there were no consistent findings in the research: attitudes were not varied consistently based on any demographic variables. Offense-specific information influenced the public's attitude: an older offender was viewed more negatively, as was a male sex offender (Gakhal & Brown, 2011; Harper, 2012). Experience with sex offenders also influenced one's attitude: police officers had highly punitive attitudes toward offenders, followed by prison officials not involved

26 Legislation and Sexual Offenders

in treatment of sex offenders, then prison officials involved in treatment of sex offenders, then probation officers and prison psychologists (Hogue, 1993). Other research supported the notion that working with sex offenders in a treatment environment increased positive attitudes (Blagden, Winder, & Hames, 2016; Gakhal & Brown, 2011; Hogue & Peebles, 1997). Research demonstrated that sex offenders were viewed as deserving of punishment instead of treatment; much of the public was not accepting of treatment in lieu of incarceration for this population of offenders (Van Kesteren, 2009). Remorse and shame by an offender may influence judgments about whether he could be rehabilitated but this did not change the public's view that punishment was necessary, though perhaps for a lesser amount of time (Hogue & Peebles, 1997; Proeve & Howells, 2006). In studies of teachers and students compared to the general public, community members tended to express the most negative attitudes (Higgins & Ireland, 2009).

While community member's negative attitudes toward sex offenders could be explained by fear (either real or imagined) for their safety or that of their children, research revealed that exposure to sex offenders in non-punitive environments increased positive attitudes. Participants in this study demonstrated highly positive attitudes on the ATS-21, likely explained by their unique, intimate relationship with the offender as husband/partner and/or father of their children. There was an 89 percent overall positive response on the Trust questions with a couple of notable exceptions. Twenty-two percent of participants agreed it was not wise to trust sex offenders generally; 11 percent felt it was necessary to be constantly on guard; and 14 percent believed sex offenders were immoral. The participants reported 97 percent positive responses on an aggregate of the sex offender Intent variables which asked questions dealing with the offender's cognitive state of mind. Examples of Intent questions included: could sex offenders be rehabilitated, if sex offenders took advantage of others, or if offenders were selfish. The Social Distance variables revealed an overall 86 percent positive response. Seventy-nine participants were of the belief that sex offenders were victims of circumstances and deserving of assistance. The other Social Distance questions dealt with sex offenders having feelings, needing praise, giving and getting respect, and being no better or worse than others. These responses ranged from 88 percent to 94 percent positive. For the entirety of the ATS-21, there was a 91 percent positive response toward sex offenders from the 94 female participants in this study.

The United States fits securely within a crime control model when dealing with sexual offenders. Numerous laws have been passed, and continue to be passed, many of which infringe on the due process rights of sex offenders. As of July 2019, Illinois became the eighth state to lift the statute of limitations on various sexual crimes. Legislators continue to focus on stereotypical cases that strike fear into the public. This diverts our attention from the structural elements in society that continue to victimize women and children.

The politics of sexual violence forces the majority of the risks of sexual violence underground, making them invisible in the political discourse. Risks that fall outside the predator template simply cannot figure into the public discourse. Because the risks must remain invisible, we are deflected from a sensible and effective fight against sexual violence.

(Janus, 2006: 144)

Community safety and the protection of the rights of women, children, and former offenders can only come from balanced policies not based on political rhetoric and pandering.

Notes

1. Other high-profile cases during the time period were not sexually related but contributed to mounting public fear. These cases included: the kidnapping and murder of the Lindbergh baby which resulted in the execution of Bruno Haumptmann in 1936; the serial Torso Killer in Cleveland who was active between 1935 and 1938, and was never caught; a 1930s serial killer called the Alligator Man of about 20 women in Texas who killed himself before he could be arrested; and between 1938 and 1942 on the border of Pennsylvania and New Jersey, six people were killed in the Lover's Lane murders by Cleveland Hill who served less than 20 years before being paroled.
2. Time's Up is an organization that promotes workplaces free of sexual harassment and is born of the MeToo movement. Three months after accepting the CEO position, Lisa Borders resigned as her 36-year-old son was accused of sexual assault.
3. www.NSOPW.gov
4. While registration requirements vary by state, it is important to note that familial offenders are not always included on the registry. The rationale behind this omission is that identification of a sexual offender, his/her photo and address, and his/her crime on a sex offense registry could also theoretically identify the victim. Victim's rights groups want to avoid the potential harm this could cause to the victim. In New Jersey, for example, the exclusion of familial offenders from the registry was advocated for by the New Jersey Coalition Against Sexual Assault. In this instance, a father described when his daughter's friends found a registry notification at school identifying her as a victim of familial sexual assault:

   > My daughters went to school and had a situation where there was a newspaper that was on the table and some of the kids came back up to my oldest daughter and basically started teasing her, saying, "You know, I heard that your daddy played sex with you." The impact of that goes beyond measure.
   > *(Zevitz & Farkas, 2000: 384)*

   While identification of the victim in such a manner is certainly harmful, to exclude familial offenders from the registry ultimately renders the registry virtually useless as familial and acquaintance offenders constitute the majority of sexual offenders. The message becomes that stranger-danger is the most devastating form of offending in terms of consequences.
5. Court decisions have not stopped some states from suggesting further legislation regarding social media. On December 22, 2019, New York's Governor Cuomo

28 Legislation and Sexual Offenders

proposed the 2020 State of the State which included legislation to prevent SOs from using dating apps, video games, and social media. The Governor said:

> Protecting New York's children is our top priority and we cannot let technological advances become entryways that allow dangerous online predators to identify and prey on new victims. Our laws must keep pace with the world around us and with this measure we will help safeguard those using these web sites and apps, and stop those who seek to harm and exploit our children once and for all.
>
> *("Governor Cuomo Unveils 11th Proposal of 2020 State of the State: Legislation to Prevent Sexual Predators from Using Social Media, Dating Apps and Video Games to Exploit Children" 2019: online)*

Currently, SOs are required to provide email addresses upon registration. The proposed legislation would require sex offenders to disclose screen names for all social media accounts and dating or gaming apps. This information would be sent to providers for review and potentially released publicly, depending on the provider's policy. It will also be a criminal offense for an SO to misrepresent himself online.

6. States with current SVP statutes are Arizona, California, Florida, Illinois, Iowa, Kansas, Massachusetts, Minnesota, Missouri, Nebraska, New Hampshire, New Jersey, New York, North Dakota, Pennsylvania, South Carolina, Texas, Virginia, Washington, and Wisconsin.

7. California, Florida, Louisiana, Georgia, Montana, Oregon and Wisconsin.

References

Benedict, Helen. (1992). *Virgin or vamp: How the press covers sex crimes*. New York, NY: Oxford University Press.

Best, Joel. (1990). *Threatened children: Rhetoric and concern about child-victims*. Chicago, IL: The University of Chicago Press.

Bevacqua, M. (2000). *Rape on the public agenda: Feminism and the politics of sexual assault*. Boston: Northeastern University Press.

Blagden, N., Winder, B., & Hames, C. (2016). "They treat us like human beings": Experiencing a therapeutic sex offender's prison. *International Journal of Offender Therapy and Comparative Criminology*, 60, 371–396.

Burick, Lawrence T. (1968). An analysis of the Illinois Sexually Dangerous Persons Act. *The Journal of Criminal Law, Criminology, and Political Science*, 59(2), 254–266.

California Welfare and Institute Code of 1955, §5501

Carringella-MacDonald, S. (1998). The relative visibility of rape cases in national popular magazines. *Violence Against Women*, 4(1), 62–80.

Chaffin, Mark, Levenson, Jill, Letourneau, Elizabeth, & Stern, Paul. (2009). How safe are trick-or-treaters? An analysis of child sex crime rates on Halloween. *Sexual Abuse: A Journal of Research and Treatment*, 21(3), 363–374.

Cohen, S. (1972). *Folk devils and moral panics: The creation of the mods and rockers*. London: MacGibbon and Kee.

Cole, Simon A. (2000). From the sexual psychopath statute to "Megan's Law": Psychiatric knowledge in the diagnosis, treatment, and adjudication of sex criminals in New Jersey, 1949–1999. *Journal of the History of Medicine*, 55, 292–314.

Cooper, Brad, & Rizzo, Tony. (September 14, 2013). Sex offender treatment programs are under scrutiny. *Kansas City Star*. Retrieved from www.kansascity.com

Cornwell, John Kip. (2003). Sex offenders and the Supreme Court: The significance and limits of *Kansas* v. *Hendricks*. In Bruce J. Winick & John Q. LaFond (Eds.), *Protecting society from sexually dangerous offenders: Law, justice, and therapy* (pp. 197–210). Washington, DC: American Psychological Association.

Corrigan, Rose. (2006). Making meaning of Megan's Law. *Law & Social Inquiry*, 31(2), 267–312.

deVogue, Ariane, & Diaz, Daniella. (June 20, 2017). Supreme Court Strikes Down Law Banning Use of Facebook by Registered Sex Offenders. *CNN*. Retrieved from www.cnn.com

DiBennardo, Rebecca A. (2018). Ideal victims and monstrous offenders: How the news media represent sexual predators. *SOCIUS: Sociological Research for a Dynamic World*, 4, 1–20.

Douard, John. (2007). Loathing the sinner, medicalizing the sin: Why sexually violent predator statutes are unjust, *International Journal of Law & Psychiatry 36*, 43–44.

Dowler, Kenneth. (2006). Sex, lies, and videotape: The presentation of sex crime in local television news. *Journal of Criminal Justice*, 34, 383–392.

Ducat, Lauren, Thomas, Stuart, & Blood, Warwick. (2009). Sensationalising sex offenders and sexual recidivism: Impact of the Serious Sex Offender Monitoring Act 2005 on media reportage. *Australian Psychologist*, 44(3), 156–165.

Gakhal, B. K., & Brown, S. J. (2011). A comparison of the general public's, forensic professionals' and students' attitudes towards female sex offenders. *Journal of Sexual Aggression*, 17, 105–116.

Galliher, John F., & Tyree, Cheryl. (1985). Edwin Sutherland's research on the origins of sexual psychopath laws: An early case study of the medicalization of deviance. *Social Problems*, 33(2), 100–113.

Gash, Alison, & Harding, Ryan. (2018). #MeToo? Legal discourse and everyday responses to sexual violence. *Laws*, 7(2). doi:10.3390/laws7020021

Governor Cuomo Unveils 11th Proposal of 2020 State of the State: Legislation to Prevent Sexual Predators from Using Social Media, Dating Apps and Video Games to Exploit Children. (December 22, 2019). *Governor's Press Office*. Retrieved from www.governor.ny.gov/news/

Grady v. North Carolina, 575 U.S. (2015)

Greer, Chris. (2012). *Sex crime and the media: Sex offending and the press in a divided society*. Portland, OR: Willan.

Group for the Advancement of Psychiatry. (1977). *Psychiatry and sex psychopath legislation: The 30s to the 80s*. New York, NY: Group for the Advancement of Psychiatry.

Harper, C. A. (2012). In pursuit of the beast: Undergraduate attitudes towards sex offenders and implications for society, rehabilitation, and British psychology education. Internet Journal of Criminology. Retrieved from www.internetjournalofcriminology.com

Higgins, Caitriona & Ireland, Carol. (2009). Attitudes towards male and female sex offenders: A comparison of forensic staff, prison officers and the general public in Northern Ireland. *The British Journal of Forensic Practice*, 11(1), 14–19.

Hogue, T.E. (1993). Attitudes towards prisoners and sex offenders. In N. C. Clark & G. Stephenson (Eds.). *DCLP occasional papers: Sexual offenders* (pp. 27–32). Leicester, UK: British Psychological Society.

Hogue, Todd E., & Harper, Craig A. (2019). Development of a 21-item short form of the attitudes to sexual offenders (ATS) scale. *Law and Human Behavior*, 43(1), 117–130.

Hogue, T. E., & Peebles, J. (1997). The influence of remorse, intent and attitudes toward sex offenders on judgments of a rapist. *Psychology, Crime & Law*, 3, 249–259.

Human Rights Watch. (2007). *No easy answers: Sex offender laws in the U.S.* New York, NY: Human Rights Watch.

30 Legislation and Sexual Offenders

International Association of Chiefs of Police. (2008). Tracking sex offenders with electronic monitoring technology: Implications and practical uses for law enforcement. Alexandria, VA: International Association of Chiefs of Police. Retrieved from www.bja.gov/Publications/iacpsexoffenderelecmonitoring.pdf

Janus, Eric S. (2006). *Failure to protect: America's sexual predator laws and the rise of the preventive state*. Ithaca, NY: Cornell University Press.

Jenkins, Philip. (1998). *Moral panic: Changing concepts of the child molester in modern America*. New Haven, CT: Yale University Press.

Kansas Rejects Buffer Zones. (February 12, 2007). *The Kansas*. Retrieved from www.thekansan.com

Kansas v. Hendricks, 521 U.S. 346 (1997)

Kansas v. Crane, 534 U.S. 407 (2002)

Karsten, Jack, & West, Darrell M. (September 21, 2017). Decades later, electronic monitoring of offenders is still prone to failure. *Brookings*. Retrieved from www.brookings.edu

Kitzinger, Jenny. (2004). *Framing abuse: Media influence and public understanding of sexual violence against children*. Ann Arbor, MI: Pluto.

Krinsky, Charles. (2016). *The Ashgate research companion to moral panics*. New York: Routledge.

Lacoursiere, Roy B. (2003). Evaluating offenders under a sexually violent predator law; The practical practice. In Bruce J. Winick & John Q. LaFond (Eds.), *Protecting society from sexually dangerous offenders: Law, justice, and therapy* (pp. 75–97). Washington, DC: American Psychological Association.

La Fond, John Q. (2000). The future of involuntary civil commitment in the U.S.A. after *Kansas v. Hendricks. Behavioral Sciences and the Law*, 18, 153–167.

Lancaster, Roger N. (2011). *Sex panic and the punitive state*. Berkeley: University of California Press.

Leon, Chrysanthi S. (2011). *Sex fiends, perverts, and pedophiles: Understanding sex crime policy in America*. New York: NYU Press.

Lieb, R., Quinsey, V., & Berliner, L. (1998). Sexual predators and social policy. *Crime and Justice*, 23, 2–49.

Lucken, K., & Latina, J. (2002). Sex offender civil commitment laws: Medicalizing deviant sexual behavior. *Barry Law Review*, 15, 1–19.

Moriearty, Perry L. (2010). Framing justice: Media, bias, and legal decisionmaking. *Maryland Law Review*, 69(4), 849–909.

No Internet for Some Sex Offenders in New Jersey. (December 27, 2007). *CNN*. Retrieved from www.cnn.com

Oklahoma Lawmaker Pushes Bill for "Chemical Castration" of Sex Offenders. (February 3, 2018). *Guardian*. Retrieved from www.theguardian.com

Pallone, Nathaniel J. (2003). Without plea-bargaining, Megan Kanka would be alive today. *Criminology & Public Policy*, 3(1), 83–96.

P.L. 1998, c.71 (S895 SCS)

Proeve, Michael J., & Howells, Kevin. (2006). Effects of remorse and shame and criminal justice experience on judgements about a sex offender. *Psychology, Crime, & Law*, 12(2), 145–161.

Reyes, Jessica Masuli. (March 8, 2017). Delaware's sex offender GPS monitoring upheld. *Delaware Online*. Retrieved from www.delawareonline.com

Russell, Josh. (May 31, 2018). Sex Offender with Undisclosed Facebook Wins Appeal. *Courthouse News Service*. Retrieved from www.courthousenews.com

Schultz, Pamela D. (2011). A rhetoric of retribution and redemption: Burke's terms for order in the drama of child sexual abuse. *International Journal of Law and Psychiatry*, 34, 168–176.

Serisier, Tanya. (2017). Sex crimes and the media. *Oxford Research Encyclopedia of Criminology*. doi: 10.1093/acrefore/9780190264079.013.118

Skinner v. Oklahoma, 316 U.S. 535 (1942)

Sullivan, S. P. (March 22, 2017). N.J. Supreme Court Tosses "Total" Internet Ban for Sex Offender. *NJ.com*. Retrieved from www.nj.com

Sutherland, Edwin. (1950). The diffusion of sexual psychopath laws. *The American Journal of Sociology*, 56(2), 142–148.

Thakker, Jo, & Durrant, Russil. (2006). News coverage of sexual offending in New Zealand, 2003. *New Zealand Journal of Psychology*, 35(1), 28–35.

The People of the State of Illinois v. *Conrad Allen Morger*, IL 123643 (2019)

The Silence Breakers. (December 18, 2017). *Time*. http://time.com/time-person-of-the-year-2017-silence-breakers/

The Unknown Sex Fiend. (February 13, 1950). *Time*. http://content.time.com/time/magazine/0,9263,7601500213,00.html

Van Kesteren, J. (2009). Public attitudes and sentencing policies across the world. *European Journal of Criminal Policy Research*, 15, 25–46.

Vetterkind, Riley. (March 4, 2018). Wisconsin doubles GPS monitoring despite five years of malfunctions, unnecessary jailings. *Wisconsin Watch*. Retrieved from www.wisconsinwatch.org

Wagner, Lindsay A. (2009). Sex offender residency restrictions: How common sense places children at risk. *Drexel Law Review*, 1(1), 175–209.

Washington State Institute for Public Policy (WSIPP). (2007). *Comparison of state laws authorizing involuntary commitment of sexually violent predators: 2006 update, revised* (No. 05–03–1101). Olympia, WA: Washington State Institute for Public Policy.

Wertham, Frederic. (1938). Psychiatry and the prevention of sex crimes. *Journal of Criminal Law and Criminology*, 28(6), 847–853.

Wolf, Richard. (June 19, 2017). Supreme Court Say Sex Offenders Can Access Social Media. *USA Today*. Retrieved from www.usatoday.com

Zevitz, Richard G., & Farkas, Mary Ann. (2000). Sex offender community notification: Managing high risk criminals or exacting further vengeance? *Behavioural Sciences and the Law*, 18, 375–391.

Zgoba, Kristen M. (2004). Spin doctors and moral crusaders: The moral panic behind child safety legislation. *Criminal Justice Studies*, 17(4), 385–404.

Zonana, Howard V., Bonnie, Richard J., & Hoge, Steven K. (2003). In the wake of *Hendricks:* The treatment and restraint of sexually dangerous offenders viewed from the perspective of American psychiatry. In Bruce J. Winick & John Q. LaFond (Eds.), *Protecting society from sexually dangerous offenders: Law, justice, and therapy* (pp. 131–145). Washington, DC: American Psychological Association.

2

TIME FOR A REALITY CHECK

As the public's fear increases alongside increasingly strict legislation targeting sexual offenders, it begs the question: what do we know statistically about sexual offending? Is there an epidemic of offenses? Are offenders becoming more predatory and violent in their attacks? A review of studies on sexual offending and offenses will give a more accurate picture of the "typical" sexual offender and victim, as well as the type of offenses committed most often. While there are many factors that contribute to under-reporting, these statistical studies viewed in combination will provide a reasonable overview of the dynamics of sexual offenses and sexual offenders.

A critical viewing of statistics is important as most of the general public simply accepts at face-value statistics presented to them by the media (Best, 2001). We are led to believe that statistics are objective facts. Regarding sex offending, this means the public buys into the moral panic and the epidemic of sexual offending presented in news articles, accepting this as truth. Statistics, however, are products of our social arrangements (Best, 2001). Specific statistics are brought to our attention for explicit purposes.

> People create statistics: they choose what to count, how to go about counting, which of the resulting numbers they share with others, and which words they use to describe and interpret those figures. Numbers do not exist independent of people; understanding numbers requires knowing who counted what, why they bothered counting, and how they went about it.
>
> *(Best, 2001: xi–xiii)*

When viewing or hearing a statistic about a social issue, it is important to evaluate three critical questions: Who was the creator of the statistic and how might their personal beliefs or professional affiliations have influenced the statistic? Why was the statistic created, and for what purpose will it be used? How was the statistic created; using what methodological design (Best 2001)? When using statistics as a basis for the consideration of policies or legislation, it is paramount that evaluation of the numbers are critical and the answers to these three questions provide a solid foundation on which to critically evaluate the usefulness of statistics (Best, 2001).

How Many Sex Offenders Are There?

Throughout history, the definition of a sexual offense has changed dramatically. Even now, there is much inconsistency between jurisdictions as to which behaviors are considered sexual offenses. For example, the age of consent for sex varies by state, between 16 and 18. As such, a state with a higher statutory age of consent would likely have a higher rate of violations. Approximately half of states have close-in-age-exemptions, which permits sex between two individuals who are both under the age of consent (also termed *Romeo & Juliet* laws). There are 13 states[1] in which public urination (especially close to a school or government building) could brand you a sex offender. Solicitation of a prostitute is considered a sex offense in a handful of states. And states are struggling with how to handle minors taking nude selfies and distributing them: should this be legally considered distribution of child pornography? Until recently, consensual sodomy was considered a sexual offense in many states. Inconsistencies in legislation have a direct impact on the measurement of sexual offenses by state, and comparisons between regions. Legally, what most jurisdictions do agree on is that a sexual offense requires a lack of consent. Lack of consent involves: (a) threats or force; (b) a statement indicating one's desire not to participate; or (c) a person who cannot consent as a result of age, mental or physical capacity, or because they are a ward of the state.

Sexual offenses are counted in two main ways. Regarding sexual offenses and offenders, the first source of knowledge comes from arrest and conviction by law enforcement. The Uniform Crime Report (UCR) in the United States counts crimes that participating agencies report to law enforcement. The UCR was updated in 1982 with the National Incident Based Reporting System (NIBRS). One drawback of NIBRS is that only the most serious offense committed in a multi-incident situation is recorded. For example, if a female is robbed, sexually assaulted, and murdered, the offense will be recorded as a murder. No robbery or sexual assault will be recorded for that victim. While only a small number of murders may also involve the victim being robbed and sexually assaulted, the method of counting offenses used in NIBRS will necessarily result in under-counting some offenses. Further, NIBRS does not include statutory sexual offenses. That said, the biggest drawback of NIBRS is that it only includes offenses reported to law enforcement. In the case of sexual offenses, there are various reasons that an individual would choose not to report to law enforcement.

34 Legislation and Sexual Offenders

To compensate for the methodological flaws of NIBRS, the second significant way in which to count sexual offenses is the use of victimization surveys. The National Crime Victimization Survey (NCVS) is conducted annually using a randomly selected population to help assess the prevalence of sexual offenses not reported to law enforcement. Victimization studies involve the self-reporting of crimes that have impacted participants during the previous 12 months. One problem with victimization surveys is participant error in the recollection of events, which may result in over-reporting of a crime. Victimization surveys ask about types of victimizations, as well as demographic information about the participant and the alleged perpetrator. These surveys suggest sexual offenses and other crimes are significantly under-reported to the authorities.

NIBRS and NCVS are the main sources of information about sexual offenses and offenders. To supplement these government data sources are studies independently conducted by researchers on the dynamics of sexual offending, impacts of treatment, residency restrictions, community integration of offenders, and other aspects of sexual offending. Finally, there are researchers who study the registered sex offender population. While there has been minimal systematic analysis of the sex offender registries and the diversity of the sex offender population, there have been a handful of state-specific studies which provide information (Adkins, Huff, & Stageberg, 2000; Freeman & Sandler, 2010; Harris, Lobanov-Rostovsky, & Levenson, 2010; Levenson, Letourneau, Armstrong, & Zgoba, 2010).

How do we know how many sex offenders there are in the United States? One method is the publicly available national registry, drawn from a phone survey that is conducted twice per year by the National Center for Missing and Exploited Children (NCMEC). This provides a jurisdictional distribution of offenders by state, however, does not provide any information regarding demographics, offense type, where the offender is residing, etc. As of December 2018, NCMEC (2018) reported a total of 917,771 registered sex offenders in the United States and its territories. This amounts to an average of 279 per 100,000 in the population. Table 2.1 provides a breakdown of registered sex offenders in the United States by state as of December 2018.

There are definite limitations to NCMEC reporting. One limitation is the aggregate nature of the data which advances the media's homogenized view of the sex offender as a repetitive and dangerous criminal. Add to that the limitation that 38 of the 57 reporting jurisdictions include in their counts some variation of registered offenders who are incarcerated, deported, or residing in another state (Harris, Levenson, & Ackerman, 2014). The registry is presumably:

> intended to facilitate tracking and monitoring of sex offenders within the community. As such, it is vital to distinguish between RSOs who are living in the community within a given jurisdiction and those who are not. Not only are such distinctions essential for planning, management, and resource allocation decisions, but the inclusion of these groups has

Time for a Reality Check **35**

TABLE 2.1 Registered Sex Offenders in the United States by State as of December 2018

State	Number of Registered Sex Offenders	Per 100,000 Population
Alabama	15,591	320
Alaska	2,426	328
Arizona	13,939	199
Arkansas	16,090	536
California	106,916	270
Colorado	19,363	345
Connecticut	5,461	152
Delaware	4,724	491
Florida	74,629	356
Georgia	31,492	302
Hawaii	3,049	214
Idaho	4,784	279
Illinois	34,010	266
Indiana	9,991	150
Iowa	5,914	188
Kansas	10,532	362
Kentucky	8,718	196
Louisiana	9,639	206
Maine	2,751	206
Maryland	7,580	125
Massachusetts	11,271	164
Michigan	43,859	440
Minnesota	18,434	331
Mississippi	10,624	356
Missouri	16,224	265
Montana	2,738	261
Nebraska	5,714	298
Nevada	6,753	225
New Hampshire	2,874	214
New Jersey	16,446	183
New Mexico	3,796	182
New York	49,114	247
North Carolina	23,227	226
North Dakota	1,637	217
Ohio	18,394	158
Oklahoma	6,917	176
Oregon	28,497	688
Pennsylvania	20,970	164
Rhode Island	3,312	313
South Carolina	16,796	334
South Dakota	3,697	425
Tennessee	24,133	359
Texas	99,511	352

Continued

36 Legislation and Sexual Offenders

TABLE 2.1 continued

State	Number of Registered Sex Offenders	Per 100,000 Population
Utah	8,186	264
Vermont	1,326	213
Virginia	23,696	280
Washington	22,193	300
West Virginia	5,930	327
Wisconsin	25,204	435
Wyoming	2,404	414
Total	917,771[1]	279

Source: NCMEC 2018.

Note

1. Total includes the territories: Northern Mariana Islands (98), St. Thomas and St. John (59), St. Croix (58), American Samoa (405), Puerto Rico (3,393), and Guam (1,115).

the net effect of inflating the number of RSOs reported as living among us. The inclusion of out-of-state registrants in the official NCMEC statistics is particularly problematic, in that it raises a fundamental question of whether and to what extent individual RSOs are being counted more than once, thus inflating the overall national estimate.

(Harris et al., 2014: 8)

A 2014 study revealed that as many as 8 percent of registered sex offenders live out of state and could therefore theoretically be counted twice on registries, thus increasing the count of sex offenders in the NCMEC data (Harris et al., 2014).

Prevalence of Sexual Offending

In data collected beginning in 1992, the number of reported sex offenses in the United States have declined by 60 percent (Finkelhor & Jones, 2012). We will overview the prevalence of child sexual abuse, adult sexual abuse, college victimization, and internet sexual offenses.

Child Sexual Abuse

There is a distinction between non-contact sexual abuse and contact sexual abuse. Non-contact sexual abuse includes actions such as inappropriate sexual comments, voyeurism, exhibitionism, acts of sexual harassment, as well as sexual acts that occur either over the telephone or the internet. Contact sexual abuse includes actions such as touching or penetration (either completed or attempted), or involvement of a minor in pornography or prostitution. Incest is either contact or non-contact sexual abuse of a child by a blood or marriage related adult. The most frequently occurring incestuous relationship is between father and daughter; mother-child incest is rarely reported to authorities.

Though the media uses the term "pedophile" synonymously with "child molester," this is technically incorrect. Pedophilia is a sexual interest in children who have not yet reached puberty. Much more common is hebephilia, an offender who is sexually interested in those who have reached puberty. While society outwardly speaks of pedophiles as mentally deranged monsters, research has found that a reasonably high percentage of men, in at least one study, have reported an attraction to children. Studying male undergraduates, researchers found that 21 percent of participants admitted a sexual attraction to children, 9 percent admitted to having sexual fantasies that involved children, 5 percent admitted to masturbating to these sexual fantasies, and 7 percent indicated they would consider engaging in sexual activity with a child if there was no fear of apprehension and punishment (Briere, 1989).

Statistics reveal that while most victims are female, regardless of the sex of the victims, most victims are abused by either adult men or male adolescents who are known to them (relatives, friends of the family, or authority figures) (NIJ, 2003). The National Child Abuse and Neglect Data System is a national data collection and analysis program that has collected data regarding the prevalence of child abuse since 1991. The data is collected annually from child protective services agencies in all states. In the 2016 Child Maltreatment report, there were 3,472,000 cases investigated, 8.5 percent of which were child sexual abuse cases (Administration on Children, Youth, and Families (ACYF), 2016). The most recent Bureau of Justice Statistics report indicates that 34 percent of sexual assaults reported to law enforcement involved a victim under the age of 12 (Bureau of Justice Statistics (BJS), 2000). When examining all sexual assault cases reported, young people accounted for 84 percent of forcible fondling reports, 79 percent of forcible sodomy reports, and 75 percent of reports of sexual assault involving an object (BJS, 2000). Of all sexual assault cases reported to law enforcement, victims were overwhelmingly female: 69 percent of victims under the age of six were female; 73 percent of victims under the age of 12; and 82 percent of victims under the age of 18 (BJS, 2000). Victims under the age of six were most likely to be victimized by a family member (97 percent) (Snyder, 2000).

Male victims under the age of 18 comprised 15 percent of those sexually assaulted with an object, 20 percent of those victimized by forcible fondling, and 59 percent victimized by forcible sodomy (BJS, 2000). National Incident Based Reporting System data reveals that a male's risk of victimization is greatest at age four, and a female's risk of victimization is greatest at age 14 (BJS, 2000). Furthermore, individuals who are sexually assaulted prior to the age of 18 are at an increased risk of being sexually assaulted as an adult, and the mental health consequences for experiencing sexual abuse are significant (BJS, 2000; MacMillan,

38 Legislation and Sexual Offenders

Fleming, Streiner, Lin, Boyle, Jamieson, Duku, Walsh, Wong, & Beardslee, 2001; Nelson, Heath, Madden, Cooper, Dinwiddie, Bucholz, Glowinski, McLaughlin, Dunne, Statham, & Martin, 2002). Abuse of a child sexually has been linked to substance use, hypersexuality, suicidality, anxiety, post-traumatic stress disorder, as well as depression (Adams, Mrug, & Knight, 2018; Gray & Rarick, 2018). Boys are at an increased risk of substance use, and girls are at an increased risk of suicidality and symptoms of depression (Gray & Rarick, 2018). Additionally, boys are at an increased risk of perpetrating child sexual abuse as an adult if they experienced frequent, serious sexual abuse at the hand of someone they shared a relationship of dependency, and this abuse began when they were 12 years of age or older (Plummer & Cossins, 2018)

Adult Sexual Abuse

Adult sexual offenses include sexual assault or rape by a stranger, acquaintance/date, a spouse, or rape that occurs in jail/prison. While laws vary from state-to-state regarding the definition of sexual assault, it generally refers to sexual behaviors that occur without consent of the victim, such as grabbing or fondling (Sinozich, & Langton, 2014). Rape definitions also vary by state, but generally involve the use or threat of force to penetrate an individual without their consent, vaginally, anally, or orally (Sinozich, & Langton, 2014).

National Crime Victimization Survey (NCVS) data from 2017 revealed 393,980 rape or sexual assaults involving a victim 12 years of age or older. This is 1.4 per 1,000 individuals in the population (BJS, 2018a). This is an increase from the 2016 rate of 1.1 per 1,000 individuals, but a decrease from the 2015 rate of 1.6 per 1,000 individuals. NCVS data from 2018 revealed 734,630 rape or sexual assaults involving a victim 12 years of age or older which is a significant increase from 2017. This is 2.7 per 1,000 individuals in the population (BJS, 2019). Reports of rape and sexual assault to law enforcement increased from 23 percent in 2016 to 40 percent in 2017 (BJS, 2018a), but fell again in 2019 to approximately 25 percent (BJS, 2019).

Because less than half of rapes and sexual assaults are believed to be reported, statistics may reveal a skewed picture of the typical victim. Studies reveal that sexual assault crosses all race and class lines. The most recent government data for which there was specific demographic details indicated that an individual's risk of rape/sexual assault or attempted rape/sexual assault decreased dramatically at the age of 25, was much higher for those that were single, and was higher among lower socio-economic groups (BJS, 2008). Some of the basic demographic data collection by governmental agencies is lacking and has not been replicated in many years. For example, the Bureau of Justice Studies put out an illustrative report on sexual violence spanning the years 1994 to 2010, however, has not replicated this study since. Findings revealed that women 34 years of age or younger, residing in rural areas or low-income households had the highest rates of sexual violence (BJS, 2013). Most sexual assaults (90 percent) involved one offender, and overwhelmingly (78 percent) the offender was known to the woman (whether a former partner, family member, or friend) (BJS, 2013). Differences in NIBRS and NCVS data remind us that the offenses most likely to be reported to law enforcement (stranger-inflicted offenses), are not the sexual offenses most likely to occur (acquaintance/family member-inflicted offenses).

Between 2002 and 2011 among individuals 12 and older, rape or sexual assault accounted for about 9 percent of victimizations among females and 1 percent among males (Catalano, 2013). Among female rape victims, just over half (54 percent) were younger than age 18 at the time of victimization, 32 percent were between ages 12 and 17, and just over 12 percent were younger than age 12 (Thoennes & Tjaden, 2000). Some studies revealed significant differences by sexual orientation. The National Intimate Partner and Sexual Violence Survey, a national, random, telephone survey completed in 2010 revealed that about 13 percent of lesbian women, 46 percent of bisexual women, and just under 18 percent of heterosexual women reported being raped at some point in their life (Walters, Chen, & Breiding, 2013). In this study, rates of rape for gay and bisexual men were too small to measure, and rates for heterosexual men were just under 1 percent over their lifetime (Walters et al., 2013). Data in the 2015 survey had not yet been separated by sexual orientation at the time of this publication; however, lifetime rates of rape had dropped overall for women to 13.5 percent (Smith, Zhang, Basile, Merrick, Wang, Kresnow, & Chen, 2018).

"Rape myths" or misconceptions surrounding sexual assault victims abound. Believed by both men and women, rape myths influence both reporting of sexual assault and responses by the criminal justice system. Examples of rape myths include: "no means yes," "subconsciously women want to be raped," "if she wants to, a woman can defend herself against a rapist," and "many women lie about being raped." Each rape myth brings shame to the victims and discourages other women from reporting assaults. In addition to rape myths, there are other reasons a woman may not report a sexual offense. An individual may experience embarrassment and not want others to know of the situation. An individual may not recognize that she was legally sexually assaulted. An individual may not want to make an allegation against someone they know or someone who is in a position of power over them. An individual may not believe there is "proof" of a sexual assault and therefore be hesitant to make a police report. An individual may be hesitant of a police investigation due to potential retribution by the accused or the stigma of being labeled a rape victim. In a nine-campus study of college students, the most frequently cited reasons for not reporting rape and sexual assault to either law enforcement or college personnel were that the victim did not believe they needed assistance, did not believe the incident was serious enough to warrant reporting, or the victim did not want any action taken (Krebs, Lindquist, Berzofsky, Shook-Sa, & Peterson, 2016). For these reasons, or a variety of other personal reasons, rape and sexual assault remain under-reported.

40 Legislation and Sexual Offenders

College Victimization

Using National Crime Victimization Data between 1995 and 2013, females ages 18 to 24 experienced the highest rates of rape and sexual victimization. Men had a 1.4 per 1,000 rate of sexual victimization among students and 0.3 per 1,000 rate of sexual victimization for nonstudents in this study. Female nonstudents were sexually assaulted at a rate of 7.6 per 1,000 and students at a rate of 6.1 per 1,000 (Sinozich & Langton, 2014). Regardless of student status, about 80 percent of women knew their offender. A mere 20 percent of student victimizations were reported to the police, compared to 32 percent of nonstudent victimizations (Sinozich & Langton, 2014).

In a study of nine colleges, researchers found a 10 percent prevalence rate for completed sexual assault among undergraduate females during the 2014 to 2015 academic year, just over 5 percent for sexual battery, and a 4 percent completed rape rate (Krebs et al., 2016). The prevalence of all offenses was higher for younger women, did not vary by race/ethnicity, and was higher for non-heterosexual women (Krebs et al., 2016). Overwhelmingly, there was one offender involved, and he was known to the victim prior to the offense. Over half of offenses were reported to a friend or family member; however, only 4 percent of sexual battery offenses and 12 percent of rape incidents were reported to authorities (either law enforcement or school personnel) (Krebs et al., 2016).

Internet Sexual Offenses

Internet sexual offenses are a burgeoning area of offending and one that is difficult to estimate the scope of statistically. It is widely under-reported and challenging for law enforcement (and even parents) to detect. The internet is used for a variety of sexual purposes, such as pornography (both adult and child), the facilitation of prostitution, as well as sites that cater to a myriad of paraphilias with the expressed goal of linking those with similar sexual preferences. The internet also provides chat rooms, where potential sexual offenders and victims can meet.

Regarding child pornography offenders, studies that conduct meta-analyses reveal distinct characteristics between online child pornography-only offenders, contact sexual offenders, and mixed offenders (with both child pornography and contact sex offenses). Based on 30 unique samples of offenders (ranging from 98 offenders to just over 2,700 offenders), research found important differences among groups. Contact sex offenders were more likely to have access to youth, than those with online-only offenses. Conversely, online offenders had greater access to the internet than contact offenders. That said, differences were not strictly the result of differential opportunities (Babchishin, Hanson, & VanZuylen, 2015). Contact offenders and mixed offenders had higher anti-sociality scores compared to online child pornography offenders. Online offenders were more likely to have psychological barriers to sexual offending (that is, they had more empathy for the victim), and they had high scores on sexual deviancy. Contact offenders had greater emotional identification with children and higher cognitive distortions. Findings of this meta-analysis suggested that mixed offenders were a particularly high-risk group, with greater paraphilic interests and increased access to children (Babchishin et al., 2015).

The public assumes that most child pornography offenders also engage in contact sexual offenses. One explanation for this expectation is the heightened sexual interest in children among child pornography offenders (Babchishin, Hanson, & Hermann, 2011). That said, the rate of contact offending is quite low among this population. One of eight child pornography offenders engaged in an officially recorded contact sexual offense against a child, and approximately half of child pornography offenders self-reported committing a contact sex offense (Seto, Hanson, & Babchishin 2011).

In an examination of three national cross-sectional telephone surveys of minor internet users, the prevalence of online sexual solicitation was found to be 2 percent among those ages 10, 11, and 12; 8 percent among those aged 13, 14 and 15; and 14 percent among those ages 16 and 17 (Jones, Mitchell, & Finkelhor, 2012). Research revealed a decline in unwanted sexual solicitation over the internet between 2000 and 2010, from 19 percent to 9 percent. In a small percentage of cases (approximately 3 percent), online solicitations are followed by an offline solicitation or attempt at a solicitation (Jones et al., 2012).

In a more recent study of offender's behavior in Germany, Sweden, and Finland, 4.5 percent of just over 2800 individuals surveyed admitted to solicitation of adolescents and 1 percent admitted to solicitation of children. Most of this solicitation occurred on pedophilia-related websites (49.1 of adolescent solicitation and 79.2 percent of child solicitation) (Schulz, Bergen, Schuhmann, Hoyer, & Santtila, 2016). Over half of those soliciting adolescents were aged 22 or younger. Almost half of the time the solicitation involved a sexual outcome, whether it be sending of sexual pictures, cybersex, or sexual activity offline. The minors' age did not affect the odds of sexual outcomes. This study found a substantial proportion of perpetrators were female: 30 percent of those soliciting adolescents and 17 percent of those soliciting children (Schulz et al., 2016).

Increasingly the world has become a detached, online society, and the anonymity of cyberspace provides an atmosphere for sexual exploration and experimentation that may lead to manipulation or coercion. Internet sexual offenses are a bourgeoning area for law enforcement. Deterrent strategies continually evolve and new laws forge ahead to prevent offenders from using the internet for sexually exploitive purposes.

Offender Profiles

Just as the "typical victim" may not be the one described by officially reported statistics like the National Incident Based Reporting System (NIBRS), we must

42 Legislation and Sexual Offenders

be cautious in suggesting that the "typical offender" is the one reported to the authorities or the one imprisoned or listed on the registry. Research shows that the type of offense most likely to be reported is that committed by a stranger and involving violence. Offenders imprisoned for sexual offenses are those that committed a crime against a stranger and/or a crime involving a higher level of violence than is "typical" of the offenses that occur most often. Therefore, we must not generalize from this data about the "typical" sexual offender who has not been caught, reported, or prosecuted.

Most studies show the sexual offender who has been brought to the attention of the authorities is overwhelmingly male (98+ percent), about 65 percent of the time is white (for forcible rape; in the case of other sexual offenses the offender is white 70 percent of the time) (UCR, 2018). Of the total 10,554,985 arrests in 2018, 23,436 were for forcible rape,[2] and 48,525 were for other sexual offenses (not including prostitution) (UCR, 2018). In 2017, an arrest was made in 34.5 percent of rape cases (UCR, 2018).

Most research suggests that offenders are male and predominantly white (Adkins et al., 2000; Freeman & Sandler, 2010; Harris et al., 2010; Levenson et al., 2010). One large study of 435,016 registered sex offenders, tried to contribute an understanding of demographics, offender status variables, as well as offense characteristics. As with other studies, the research found most offenders were white (upwards of two-thirds in this study), and this research found a mean age of almost 45 (Ackerman, Harris, Levenson, & Zgoba, 2011). Where a specific offense was indicated, 55 percent of offenders had committed an offense against a child. About 28 percent of offenders listed on the registry were institutionalized (Ackerman et al. 2011). Given that the sex offense registry was designed to alert the public to sex offenders in their neighborhood, this finding was somewhat curious.

Juvenile Sexual Offenders

Research on juvenile sexual offenders remains in its early stages, though it really accelerated in the early 1980s. There are many contradictory findings, with few large-scale studies regarding the characteristics of juvenile sex offenders, the patterns of juvenile offending, motivations, and proper treatment methods. Researchers and treatment practitioners still debate whether we are dealing with "children at risk" or "risky children." Are juvenile sexual offenders "risky children" destined to mature into the monstrous predators portrayed by the media? Or are juvenile sexual offenders "children at risk" who are acting out due to a series of social problems in their home environment and their community, such as domestic violence or substance abuse?

Research reveals that juveniles are just over one-third of those reported to police for committing sex offenses against a minor, with early adolescence the peak age for offenses against young children and offenses against teenagers increasing during mid-to-late teen years (Office of Juvenile Justice and Delinquency Prevention (OJJDP), 2009). Juveniles constitute approximately 25 percent of all sex offenders. Offenses are mainly committed by male offenders (93 percent) and victims are likely to be family members. Compared to adult offenders, offenses are more likely to involve episodes that are multiple victims and multiple-perpetrators (OJJDP, 2009).

While there are many studies discussing the factors that contribute to juvenile sex offending, research shows that most victims of sexual abuse do not perpetrate sexual abuse in adolescence or adulthood (Widom & Ames, 1994). Among juvenile sexual offenders, there is both a diversity of backgrounds and a diversity in motivation. While some offenders are motivated simply by sexual curiosity, other offenders are motivated by a desire to violate another individual and their offense is part of a larger pattern. Some behaviors occur in conjunction with mental health issues, other behaviors are compulsive, but perhaps most frequently, juvenile behavior is impulsive and the result of poor judgment (Becker, 1998; Center for Sex Offender Management (CSOM), 1999; Hunter, Figueredo, Malamuth, & Becker, 2003). Risk of reoffending is also variable, though follow-up studies of juvenile sex offenders indicate a sexual recidivism rate between 5 and 15 percent (OJJDP, 2009).

Despite not knowing a lot about the juvenile sex offender population, there are hundreds of specialized treatment and management programs geared to juvenile offenders across the country. Additionally, juveniles are forced into many of the same legislative rules as adult sexual offenders, such as registration and community notification. This means succumbing to the stigma of the "sexual offender" label for an act a young person committed at the age of 12 or 13. While select states permit a juvenile to petition to get off the sex offense registry when they are 18 years old, many more states require a juvenile to be on the registry for a minimum of 15 years.

Female Sexual Offenders

Overwhelmingly sexual offenders are male, so little is known about the female sexual offender. Regarding juveniles, female juvenile offenders constitute approximately 7 percent of the population (OJJDP, 2009). There are several distinguishing characteristics of the female juvenile offender: one-third are younger than 12 years old, more than one-third offend with another individual, 13 percent offend with an adult, and female juvenile offenders are more than twice as likely as a male juvenile offender to have multiple victims (23 percent versus 12 percent), as well as victims under the age of 11 (OJJDP, 2009).

When looking at the adult female sex offender population, perhaps the most widely known study was conducted in the 1980s. This research used the National Incidence Study on child abuse and integrated it with two other surveys: results revealed 20 percent of males and 5 percent of females experienced abuse by

44 Legislation and Sexual Offenders

a female offender (Finkelhor, 1984). Self-report studies in the 30 years since this research support the notion that female sex abuse is underestimated in official arrest and conviction data (Denov, 2004). Female-perpetrated sexual abuse could be under-reported because these events disproportionately involve a familial victim, which is the least reported type of sexual violence (Elliott, Eldridge, Ashfield, & Beech, 2010). Further, women's involvement in caretaking roles involves legitimate touching, which may bring confusion as to the appropriateness regarding types of touching. Indeed, some acts that are sexually abusive may be "dismissed" as part of routine childcare. Investigations into allegations of sexual abuse by women are three times as likely to be determined "unfounded" as allegations of male sexual abuse (Denov, 2004).

There exists the stereotype of "woman as caregiver" who would not intentionally harm a child. An alternative explanation is an adolescent male victim with an older woman. The authorities may be reluctant to define such an incident as abusive, instead viewing the situation as "sexual experimentation." Numerous encounters between adolescent boys and adult women are portrayed in films such as *The Graduate* (1967) and *American Pie* (1999).

> Society romanticises and minimizes the impact female molesters have on their young male victims. If a boy discloses abuse, he may not be believed. If he physically enjoyed the molestation, he does not perceive himself as a victim, despite the fact that he may be suffering from the effects of abuse. Many will suggest that he should have enjoyed the experience. If he did not enjoy aspects of the abuse, he may fear that he is homosexual. Either way the young male victim of the older female is placed in an untenable position.
>
> *(Mayer, 1992: 49–50)*

Because of the small number of female offenders studied, care needs to be taken in drawing generalizations.

Female sexual offenders comprise a small percentage of offenders: just over 2 percent of arrests for rape and approximately 10 percent of arrests for all other sex offenses (UCR, 2018). In a study of female registered sex offenders, records revealed that offenders were almost exclusively white, and females were the victim just over half of the time (55 percent), and almost all offenders (94 percent) were related to the victim (Vandiver & Walker, 2002). What research has been conducted in this area has found female offenders to be a diverse group, with variation in age, background characteristics, mental health history, and offense behavior (Marshall & Hall, 1995; Ward, Polaschek, & Beech, 2006). A common thread running through what research has been conducted on female sexual offenders is that they have experienced a history of sexual abuse (Fehrenbach & Monastersky, 1988; Lewis & Stanley, 2000; Travin, Cullen, & Protter, 1990). Another common thread is the presence of a co-offender who is typically male and is present in more than half of cases involving a female sexual offender (Grayston & DeLuca, 1999), though some research challenges this claim (Ferguson & Meehan, 2005).

Probably the largest summary of studies to date on female sex offenders involves the analysis of data from four federal agency surveys (the National Intimate Partner and Sexual Violence Survey, the National Crime Victimization Survey, incarcerated populations, and data from the Prison Rape Elimination Act) from 2008 through 2013 (Stemple, Flores, & Meyer, 2017). This research suggests the need to overcome stereotypes regarding female offenders and move past preconceived ideas of victimization. The complexity that accompanies disclosure of sexual assault seems to be magnified when the offender is female; an offender who society still perceives to be relatively harmless and sexually innocent. Even professionals sometimes remain ambivalent and dismissive as they learn to deal with this under-reported aspect of sexual offending.

Virtually all the research on sex offender recidivism examines the male population. Research on the female population reveals that female sex offenders have a significantly lower re-offense rate than male sex offenders. In a study of 380 female sex offenders, the average sexual recidivism rate was 1 percent, the violent recidivism rate was 6 percent, and the overall recidivism rate was 20 percent at a follow-up period of five years (Cortoni & Hanson, 2005). A meta-analysis involving 2,490 female sex offenders across ten studies determined an average sexual recidivism rate at a follow-up period of 6.5 years of approximately 3 percent (Cortoni, Hanson, & Coache, 2010).

Incarceration and Recidivism

From 2005–2010, 36 percent of sexual assaults/rapes were reported to the police. The most common law enforcement response was to take a report from the victim (85 percent of cases), question witnesses, and conduct a search for the offender (48 percent of cases) (BJS, 2013). In 19 percent of cases, the police also collected evidence. Between 2005 and 2010, approximately 12 percent of cases resulted in an arrest (BJS, 2013). Those imprisoned for rape/sexual assault represented 12.5 percent of the state prison population; a total of 161,900 prisoners. This was 2 percent of the female state prison population and 13 percent of the male state prison population (BJS, 2018b). While a select few states have Special Sex Offender Sentencing Alternatives (SSOSA), these programs are used very selectively and permit an offender to get treatment in the community as opposed to imprisonment. This type of alternative is sparingly approved by the courts and many sexual offenders receive a prison term. At that point, criminal justice authorities, policymakers, and the community are concerned with recidivism.

Findings vary dramatically in studies of recidivism of sexual offenders for a variety of reasons, most notably a variation in methodology of the research design. From study to study, researchers do not use a consistent period of measurement (the longer the period of study, the higher the rate of recidivism), studies vary what they consider recidivism (some studies only count new sexual offenses, other studies count any offense, and still other studies measure technical violations, such as failure to notify a change of address within the specified time limit). Additionally, the type of data used to measure recidivism impacts the rate found: self-reports, arrest data, versus conviction data. This adds to the already mentioned complexity that sexual offending is under-reported.

Regardless of the type of study used, what is clear is that the public believes sex offenders have a significantly higher recidivism rate than they do. Less than a year after Jessica Lunsford and Sarah Lunde were murdered, a study was conducted in Florida regarding public perceptions of sexual offenders. Study participants estimated sexual offender recidivism at about 75 percent (Levenson, Brannon, Fortney, & Baker, 2007). This misperception is common among the public and reinforced by politicians. For example, Rep. Randy Wood in Alabama suggested that "if there's any way to rehabilitate anyone on any crime, they need to be rehabilitated, but our information shows us that they [sex offenders] can't be rehabilitated" (Kiszla, 2017).

In 2018, a gross misrepresentation of recidivism data appeared in *The Atlanta Journal-Constitution* in an article discussing the failure of Georgia to assess the tier level of sex offenders and the potential risk to the state's federal funds as a result. The article stated:

> Level 1 offenders have a 4 percent to 13 percent chance of committing another sex crime, while those at Level 2 have a 34 percent chance of committing another sex offense. Level 3 offenders – 'sexually dangerous predators' – have a 65 percent chance of committing more sex crimes
> *(Cook, 2018: online)*

These statistics were presented to readers without any supporting evidence and are grossly inaccurate.

This was in the same vein as an earlier 1986 article in *Psychology Today* which stated: "Most untreated sex offenders released from prison go on to commit more offenses – indeed, as many as 80% do" (Freeman-Longo & Wall, 1986: 64). This unsubstantiated statistic was the only reference provided in *A Practitioner's Guide to Treating the Incarcerated Male Sex Offender* published by the Department of Justice (DOJ). The DOJ guide was cited many years later in 2002 by Supreme Court Justice Anthony Kennedy when he argued for mandatory treatment of sex offenders, due in part to their alleged high recidivism rates (Ellman & Ellman, 2015). Yet another example of the influence of such unverified data on the judiciary is the 2010 Supreme Court ruling *United States* v. *Comstock* which addressed the court's power to act in protection of communities from the alleged future danger posed by offenders. What is of special note is that three of the five "sexually dangerous persons" whose appeals were addressed in *United States* v. *Comstock* were imprisoned on offenses of child pornography, not contact offenses. A similar opinion was delivered by Supreme Court Justice Samuel Alito Jr. in *Packingham* v. *North Carolina* (137 S.Ct. 1730) in 2017 when he stated: "When convicted sex offenders reenter society, they are much more likely than any other type of offender to be rearrested for a new rape or sexual assault." In *McKune* v. *Lile* in 2002, Justice Kennedy Smith in Alaska wrote:

> a conviction for a sex offense provides evidence of substantial risk of recidivism. The legislature's findings are consistent with grave concerns over the high rate of recidivism among convicted sex offenders and their dangerousness as a class. The risk of recidivism posed by sex offenders is frightening and high.
>
> *(536 U.S. 24)*

However, these allegations of "substantial risk of recidivism" are not what research demonstrates.

In a large study of male sex offenders (9,691) released from prisons across 15 states in 1994, researchers found a 5.3 percent recidivism rate during the three-year follow-up based on an arrest for a new sexual offense (Langan, Schmitt, & Durose, 2003). When considering re-arrests for any type of crime, the research found that 43 percent of the released sex offenders were rearrested (compared to 68 percent among the non-sex offending released population). Almost 40 percent of the sex offenders who had been released were returned to prison within three years, due either to the commission of a new crime or to a technical violation of their release (Langan et al., 2003). A study conducted in 2000, using a sample of sexual offenders on probation, with a follow-up period of almost five years, found a re-arrest rate of 35 percent for non-sexual offenses, and a re-arrest rate of 5.6 percent for sexual offenses (Kruttschnitt, Uggen, & Shelton, 2000). Other studies have found slightly higher rates of sexual recidivism from between 9 percent (Zgoba & Simon, 2005) and 12 percent (Meloy, 2006).

A large study examining the data of 146,918 offenders originally arrested in Illinois in 1990, authors found sexual re-arrest rates for sexual offenders at one year post-release to be 2.2 percent, three years post-release to be 4.8 percent, and five years post-release to be 6.5 percent (Sample & Bray, 2003). Non-sexual offense re-arrest rates at the same follow-up periods were approximately 21 percent, 37 percent, and 45 percent (Sample & Bray, 2003). In another large study conducted by the California Department of Corrections and Rehabilitation, the 8,989 sex offenders who were released from prison between 2010 and 2011 were examined for recidivism over a three-year period. The offenders required to register as sex offenders represented almost 10 percent of the release cohort for that year and were found to have a higher recidivism rate at 56 percent than non-sex offenders at 43 percent. That said, 91 percent of returns to prison

48 Legislation and Sexual Offenders

for sex offenders were for parole violations (CA Department of Corrections and Rehabilitation, 2015). For sex offenders, less than 1 percent were re-incarcerated for a new sex offense, 2 percent of offenses involved a violation of the sex offense registry rules (example: failure to update the information on the registry when scheduled, failure to notify police of a change in address, etc.), and the remaining 5 percent of offenders were re-incarcerated for a non-sexual offense (CA Department of Corrections and Rehabilitation, 2015).

Another meta-analysis combined data from 21 studies that tracked almost 8,000 offenders for just over 8 years on average. Sixteen of these studies were conducted in Western countries other than the United States (most typically Canada), where there are often shorter sentences for sex offenders and no use of the registry. Findings were analyzed by risk level of the offender (low, medium, and high) (Hanson, Harris, Helmus, & Thornton, 2014). Almost 20 percent of high-risk offenders committed a new sexual offense within five years of release, and 32 percent of high-risk offenders had committed a new sexual offense within 15 years of release. However, high-risk offenders who remained offense-free at the 15-year post-release mark, rarely committed a later sexual offense. In the meta-analysis, there was no instance of a high-risk offender remaining offense-free for 15 years and committing a sexual offense after that time (Hanson et al., 2014). When examining low-risk offenders, the meta-analysis revealed that approximately 97 percent were offense-free at the five-year mark, and 95 percent remained offense-free at the 15-year point (Hanson et al., 2014). Given the negative relationship between age and offending found in much of the research, the 15-year finding of very low or no recidivism among offenders should not be surprising given the decline of testosterone and the decrease in a man's libido as they age (Barbaree, Blanchard, & Langton, 2003). A recent study found that approximately 3 percent of felons with no previously known history of sex offenses committed a sexual offense within 4.5 years of their release from prison. This recidivism rate for a sexual offense by an offender was higher than many recidivism rates found for a new sexual offense by an individual released for a sex crime … even when examining 15-year follow-up data (Wormith, Hogg, & Guzzo, 2012).

Some research indicates that different categories of sexual offenders have different rates of reoffending, with offenders who commit rape against adult women having the highest rate of recidivism. In a study with a three-year follow-up of 3,115 rapists, researchers found a 5 percent sexual recidivism rate, a 19 percent re-arrest rate for a violent crime, and 46 percent re-arrest rate for any crime (Langan et al., 2003). These re-arrest statistics were higher than other types of sexual offenders. A study, significant due to its 25-year follow-up period, also revealed differences among rapists and other sexual offenders (though generalization can be somewhat problematic given that treatment and management of sexual offenders is significantly different today than in the period of study, which was from 1959 through 1985) (Prentky, Lee, Knight, & Cerce, 1997). This study involved 136 sexually dangerous offenders (rapists). Researchers found

Time for a Reality Check **49**

some offenders remained at risk to reoffend well beyond their release. The sexual recidivism follow-up at 25 years was 39 percent and the overall recidivism rate was 74 percent (Prentky et al., 1997). Compare this to a 23 percent sexual recidivism rate among child molesters at a 15-year follow-up in a more recent study (Harris & Hanson, 2004). So, while there are cautions to read from these studies, there are also lessons to be learned.

When examining the effect of treatment on recidivism, most studies point to a decreased level of recidivism with provided treatment compared to no treatment. Effectiveness of treatment, however, is dependent on a number of factors, such as program delivery, treatment climate, and response of the participant (Friendship, Mann, and Beech, 2003). Offenders who are responsive to treatment, as measured by a change in attitude, are less likely to recidivate sexually (Beech, Erikson, Friendship, & Ditchfield, 2001). Examination of a prison-based treatment program in Colorado and its impact on recidivism indicated a positive impact. Sexual offenders who completed a treatment program as well as participated in an aftercare program had parole revocation rates that were three times lower than sexual offenders who did not participate in treatment (Lowden, Hetz, Harrison, Patrick, English, & Pasini-Hill, 2003). Each additional month an offender spent in treatment increased the likelihood of success after release by 1 percent (Lowden et al., 2003). Similarly, in a study examining the impacts of a cognitive-behavioral treatment in a Canadian prison, significant reductions in recidivism were found. Follow-up periods were five years and ten years, comparing sex offenders who had treatment to sex offenders who did not participate in treatment. Sexual reconviction rates in the treatment group after five years were just under 17 percent, and about 22 percent after ten years. In the nontreatment group, sexual reconviction after five years was just under 25 percent, and about 32 percent after ten years (Oliver, Wong, & Nicholaichuk, 2008).

A Minnesota study suggested that lowered recidivism extended beyond sexual recidivism. For sexual offenders who completed treatment, sexual recidivism as measured by re-arrest was about 13 percent, violent recidivism 29 percent, and general recidivism about 55 percent. Compare this to the nontreatment group with sexual re-arrest rates of almost 20 percent, violent recidivism at about 34 percent, and general recidivism at 58 percent (Duwe & Goldman, 2009). One of the largest meta-analyses involved an examination of 69 studies with just over 22,000 participants. With an average follow-up of 5 years, the recidivism rates for the treatment group were 11 percent for sexual offenses, just over 6 percent for violent offenses, and just over 22 percent for any crime. The recidivism rates for the offenders who had not received treatment were just over 17 percent for sexual offenses, almost 12 percent for violent offenses, and just over 32 percent for any crime (Lösel and Schmucker, 2005). The impact was clearly greater for individuals who completed treatment.

Research has found that type of treatment method can make a difference in recidivism as well. MacKenzie (2006) found cognitive-behavioral programs

50 Legislation and Sexual Offenders

that focused on relapse prevention treatment, behavioral treatment, as well as hormonal medication, were the most successful in the reduction of sexual recidivism. Other researchers have found that in populations of high-risk sex offenders, those who completed intensive residential treatment were significantly less likely to recidivate (more than two times less likely) than high-risk offenders who did not complete intensive treatment (Lovins, Lowekamp, & Latessa, 2009). In a surprising finding, such intensive treatment increased the likelihood of recidivism for low-risk offenders compared to low-risk offenders who were not provided intensive treatment at the rate of a 21 percent increase (Lovins et al. 2009).

While recidivism rates vary in the research, and are influenced by a myriad of factors, what is clear is that the longer an individual remains in the community offense-free, the less likely they are going to recidivate (Langan et al., 2003). Additionally, factors such as community-based treatment, intensive supervision programs, and broad-based community notification for the highest risk offenders, and the reduction of transience can reduce the likelihood of sexual recidivism (Duwe & Donnay, 2008). Releasing sexual offenders into the community after incarceration without proper reintegration skills sets them up to reoffend and subjects society to a cycle of revictimization.

Because public fear increases alongside increasingly strict legislation targeting sexual offenders, it is important to have a clear statistical understanding of sexual offenses and offenders. Using UCR and NCVS data, this chapter has provided a review of studies on sexual offending and offenses to give a more accurate picture of the "typical" sexual offender and victim. While there are many factors that contribute to under-reporting, this research viewed in combination can provide a critical overview of the dynamics of sexual offenses and sexual offenders and a solid foundation on which to analyze this social issue.

Notes

1. Arizona, California, Connecticut, Georgia, Idaho, Kentucky, Massachusetts, Michigan, New Hampshire, Oklahoma, South Carolina, Utah, and Vermont
2. As of 2013, the UCR definition of rape is:

> penetration, no matter how slight, of the vagina or anus with any body part or object, or oral penetration by a sex organ of another person, without the consent of the victim. Attempts or assaults to commit rape are also included.
> (UCR 2018: https://ucr.fbi.gov/crime-in-the-u.s/ 2017/crime-in-the-u.s.-2017/topic-pages/rape)

Excluded from this definition are statutory rape and incest.

References

Ackerman, Alissa R., Harris, Andrew J., Levenson, Jill S., & Zgoba, Kristen. (2011). Who are the people in your neighborhood? A descriptive analysis of individuals on public sex offender registries. *International Journal of Law & Psychiatry*, 34, 149–159.

Adams, Jonathan, Mrug, Sylvie, & Knight, David K. (2018). Characteristics of child physical and sexual abuse as predictors of psychopathology. *Child Abuse & Neglect* 86, 167–177.

Adkins, Geneva, Huff, David, & Stageberg, Paul. (2000). *The Iowa sex offender registry and recidivism.* Des Moines, IO: Iowa Department of Human Rights, Division of Criminal and Juvenile Justice Planning and Statistical Analysis Center.

Administration on Children, Youth, and Families (ACYF). (2016). *Child maltreatment 2016.* Washington, DC: U.S. Department of Health and Human Services.

Babchishin, K. M., Hanson, R. K., & Hermann, C. A. (2011). The characteristics of online sex offenders: A meta-analysis. *Sexual Abuse: A Journal of Research and Treatment*, 23, 92–123.

Babchishin, Kelly M., Hanson, R. Karl, & VanZuylen, Heather. (2015). Online child pornography offenders are different: A meta-analysis of the characteristics of online and offline sex offenders against children. *Archives of Sexual Behavior*, 13, 45–66.

Barbaree, Howard E., Blanchard, R., & Langton, C. M. (2003). The development of sexual aggression through the life span: The effect of age on sexual arousal and recidivism among sex offenders. *Annals of the New York Academy of Science*, 989, 59–71.

Becker, J. V. (1998). What we know about the characteristics and treatment of adolescents who have committed sexual offenses. *Child Maltreatment 3*, 317–329.

Beech, Anthony R., Erikson, Matt, Friendship, Caroline, & Ditchfield, John. (2001). *A six-year follow-up of men going through representative probation-based sex offender treatment programmes* (Findings 114). London, England: Home Office.

Best, Joel. (2001). *Damned lies and statistics: Untangling numbers from the media, politicians, and activists.* Berkeley, CA: University of California Press.

Briere, J. (1989). University males' sexual interest in children: Predicting potential indices of "pedophilia" in a nonforensic sample. *Child Abuse and Neglect*, 13, 65–75.

Bureau of Justice Statistics (BJS). (2000). *Sexual assault of young children as reported to law enforcement: Victim, incident, and offender characteristics* (NCJ 182990). Washington, DC: U.S. Department of Justice.

Bureau of Justice Statistics (BJS). (2008). *Criminal victimization in the United States 2008: Statistical tables* (NCJ 231173). Washington, DC: U.S. Department of Justice.

Bureau of Justice Statistics (BJS). (2013). *Female victims of sexual violence, 1994–2010* (NCJ 240655). Washington, DC: U.S. Department of Justice.

Bureau of Justice Statistics (BJS). (2018a). *Criminal victimization, 2017* (NCJ 252472). Washington, DC: U.S. Department of Justice.

Bureau of Justice Statistics (BJS). (2018b). *Prisoners in 2018* (NCJ 251149). Washington, DC: U.S. Department of Justice.

Bureau of Justice Statistics (BJS). (2019). *Criminal victimization, 2018* (NCJ 253043). Washington, DC: U.S. Department of Justice.

CA Department of Corrections and Rehabilitation. (2015). *2015 outcome evaluation report: An evaluation of offenders released in fiscal year 2010–2011.* Sacramento, CA: California Department of Corrections and Rehabilitation. www.cdcr.ca.gov/Adult_Research_Branch/Research_Documents/2014_Outcome_Evaluation_Report_7-6-2015.pdf

Catalano, Shannan. (2013). *Intimate partner violence: Attributes of victimization, 1993–2011* (NCJ 243300). Washington, DC: Bureau of Justice Statistics.

Center for Sex Offender Management (CSOM). (1999). *Understanding juvenile sexual offending behavior: Emerging research, treatment approaches and management practices.* Silver Spring, MD: Center for Effective Public Policy.

Cook, Rhonda. (May 28, 2018). GA sex offender registry problems cost the state federal funds. *The Atlanta Journal-Constitution.* Retrieved from www.ajc.com

Cortoni, Franca, & Hanson, R. Karl. (2005). *A review of the recidivism rates of adult female sex offenders* (No. R-169). Ottawa, Ontario, Canada: Correctional Service of Canada.

Cortoni, Franca, Hanson, R. Karl, & Coache, Marie-Ève. (2010). The recidivism rates of female sex offenders are low: A metaanalysis. *Sexual Abuse: A Journal of Research and Treatment*, 22, 387–401.

Denov, M.S. (2004). *Perspectives of denial on female sex offending: A culture of denial.* Aldershot: Ashgate Publications.

Duwe, Grant, & Donnay, William. (2008). The impact of Megan's Law on sex offender recidivism: The Minnesota experience. *Criminology*, 46(2), 411–446.

Duwe, G., & Goldman, R. (2009). The impact of prison-based treatment on sex offender recidivism: Evidence from Minnesota. *Sexual Abuse: A Journal of Research and Treatment*, 21, 279–307.

Elliott, Ian A., Eldridge, Hilary J., Ashfield, Sherry, & Beech, Anthony R. (2010). Exploring risk: Potential static, dynamic, protective and treatment factors in the clinical histories of female sex offenders. *Journal of Family Violence*, 25, 595–602.

Ellman, Ira Mark, & Ellman, Tara. (2015). "Frightening and high": The Supreme Court's crucial mistake about sex crime statistics. *Constitutional Commentary*, 30(3), 495–508.

Fehrenbach, P.A., & Monastersky, C. (1988). Characteristics of female adolescent sexual offenders. *American Journal of Orthopsychiatry*, 58, 148–151.

Ferguson, Christopher J., & Meehan, D. Cricket. (2005). An analysis of females convicted of sex crimes in the state of Florida. *Journal of Child Sexual Abuse*, 14(1), 75–89.

Finkelhor, D. (1984). *Child sexual abuse: New theory and research.* New York, NY: The Free Press.

Finkelhor, David, & Jones, Lisa. (2012). *Have sexual abuse and physical abuse declined since the 1990s?* Crimes Against Children Research Center, University of New Hampshire. Also available at www.nsopw.gov/enUS/Education/FactsStatistics

Freeman-Longo, Robert E., & Wall, R. (March 1986). Changing a lifetime of sexual Crime. *Psychology Today*, 58–64.

Freeman, N., & Sandler, J. (2010). The Adam Walsh Act: A false sense of security or an effective public policy initiative? *Criminal Justice Policy Review*, 21, 31–49.

Friendship, Caroline, Mann, Ruth E., & Beech, Anthony R. (2003). *The prison-based sex offender treatment programme: An evaluation.* London, England: Home Office.

Gray, Sandra, & Rarick, Susan. (2018). Exploring gender and racial/ethnic differences in the effects of child sexual abuse. *Journal of Child Sexual Abuse*, 27(5), 570–587.

Grayston, A. D., & DeLuca, R. V. (1999). Female perpetrators of child sexual abuse: A review of the clinical and empirical literature. *Aggression and Violent Behaviour*, 4, 93–106.

Hanson, R. Karl, Harris, Andrew J. R., Helmus, Leslie, & Thornton, David. (2014). High-risk sex offenders may not be high risk forever. *Journal of Interpersonal Violence*, 29(15), 2792–2813.

Harris, Andrew J. R., & Hanson, R. Karl. (2004). *Sex offender recidivism: A simple question.* Ottawa, Ontario, Canada: Public Safety and Emergency Preparedness Canada.

Harris, Andrew J., Levenson, Jill S., & Ackerman, Alissa R. (2014). Registered sex offenders in the United States: Behind the numbers: *Crime and Delinquency*, 60(1), 3–33.

Harris, A. J., Lobanov-Rostovsky, C., & Levenson, J. S. (2010). Widening the net: The effects of transitioning to the Adam Walsh Act classification system. *Criminal Justice and Behavior*, 37, 503–519.

Hunter, J. A., Figueredo, A. J., Malamuth, N. M., & Becker, J. V. (2003). Juvenile sex offenders: Toward the development of a typology. *Sexual Abuse: A Journal of Research and Treatment* 15(1), 27–48.

Jones, L. M., Mitchell, K. J., & Finkelhor, D. (2012). Trends in youth internet victimization: Findings from three youth internet safety surveys 2000–2010. *Journal of Adolescent Health*, 50, 179–186.

Kiszla, Cameron. (July 15, 2017). As some states reconsider sex-offender registries, an Alabama resident argues the state's for-life requirements are too much. *Anniston Star*. Retrieved from www.annistonstar.com

Krebs, Christopher, Lindquist, Christine, Berzofsky, Marcus, Shook-Sa, Bonnie, & Peterson, Kimberly. (2016). *Campus climate survey validation study: Final technical report* (NCJ 249545). Washington, DC: Bureau of Justice Statistics.

Kruttschnitt, C., Uggen, C., & Shelton, K. (2000). Predictors of desistance among sex offenders: The interaction of formal and informal social controls. *Justice Quarterly*, 17, 62–87.

Langan, Patrick A., Schmitt, Erica L, & Durose, Matthew R. (2003). *Recidivism of sex offenders released from prison in 1994* (NCJ 198281). Washington, DC: U.S. Department of Justice.

Levenson, Jill S., Brannon, Yolanda N., Fortney, Timothy, & Baker, Juanita. (2007). Public perceptions about sex offenders and community protection policies. *Analysis of Social Issues and Public Policy*, 7(1), 1–25.

Levenson, Jill S., Letourneau, E., Armstrong, K., & Zgoba, K. (2010). Failure to register as a sex offender: Is it associated with recidivism? *Justice Quarterly*, 27, 305–331.

Lewis, Catherine F., & Stanley, Charlotte R. (2000). Women accused of sexual offenses. *Behavioral Sciences and the Law*, 18, 73–81.

Lösel, Friedrich, & Schmucker, Martin. (2005). The effectiveness of treatment for sex offenders: A comprehensive meta-analysis. *Journal of Experimental Criminology*, 1, 117–146.

Lovins, Brian, Lowenkamp, Christopher T., & Latessa, Edward J. (2009). Applying the risk principle to sex offenders: Can treatment make some sex offenders worse? *The Prison Journal*, 89, 344–357.

Lowden, Kerry, Hetz, Nicole, Harrison, Linda, Patrick, Diane, English, Kim, & Pasini-Hill, Diane. (2003). *Evaluation of Colorado's prison therapeutic community for sex offenders: A report of findings*. Denver, CO: Office of Research and Statistics, Division of Criminal Justice, Colorado Department of Public Safety.

MacKenzie, Doris Layton. (2006). *What works in corrections: Reducing the criminal activities of offenders and delinquents*. New York, NY: Cambridge University Press.

MacMillan, H. L., Fleming, J. E., Streiner, D. L., Lin, E., Boyle, M. H., Jamieson, D., Duku, E. K., Walsh, C. A., Wong, M. Y., & Beardslee, W. R. (2001). Childhood abuse and lifetime psychopathology in a community sample. *American Journal of Psychiatry*, 158(11), 1878–1883.

Marshall, W. L., & Hall, G. C. N. (1995). The value of the MMPI in deciding forensic issues in accused sexual offenders. *Sexual abuse: A Journal of Research and Treatment*, 7, 205–219.

Mayer, A. (1992). *Women sex offenders: Treatment and dynamics*. Holmes Beach, FL, Learning Publications.

McKune v. *Lile*, 536 U.S. 24 (2002)

Meloy, Michelle L. (2006). *Sex offenses and the men who commit them: An assessment of sex offenders on probation*. Boston, MA: Northeastern University Press.

National Center for Missing and Exploited Children (NCMEC). (2018). Registered sex offenders in the United States. Retrieved from www.missingkids.org/content/dam/pdfs/SOR%20Map%20with%20Explanation_10_2018.pdf

National Institute of Justice (NIJ). (2003). *Youth victimization: Prevalence and implications*. Washington, DC: U.S. Department of Justice.

Nelson, E. C., Heath, A. C., Madden, P. A., Cooper, M. L., Dinwiddie, S. H., Bucholz, K. K., Glowinski, A., McLaughlin, T., Dunne, M.P., Statham, D. J., & Martin, N. G. (2002). Association between self-reported childhood sexual abuse and adverse psychosocial outcomes: Results from a twin study. *Archives of General Psychiatry*, 59(2), 139–145.

Office of Juvenile Justice and Delinquency Prevention (OJJDP). (2009). *Juveniles who commit sex offenses against minors* (NCJ 227763). Washington, DC: U.S. Department of Justice.

Oliver, M., Wong, S., & Nicholaichuk, T.P. (2008). Outcome evaluation of a high-intensity inpatient sex offender treatment program. *Journal of Interpersonal Violence*, 24, 522–536.

Packingham v. *North Carolina*, 137 S.Ct. 1730 (2017)

Plummer, Malory, & Cossins, Annie. (2018). The cycle of abuse: When victims become offenders. *Trauma, Violence & Abuse*, 19(3), 286–304.

Prentky, R.A., Lee, A.F., Knight, R., & Cerce, D. (1997). Recidivism rates among child molesters and rapists: A methodological analysis. *Law and Human Behavior*, 21(6), 635–659.

Sample, Lisa L., & Bray, Timothy M. (2003). Are sex offenders dangerous? *Criminology & Public Policy*, 3(1), 59–82.

Schulz, Anja, Bergen, Emilia, Schuhmann, Petya, Hoyer, Jurgen, & Santtila, Pekka. (2016). Online sexual solicitation of minors: How often and between whom does it occur? *Journal of Research in Crime and Delinquency*, 53(2), 165–188.

Seto, M. C., Hanson, R. K., & Babchishin, K. M. (2011). Contact sexual offending by men with online sexual offences. *Sexual Abuse: A Journal of Research and Treatment*, 23, 124–145.

Sinozich, Sofi, & Langton, Lynn. (2014). *Rape and sexual assault victimization among college-age females, 1995–2013* (NCJ 248471). Washington, DC: Bureau of Justice Statistics.

Smith, S. G., Zhang, X., Basile, K. C., Merrick, M. T., Wang, J., Kresnow, M., & Chen, J. (2018). *The national intimate partner and sexual violence survey (NISVS): 2015 data brief*. Atlanta, GA: National Center for Injury Prevention and Control, Centers for Disease Control and Prevention.

Snyder, H. (2000). *Sexual assault of young children as reported to law enforcement: Victim, incident, and offender characteristics*. Washington, DC: Bureau of Justice Statistics, U.S. Department of Justice.

Stemple, Lara, Flores, Andrew, & Meyer, Ilan H. (2017). Sexual victimization perpetrated by women: Federal data reveal surprising prevalence. *Aggression and Violent Behavior*, 34, 302–311.

Thoennes, Nancy, & Tjaden, Patrick. (2000). *Full report of the prevalence, incidence and consequences of violence against women: Findings from the National Violence Against Women Survey* (NCJ 183781). Washington, DC: U.S. Department of Justice.

Travin, S., Cullen, K., & Protter, B. (1990). Female sexual offenders: Severe victims and victimizers. *Journal of Forensic Sciences*, 35, 140–150.

Uniform Crime Report (UCR). (2018). *Crime in the United States, 2017*. Washington, DC: U.S. Department of Justice.

United States v. *Comstock*, 560 U.S. 126 (2010)

Vandiver, D.M., & Walker, J.T. (2002). Female sex offenders: An overview and analysis of 40 cases. *Criminal Justice Review*, 27(2), 284–300.

Walters, M.L., Chen J., & Breiding, M. J. (2013). *The national intimate partner and sexual violence survey (NISVS): 2010 findings on victimization by sexual orientation*. Atlanta, GA: National Center for Injury Prevention and Control, Centers for Disease Control and Prevention.

Ward, T., Polaschek, D., & Beech, A. R. (2006). *Theories of sexual offending*. Chichester, UK: Wiley.

Widom, C. S., & Ames, M. A. (1994). Criminal consequences of childhood sexual victimization. *Child Abuse and Neglect*, 18(4), 303–318.

Wormith, J. Stephen, Hogg, Sarah, & Guzzo, Lina. (2012). The predictive validity of a general risk/needs assessment inventory on sexual offender recidivism and an exploration of the professional override. *Criminal Justice and Behavior*, 39, 1529–1532.

Zgoba, Kristen M., & Simon, Leonore, M. J. (2005). Recidivism rates of sexual offenders up to 7 years later. *Criminal Justice Review*, 30(2), 155–173.

PART II

Life With a Registered Sex Offender

3

RELATIONSHIP AND REVELATION

Of the 94 women interviewed for this study, 56 (60 percent) began a relationship with a man after he had committed a sexual offense and become a registered sexual offender (RSO), and 38 (40 percent) were involved with a man (either dating or married) when the offense occurred. Because the motivations and reactions varied depending on when the relationship began in timeline with the offense, these groups of women will be discussed separately.

Generally, not all offenders convicted or who plea to a sexual offense spend time in prison. Of all state prisoners, approximately 95 percent are released, and once in society RSOs seek to integrate (or reintegrate) with family, friends, and an intimate partner (Martinez & Christian, 2009). In this study, 70 of the men (74 percent) spent time in prison (either on the initial sex offense charge or on a violation).[1] Research consistently demonstrates that family and close friends provide integral support for offenders post-incarceration in successful reintegration into society and in keeping individuals offense-free. Partners provide emotional and financial support, as well as access to tangible items, such as transportation (Braman, 2004; Comfort, 2007a; Herman-Stahl, Kan, & McKay, 2008; Petersilia, 2003). However, the obstacles offenders face in society are often shifted to their partners, and this is obvious when dealing with RSOs. Having a history with a sex offense provides specific challenges that add complications to the maintenance of a healthy relationship and may weaken marital bonds (Lindquist, Landwehr, McKay, Feinberg, Comfort, & Anupa, 2015). These changes may be the result of the partner's absence if he was incarcerated, psychological stressors, economic stressors, rigid routines from probation/parole requirements, and depression or anxiety, all of which may have negative consequences for an intimate relationship (Lopoo & Western, 2005; Christian, 2005; Wildeman, Schnittker, & Turney, 2012).

60 Life With a Registered Sex Offender

Of the 94 women interviewed, only three women (3 percent) were no longer with their partner at the time of the interview. These three women became involved in their relationships after the men had committed the offense. Vanessa's relationship with her RSO boyfriend ceased after a year of their involvement at the advice of her attorney. Vanessa's ex-husband threatened to seek sole custody of her two children as a result of her dating an individual who accepted a plea for a familial child sexual offense that he asserted was a false accusation. She explained:

> Yeah, I actually consulted my attorney because of what the baby's dad is saying he'll do and so [the lawyer] told me it's easier in court to say there is no contact with him then to try to fight and be with him. I love him, but even when he gets off parole it's always a stigma that's attached to him and the kid's father is never gonna change his opinions. I think it's just gonna make it too hard and so it's kinda just one of those things that we have to do what we have to do, and it sucks real bad but, it's not worth losing my kids.

Misty spent ten years in a relationship with a man who pled to a statutory rape charge. She said they simply grew apart over the years and the demise of the relationship had nothing to do with his status as an RSO. At the time of the interview, they continued to remain friends. Finally, Kristy was no longer with her husband, although their lack of involvement was not voluntary, but was instead the result of a court-ordered no-contact order from a domestic violence charge. They married after her husband was sentenced to 15 years for two attempted rape charges and molestation of a minor, for which he served seven years in prison. Kristy had been involved with her husband for 20 years and expressed an interest in resuming their relationship in two years once the no-contact order expired. These were the only women, of the 94 interviewed, who were no longer in intimate relationships with the offenders of interest for this research. Ninety-seven percent of the women chose to face the consequences that an RSO status brings with their partner.

New relationships bring challenges. A relationship with an individual reintegrating into society post-incarceration brings greater challenges. A relationship with an individual on the sex offense registry, stigmatized by society brings yet further challenges. So, if you are a single woman, or a single mother, what are the motivations for beginning a relationship with an RSO?

Beginning a Relationship After the Offense Occurred

Motivations for Beginning the Relationship

When the world is full of single men, and you are free to choose your next partner, it raises the question as to why someone with a sex offense conviction may be viewed as a good potential partner, especially for a woman with children? Some of the women in the study admitted to sharing the same types of stereotypes regarding RSOs that society at large possesses, prior to meeting their partner. Cheryl was involved with a man who pled guilty to possession of child pornography prior to meeting her:

> Before I met him, I assumed that everyone on the registry was someone awful, someone you couldn't trust, someone to be afraid of who had done something really heinous, but that's not the case. There are people who are on there that are really bad but you just have to look at them as individuals and yes, they did something illegal and you think of him as someone who did the worst of the worst, and he didn't do the worst of the worst. That sounds like you know, like I could be dating somebody worse than [him], but no. Just that it's not, that [people] need to understand what it means to be a sex offender in the U.S. these days, and it's not what everybody thinks from what the media says.

In moving past these stereotypes, what many of the women spoke about was the role of forgiveness and the importance of judging an individual on their present instead of their past. Angela married a man who pled guilty to possession and distribution of child pornography prior to their involvement. She spoke about her ability to forgive the past, provided it did not repeat itself:

> I'm a very forgiving individual. I understand what happens in the past is the past. You need to look to the future and people make mistakes. But he knows if he messed up now there's gonna be some issues. I trust him now and trust is the most important thing in a relationship. Because honestly, knowing that about him made me trust him more. That's always a very difficult thing to explain to people. I have this irrational fear that any man I would be dating would be basically, potentially, a child molester because of my past experience.

Alison married a man who spent almost two decades in prison. At trial he was found guilty of sexual contact with a minor, and likely received a lengthy sentence due to a previous violent conviction of a non-sexual nature. Alison suggested:

> Everyone should be judged on what they are now and what they're trying to be and do and not on something that happened in their past because all of us have things in our past that we would love to not have known, even if they're not quite that serious.

Diana echoed Alison's sentiments about focusing on the here and now. Diana's husband was found guilty at trial for rape and attempted rape prior to their

62 Life With a Registered Sex Offender

involvement. He was sentenced to 15 years and had a violation for solicitation of a prostitute while on probation. Diana focused instead on what he was trying to do with his life:

> [I'm with my husband because] he is a very intelligent man. He's very smart, funny, caring. I mean, he just wants to be a better person. He's made mistakes, but he tries to be a better person each day and knows he isn't perfect at it, and he realizes that, and starts all over again.

For some women, like Patricia, the attraction to their partner was as a result of his total and complete acceptance of her: "[He] was the first one to say I'm willing to accept you as you are, I like you for who you are, you're free to be who you are." For most women, however, the motivation for being with their partner came down to love, as it does in many relationships. Carrie said of her husband: "I love him with my whole heart, and I think he's beautiful on the inside and out, and just because his consequences are a little more outstanding and visible to others, it doesn't make his sins any worse than mine."

Sheila married a man who pled guilty to two charges of molestation of a minor. His sentence was five years on probation and 25 years on the registry. Sheila did not know about his history until a year into the relationship, and by that time she was in love with her partner, who she had been with for seven years at the time of our interview. Sheila expressed her love for her partner, mixed with her lack of knowledge of the implications of being with an RSO:

> I mean, I just love the guy, you know. Whatever, I just don't know how to say it. I loved him and I just didn't think about it. I mean, that's how little I knew about how bad it is out there. Maybe if I had just realized I would have walked away … I had no idea.

While women were willing to look beyond mistakes of the past, many of them did so with some understanding of what being with an RSO would mean for their future, though none of them could truly understand the full implications. Natasha knew her eventual husband in a friend capacity prior to their intimate involvement and before to his offense. He accepted a plea to a charge of statutory rape and was sentenced to 16 years. Additionally, because of the minor status of the female, he will serve a lifetime on the sex offense registry. Natasha explained:

> I really had to think about it and honestly, did some soul searching and realized that people do make mistakes and it doesn't necessarily mean that you have to just write them off. You know, the way I believe is that, you know, God looks at all of us the same. We've all done things that we don't want posted on the internet, we've all done things that we would not want our mom to know, and his just so happens to be something that

is very, very public and very taboo and very gruesome in society's eyes, but there are plenty of people out there who have done similar things and haven't gotten in trouble for it, or done worse things and haven't gotten in trouble for it. So, who am I to sit here and judge him when I've done things that are wrong too.

Carrie discussed the significance of trust in her relationship. Her husband was found guilty at trial of sexual contact with a minor prior to their marriage. He revealed this on their second date. He served 11 months in prison plus 10 years on probation and will spend his life on the sex offender registry. Carrie said:

And I don't think that we could do this, if [we] didn't trust each other. I mean, trust is probably more important than love in a marriage. Because if you don't trust the other person, it doesn't matter how much you love them. Like I said, love is not always a warm, fuzzy feeling. It's a choice. And every day I have to say to myself, "Even if I don't feel like it, I choose to love him." And he chooses to love me. I'm not perfect either.

Despite the forgiveness women have, and as much as they love their partners, hesitations regarding the relationship are normal. Some of women's misgivings deal with restrictions that come from the sex offense registry and other legal controls, some indecision is from society's stereotypes, and some reluctance is from potential fears of their partners reoffending.

Hesitations Regarding the Relationship

As the relationship evolves, as the laws change and the partner and family are subjected to increasingly punitive sex offender legislation, there are bound to be doubts about whether getting involved with an RSO was the most prudent decision. Overwhelmingly, the women interviewed expressed that they would choose their partners again, despite the many legal complications they experienced; however, they did convey some misgivings. One hesitation had to do with society's perception of her as the wife/partner of a sex offender. Catherine married a man who will spend a lifetime on the registry as part of his punishment for pleading guilty to an alleged false claim of familial molestation of a minor.

I thought long and hard about dating him because I didn't know him well enough to know what had actually happened. I didn't think it had happened but I didn't know for sure. I didn't know him like I know now you know? And I took even longer to marry him and that's horrible of me, I hate to say it. My husband is not a child molester, but the world looks at him like he is. And I didn't want to be looked at like the wife of a child molester.

64 Life With a Registered Sex Offender

Mary had been in a relationship for almost a decade with a man who accepted a plea to a charge of statutory rape. He told her about his history on their first date. Mary admitted that she participated in judgments of RSOs prior to meeting her partner:

> I didn't know all the restrictions and everything. I mean, certainly I know that being a sex offender is something society is going to judge very harshly and so that was no surprise, that was nothing that I didn't know, because I did that, so I knew that.

Depending on what the partner's offense was, a select group of women also experienced fleeting concerns about their partners reoffending and how a re-offense may impact their future. None of the women in the study had a serious fear of their partners reoffending. In fact, most women said it wasn't a fear at all. Sabrina said her husband would never risk the life he has now to commit another offense:

> So, there's no [chance he would ever commit another offense] ... he would lose both of us and he's so happy and he loves both of us so much. He wanted a family before he met me and had given up on having a family and then, when we met, that was all given back to him. The chance of having a family and having a wife was all given back to him, so I just, I don't honestly think ... and he risks going to jail for life. And I don't think that he would risk that. I think he made a mistake when he was young and I think the consequences, if nothing else, kept him away from doing something. I think the consequences of doing something would be so dramatic that he wouldn't even think about it.

And for those that did mention it, like Jessica, the risk was perceived as minimal. Jessica's husband accepted a plea to an alleged false charge of molestation by his daughter. For her, there seemed a small risk in the beginning, though not so real as to forgo the relationship:

> Yeah, of course I thought about [the risk of re-offense], I have two girls. Of course I thought about it, we talked about it. We talked about house rules and all kinds of things, and I even said, if I even suspect you touch one of my girls, I'll shoot you and I'll go to prison. Matter of factly, that's the ... I'm the type of person ... he knows that I would.

As most women reflected on their motivations for beginning a relationship with an RSO, and the hesitations during the beginning of the relationship, the hurdle most frequently mentioned were the legal restraints. And perhaps most inter-estingly, while women knew that sex offender legislation was strict, they really had no idea of the extent of those restrictions until their intimate involvement with a legally-controlled individual. Honesty between partners helped Carrie get through some of the pressures from society and the stressors of the legal requirements:

> There's never been any secrets between us. I've been there for him during polygraphs and the general assemblies, um, new laws, and I've never had a hesitation with wanting to have a family with him and you know, it's just part of our lives and we deal with it. It's really easy to forget sometimes until something happens and then it all comes crashing down and you realize what you have to deal with. But, even in those moments it brings us closer together. Before we got married I received an anonymous letter in the mail and all it was a picture of him from the registry with a pen scratching on the back that said, "Do you know who you're marrying?" And I thought, "Well, duh, how could you be marrying somebody and not know something this big about them?"

Part of honesty is believing the account of events that one's partner was told regarding the offense. Samantha married a man who claimed he was falsely accused of sexual contact with a family member. He took a plea at the advice of his public defender and was sentenced to 15 years on probation. During his probationary period, he served 5 years on a drug violation. Due to the minor status of the victim, he will be on the sex offense registry for life. The minor victim later recanted, but at the beginning of the relationship Samantha had her doubts:

> The first year, once in a while, I would think, "What if some of this isn't true and all this time has passed and he lied, but he feels really bad about it now?" You know, we're married and have a kid. I mean, what would I do? Would I divorce him? Now we're married and we have this kid … every now and then, you know when you wake up in the middle of the night you think weird things? That used to happen the first year, but I never think about it anymore.

Even with honesty between partners, the sacrifices required in a relationship between an RSO and his partner are often exceptional and strain the relationship in ways more demanding than in other relationships. Diana said:

> We actually had a point in our relationship, probably about 6.5 months dating that I thought that we were going to have to just walk away and wipe our hands clean. And it kind of felt like mourning for someone who has just passed away, kind of like going through that. And I was like, "This is too much stress on my kids and my ex-husband is not happy …

and I can't just take a job somewhere because I have to think about where we're going to live in that area and can you come to my work?" and I just thought I would wash my hands of it and he did too because he didn't expect me to deal with all this baggage. And then I just prayed about it and stepped away from the situation for a couple of weeks and put things back and thought, "No, I want to be with this person and I'm going to have to do what it takes to make it work and I'm going to have to sacrifice some things." But, don't we all in our relationships have to sacrifice something? So, that's when I decided to go ahead with the relationship.

Upon consideration of what life would be like with an RSO, most women stood firm in their decision to be with their partner. Courtney decided she made the right decision to marry the man she loved. Prior to meeting, he was found guilty at trial of molestation of a minor family member and was sentenced to 10 years. He will serve a lifetime on the sex offense registry. Courtney said:

> I don't ever question myself … I really don't ever question myself about it because I know I did the right thing, but I worry about it long-term as far as the kids are concerned because people can be so cruel. But I don't regret it. I can't change people and there's not a whole lot about this that I can change, so I deal with it.

Like Catherine, the women did not blame the stress they experienced on their partners, but instead deemed laws dealing with RSOs as too far-reaching:

> No. I might not have married him, maybe. I don't know. But it's not fair, he didn't do this … he didn't do anything wrong, I can't see not getting involved with someone because society has gone crazy with what's illegal and what's not.

Janet still struggled with being involved with an RSO and what that may mean legally for her down the road. At the time of the interview, Janet had been involved with her partner for 18 months. She explained:

> [I still think about whether I should stay with him.] I think it's more of a selfish thing. I think my life might be easier if I didn't stay with him. Because I think about in the long run, and we've discussed getting married and we've discussed moving in, and those things make me nervous. You know, what if I want to have a child? The laws have messed things up so badly that I would pretty much be a single parent. But then I'm a little defiant … he's not a monster and legislation needs to change and if I leave him, you know, for what?

To combat the frustrations, some of the women, like Katherine, spent their energy working toward legal change, and encouraging their partner to do the same:

> I wish more people would get involved, and believe me I kept telling my husband, "You need to get involved, you need to get involved," and I want him to be involved doing more things to influence and make a difference. And he's working up to it, but he says it's been very difficult, because no matter how you cut it, there's still scars every day when you can't do what you want to do. So, that's my sadness and the hard part as a wife, when you make a decision to really, truly look at a person for who they are, and not judge them on a bad situation that they had in their lives. Because I don't care who you are in this world, you have some story behind your life, and it can be good, bad, and ugly.

Sixty percent of the women in this study were able to look beyond the past of a man who had committed a sex offense prior to meeting them and move forward in a relationship without judgment. Forty percent of the study's participants were involved with a man in either a dating relationship or a marriage when the offense occurred; all of these women decided to remain in the relationship. How are the motives different for remaining in a partnership when a sexual offense occurs within the context of a committed relationship?

Being Together When the Offense Occurred

The family is a critical support for offenders and most often one's partner aids in keeping the offender crime-free. A partner may play a role in mediating stressful interactions, such as with supervisory agents like parole officers. Additionally, the upheaval and restructuring of the partner's life and patterns cannot be overlooked. It takes a strong couple and family to be able to re-evaluate how to successfully live together (Shapiro & Schwartz, 2001). The reintegrating offender often views the woman as a source of material resources, significant emotional support, and acceptance, and recognizes that they are typically unable to provide much in return (Scheyett & Pettus-Davis, 2012). A former offender returning to the family places serious stressors on family resilience, and the family must learn new modes of adaption to these stressors, often exacerbating pre-existing relational tensions (Farkas & Miller, 2007; Martinez, 2006; Patterson, 2002). When a sex offense occurs during the relationship, the woman needs to consider her motives for remaining in the relationship and the stressors that will ensue postconviction. Research finds that providing support to released prisoners can be considered one way in which women are expected to care for vulnerable populations; a role that is filled with stress and generally discounted by the larger society (Comfort, 2007b).

68 Life With a Registered Sex Offender

> Family and kinship ties can be irreparably broken by the nature of the sex offense committed by a family member, especially if there are victims in the family itself. Those families who choose to reunite with convicted sex offenders bear an enormous burden.
>
> *(Farkas & Miller, 2007: 89)*

If the female partner is not appreciated as the significant source of support that she is, what are her motivations for remaining in such a relationship?

Motivations for Staying in the Relationship

All of the women in this study decided to remain in the relationship after the offense occurred when it occurred within the context of a dating relationship or marriage. That does not mean they did not question their relationship and the foundation of honesty and trust between themselves and their partners. When the offense occurs inside of a relationship, this represents a betrayal. As a result, for some women, there were temporary separations. This was the case for Melissa. Melissa's daughter revealed incidents of abuse by her step-father two years after the abuse had ceased. Melissa reported the incidents to the child welfare agency in her state and her husband pled guilty and was sentenced to six years in prison and 18 months on probation. After her husband served his sentence and participated in sex offender therapy, and Melissa and her daughter participated in therapy, the family decided to reunify. Melissa discussed the reunification decision:

> Oh yeah, oh yeah, but it wasn't until about 3 years ago or so that I really just, I had to stop, I mean, it was almost like every day, "Did I do the right thing? Did I do the right thing?" Yeah, and I tortured myself terribly about whether or not to stay with him and you know, I'm going through a lot of therapy, we were getting, I mean it was, it was getting good results with the therapy and the family was very supportive. It was like, okay, well, I can either break up this marriage, break up this family. [My daughter's] already been through a broken family and her father was going through his second divorce, her world was upside down or I could try to stay and make it work because I really love this guy and we get along perfectly except for this and we still do. I can either stay and make this work and give her some stability because god, she was [a young teenager] and would really need stability for the next several years with high school and stuff and the teenage years and you know, all signs pointed to us being together so we did, we made a go of it. I made the best choice I could at that time, taking direction from [my daughter], seeing how she was acting and reacting and how he was doing. Yeah, he eventually did end up moving back into the house and um.... How long was he gone for? 7 months. It was 7 long months.

Relationship and Revelation **69**

For Crystal, her husband was serving a 31-month prison sentence for possession of child pornography at the time of the interview, and she struggled with the idea of divorce upon his release due to the potential impact his RSO status would have on her chosen career:

> Well, yeah … I mean we knew that I was going to be a teacher, so from very early on we knew that we might have to get a divorce. Another side of me is very … survival oriented. And I was very fast, not just at this point, but at any crisis … I am very fast at trying to fix the problem to prevent the boat, my personal boat, from tipping over. In this case there wasn't anything I was going to be able to do to protect [my husband]. I knew I couldn't keep him from going to prison … and that was kind of the hardest part about this … it was kind of like death … there was no way to get away from this happening.… And I couldn't go down with the ship. If I was going to be a teacher, I couldn't be married to a registered sex offender. And at the time I was absolutely unwilling to live the life of a sex offender's wife. But, do I want to be divorced? God, I'm just so ambivalent about it now. I really, really, really do not know. [My husband] feels that we need to be divorced because he doesn't want to bring any more of this into my life. For me, I'm ambivalent because this is the person I love more than anyone else in the world and I don't have high hopes of meeting anyone … well, actually I don't even want to meet anyone. I don't want to meet someone new, I want my husband back. And I know I won't have him back under the old paradigms … we will always have this hanging over our heads, this thing that changed our lives. We will never be normal like other couples are. So … I … I don't know if I want the divorce. I do want a normal life, but I guess I haven't defined yet what that means to me. And I'm also extremely bonded to his family and have no family of my own. So, I don't want to go off into this scary, amorphous future with no family. And that's another part of my anger at [my husband]: this is going to cost me a family. And how could he do that to me?

In thinking about whether or not to remain with her husband, Sarah, whose husband was serving 5 years in prison for one count of possession of child pornography, struggled with society's perception of her as a partner of an RSO:

> I did, like I said, I talked to an attorney about what my options were as far as divorce. What was available, how much it would cost. I went through every possible scenario in my head … and I don't know … knowing that he needed us to be there … I decided to stay. But I will tell you, leaving him would have been the easier choice. It would have been so much easier to walk away because to this day, I still get questions from people,

70 Life With a Registered Sex Offender

> are you going to leave him, are you gonna stay? You know, they constantly
> want to know and there are people in the community who wonder, who
> are not friends of mine, and so they can't ask. Why are you staying with
> him? They want to know that. I've known him for 20-plus-years and for
> 20 years, 95 percent of the time, he's my best friend. He's a great father
> and a good individual. Why is it okay to walk away from that? I mean,
> he could have been charged with drunk driving and no one would have
> asked me if I was gonna leave him. You know, you could have a DUI and
> injure somebody or hurt somebody, kill somebody, and people don't ask
> that spouse, well are you gonna leave him? And you just committed mur-
> der. He was charged with one count of possession [of child pornography]
> and you're asking me if I'm going to leave him? I couldn't make that
> work in my head. My in-laws actually gave me permission to leave him.
> Not that I need their permission or want it. I mean, these are the types
> of things you're dealing with in society from other people and his own
> parents for goodness sakes were telling me I should leave.

While women did consider leaving their partners, all of the women in the
study decided to remain in the relationship, and when they discussed motivations
for doing so, they talked about the fact that their partners owned up to their
offenses and changed their behaviors or were working toward changing their
behaviors, the effect that an absent father would have on the children, the partner's need for support during this difficult time, and, perhaps most frequently, the
love they had for them. Admitting to the offense and asking for forgiveness played
a key role in many women's decisions to stay in the relationship. Maria's husband
was charged with sexual misconduct with a minor. She found out about the
offense when her husband confessed to her and requested forgiveness. There was
no attempt to hide the behavior, and for Maria that carried a lot of weight. Her
husband served 8 years in prison and 6 years on parole after being found guilty in
a jury trial. Maria said:

> I really didn't [think about leaving] because he was devastated himself
> and expressed such remorse and asked for forgiveness that I felt I should,
> I wanted to extend that to him. Although it was a wait and see, you
> know, you have to prove it to me that you really have changed. He has
> changed, I wouldn't just say that, just like anyone, I wouldn't trust anyone
> 100 percent, but I do trust him for the most part.

And in searching for guidance about whether to remain in the relationship, many
women, like Stacey, turned to religion for insight:

> I'm actually a really spiritual person so I spent a lot of time searching
> God and praying and every time I turned around to a different answer,

the answer was: don't leave. And I had decided that as long as he gave me 100 percent, all he had, that I was gonna allow him to try to do that.

Stacey's husband confessed to her after an incident of sexual contact with a minor during their ten-plus-year marriage. He pled guilty and received a six-month sentence in addition to five years on probation.

Several women in the study had children and spoke of their children and the additional ramifications on their children if they left the relationship. Erica's husband confessed to molestation of a minor that occurred 20 years prior. He was sentenced to five years on probation in a plea agreement but served one year in prison for a violation because he failed to participate in sex offender therapy. Erica discussed the impact her leaving would have had on the children:

> [Leaving] hadn't occurred to me at that time. And when I realize it was a possibility, I knew I had plenty of grounds, but I had no intention of doing it. One factor was that, the effect on our kids, I had a strong feeling that the only thing we can do to repair the damage for our children was to show them that it was possible to get through this. Basically, we've had so much good going for us that I wasn't gonna throw that away. Plus, the fact that once he was caught, he admitted everything and he was willing to do what he had to do. You know, if he had stayed in denial at that point, things might have been different then.

Maria had been with her husband for more than 30 years at the time of the interview. The crime in question was sexual misconduct of a minor, and at jury trial and he was found guilty and served eight years and six years on parole. Maria articulated that part of her motivation in staying with her husband was teaching the children that individuals deserved a second chance:

> I just feel like people deserve a second chance and you know by the grace of God it could've been me that messed and I'd want a second chance. I want to make our marriage work, and I do think it's the best thing for the children if the parents can figure out a way to make it work and I don't know if there's somebody else out there for me.

For Felicia, whose husband was charged with molestation of his children, it was an underlying need to fight for the family, no matter how long the battle:

> I felt like my world was just shattered. You know and I really didn't know what the future was going to hold for us. I always had this feeling that I wanted to fight for my family though. But it took about 6 years before he could come home.

72 Life With a Registered Sex Offender

Criminological literature speaks clearly about the need for family support in reintegrating offenders into society, and the women in this study echoed that theme repeatedly. Several of the women, however, recognized that their support may have been entangled with issues of co-dependency. Cindy's husband was charged with online solicitation of a minor, who was an undercover law enforcement officer. He accepted a plea to five years on probation, but Cindy discussed this incident as a small part of a larger issue of sexual addiction:

> You know, for our family. For him. I felt like he had the best chance of recovery, surrounded by his family. I also now have realized that that's part of my contribution to this mess. It's me, you know, my co-dependence and stuff. And I just trusted God to tell me what I was supposed to do, and I haven't been told I'm supposed to leave yet. I say yet. Our marriage right now is in a really, um, it's at a very critical point. Well, when I looked at both of our families very early in this journey, both of our families are filled with addiction and co-dependency. And that's what we were living in. The others just so happened to be a little bit more socially acceptable … food, alcohol, um, things like that. But, his manifested sexually and his brothers did as well.

Carolyn discussed similar entanglements:

> I'm prepared to say good-bye to our marriage if I need to, but I'm just giving him this chance because if he screws up it'll be jail for the rest of his life and loss of all of his support. I will support him now, but I can't be a doormat anymore. I don't deserve that. I grew up with standing by somebody at their worst if you love them. I really do believe that I am a person who places such a high value on marriage and that when there's a true love, you stand there with somebody no matter what. Is that co-dependency or enabling?

Carolyn had been with her partner for more than 30 years at the time of the interview. At that time, her husband was in prison, serving a ten-year sentence for rape with a weapon, to be followed by five years of supervised probation. Women who chose to stay with partners, especially when sentenced to prison, recognized the tough choice they were making; the fork in the road their lives had brought them to. And for some women, they stayed and provided support because that was how they were raised. April, whose husband said child pornography was planted on his computer by a bitter ex-wife said:

> My crossroad was, is it easier to just walk away from this and say sorry, or move forward? So that was the kind of soul searching that you just have to lay it all out. You have to make a really tough choice. And I thought,

Relationship and Revelation **73**

well, you know, he's always been a really great person. Would you really just leave them when they're down and out? Is that how you're raised, is that what you do? And so, you know, we had agreed, because he kept saying, "You know what, you need to just enjoy your life and I'm good. I'll serve the time and when I'm done, you know, I'll look you up." And I thought, oh that's a really great thing to say and I knew. I just knew, when you're accused of something like this, you don't have friends. You have nobody. So, I stayed.

Robin decided to stay and provide support because her partner had provided her support in the past. At the time of the interview, Robin's boyfriend was serving a prison sentence of just over six years for charges of sexual assault at his workplace.

I was not happy at all. I mean, I was really angry when he didn't fight [the charges]. I was also just angry with all the stuff that had happened. I was angry and I still am. I'm not happy in any way, shape or form about any of it to be completely honest. He's got a long sentence and right now we're still in a relationship but, you know, I mean, we don't know where we're going and the truth is, we probably won't until he gets out. [I have decided to stay by him] mostly because I know the person that he is. He really stuck by me through my disability process and my own challenges. I also really feel like, he really got shafted. I feel like that's really wrong, really, really, really, wrong. And I mean, I know no matter even if we end up going our separate ways … he will be a registered sex offender for the rest of his life. I mean, he helped me in all kinds of ways when I was going through my own challenges. I will stick by him because that's what he did for me. We've been through hell together and no matter what happens I will always be supportive of him.

What women discussed as the main rationale for remaining in the relationship was love. Love was more significant than stability for the children, or support of their partners, or the partner accepting responsibility. Love was the prime motivation for remaining in the relationships after the offense occurred. Victoria talked about the importance of one main element in a marriage: Commitment.

You know, it takes two to tango and my success, our success in this marriage is not just because of me, it's because of us. Communicating through the challenges and issues … I've never doubted that commitment to this marriage on his part or my part and that's huge. You can't experience the highs until you know the lows and we've seen more in 15 years of marriage than most people do in a lifetime. And, you know, people who see us walking in Walmart and stuff, they still think that we're newlyweds a lot of the time because we have a relationship built on … the trust issues we're still working on, we still have some trust issues, but we have a commitment to each other and we have a commitment to God and what the institution of what marriage is and should be and we've had good role models. And that's part of that decision: you make the decision, you work through it, you don't take the easy way out.

Repeatedly, the participants talked about the fact that: "You can love someone and not like their actions" (Sarah) and "then you would choose the love, that's what I chose to do" (Melissa). And some of the women talked about their love for their partners as if it was simple, even though I know from the long conversations I had with them that it was anything but simple and uncomplicated. Leah spoke of her commitment to her marriage after her husband's plea to molestation of his daughter:

I, my biggest thing is that I want everybody to realize how this does affect … well I guess you could say, "If you'd just divorced him you would have been better off," and what start over again? Financially better off? You know, if he wasn't changing, yes. I would have left, but would I want someone to quit on me? No. I'm human, I make mistakes. But I wouldn't want anybody quitting on me and I couldn't do it with him. I mean, like I said, if he wasn't changing, but even now a lot of people say, "Well why are you still married with him when you have to deal with all this stuff?" And it's like, well, okay … for what? To start over? I married for better or worse.

And Stephanie spoke of the importance of unconditional love for her husband who was serving a 16-year prison sentence at the time of the interview for manufacture and distribution of child pornography:

Um, because I love him. I don't know how else to describe it, I love him unconditionally. I love the person that he is, the real person, I don't love the addiction, I love the person he can be and he doesn't have many people right now, you know the longer you stay in prison, the numbers dwindle of people who write to you, remember you and he's expressed multiple times that he's suicidal and I don't feel responsible for keeping his mental health up but I definitely play a part in it and I just, I just love him.

Even in a loving relationship, the women in the study were keenly aware that life was not normal after having a partner designated as an RSO. Tara stated: "I keep hoping that it's going to get better. At one point or another, I keep hoping that we'll have a normal life." This lack of normalcy is part of what causes changes as the relationship moves forward.

Changes in the Relationship

The main changes in the relationship that were expressed by women in this research dealt with the end of the cycle of violence; changes to the family; impacts on closeness within their partnerships; and personal issues of guilt and trust in the relationships. A handful of women in the study talked about the revelation of the offense as a breakthrough because it finally stopped a family cycle of sexual violence. Yolanda's husband confessed to her immediately after he touched his son inappropriately. Yolanda spoke about her husband's secrets of his own history of child sexual abuse:

> The cycle has stopped and that was one of the most important things that we could have done for the family itself. And I don't think that my husband meant to keep it a secret from me, but after so many years of therapy and talking and discussing and wondering, "Why didn't he just tell me?" I have realized that this is the way it was going to be and that you can't control everything. [He] is a better man ... and this is a sad, well not sad, but interesting thing, is that he is a better man because of some of the things that happened. He knows himself better now than he ever has and it's because there were things that he had to deal with that he never dealt with in his life before. So, for him, when we went to ... he had to see a Forensic Psychiatrist ... and for 45 minutes I sat outside of the room and all I heard was crying. And when we were on the way home he said, "I cannot believe how much I feel better. I can't even tell you how I feel, but I know now that those things happened to me, they weren't just dreams. These were things that I always blocked out and never really dealt with." And then, down the road, he was also able to speak with some of his siblings and find out that they were victims too. In some ways this event had to happen in order to stop the cycle.

Colleen's husband was serving 15 years in prison at the time of the interview for molestation of his daughter and receipt of child pornography. Colleen recounted a similar reaction to her husband's history of child sexual abuse:

> I mean, he couldn't explain it. Between that day and the day he was formally arrested he tried to commit suicide twice. Or he, I shouldn't say "tried to commit," I should say he contemplated committing suicide. But, as the year's gone by, he's in his own healing place and we're in our own healing place. So much different and so much healthier and we're able to see the big picture as it is and also each person individually, and

we want to heal and we're truthful about everything in the past and not lying about things and hiding things. I know it sounds bad, but I'm so thankful that it came out because now there's no lies.

Both Yolanda and Colleen recognized the importance of ending the cycle of child sexual abuse and having both husband and children participate in therapy. Research has demonstrated that the sex of child sexual abuse victims may result in different psychosocial impacts. The impact on boys may involve risk factors for social and sexual development that may heighten their likelihood of becoming an offender in adulthood (Plummer & Cossins, 2018).

Other women in the study discussed additional impacts on the family. Sandra's husband was found guilty in a bench trial of sexual contact with a minor that was reported more than a decade after its occurrence. He was sentenced to 10 years and served 6 months. He will spend a lifetime on the sex offense registry. Sandra said:

So yes, it was, yes, [our relationship] did change. My husband was, I think, believe it or not, I think it strengthened us. Once we came to grips with us, it strengthened us. There was a few rough years, about 3 years out that were really rough that initially I think I was in a state of preserving the family situation. And my mind was just on that, keeping the family together.

Stacey also discussed a greater focus on her family and relationship of 12 years since the offense:

I had always desired for him, like I think most women do, for their husbands to be more in tune with their emotions and how important it is to spend time with family, which is something I think most men don't realize. So I had always wished for that – so we weren't gonna let the situation define us and decided to work together, we hadn't always been working in each other's best interest, so we had seen … every day [people] whose lives were torn apart by making dumb decisions … and not trying to work things out and we decided we didn't want our family to be a broken family. So we decided that we wanted to go forward every day and make the best of every day and so now we're a lot more honest with each other and now we're a lot more aware of things that push each other's buttons and what pushes us apart rather than pulling us together. I guess, we're more in tune with our family now than we were before.

When a sexual offense occurs within a long-term dating relationship or marriage, the shock of the event often puts women into a fight or flight situation. The women in this study chose to stay with their partners, and many discussed initially entering survival mode which can serve to bring the couple closer. Victoria's husband pled guilty to two counts of molestation of a minor. She discussed her fight or flight response:

> Initially [our relationship did not change]. I mean, when you're thrown into a situation like this ... I tell people you make a choice to survive or you don't and we went into survival mode. Which included me not dealing with the emotions at the time. We had too much legal stuff to deal with, and we had house stuff ... so you shut down all of the other thoughts so you can deal with the logistics of what's going on. So, in a way we grew closer together initially because in my opinion we were in it together. Like, the rest of the world was against us. So, we were working as a team trying to figure out how we were going to get through this, how do we do this? And even within our own families, there were a lot of mixed emotions. Initially my parents ... because they were scared for their daughter and wanted what was best for their daughter ... my mother and I had a lot of conversations about whether it would be best just for me to leave. But I put it out of my mind. At that point you just go into survival mode and that brings you closer together. So, our relationship actually grew a lot stronger in the months and years that followed ... until I moved ... then, the emotions started hitting me and I had to deal with them.

For women like Brandi, part of what brought her greater closeness to her partner was the stigma she received from the larger society:

> I don't think I'm any less of a person, I just feel like in the eyes of the state and my neighbors I don't matter. I know who I am, and as a matter of fact, I think in some cases I'm a better person than others. I look at the women around me and I think that there's no way that my neighbor's wives, that they would look at their husbands and stick up for them. What would they do if they were walking in my shoes? Then again, they don't know what I know.

The closeness and rebuilding of the relationship doesn't come without questions for a lot of the women, however, and some experienced personal guilt, as well as issues with trust. Though there is significant research to the contrary, society continues to lay the blame for familial sexual abuse at the feet of the adult female partner (Philpot, 2009). There exists the notion that women are responsible if their partners act in ways that are sexually deviant, and this is somehow a result of the females' lack of sexual availability (McLaren, 2013). Melissa explained:

> I had a lot of guilt, I had a lot of guilt that I didn't know this was happening and I mean, it was bad for a while. It was almost, like every other

78 Life With a Registered Sex Offender

> week, we were talking about splitting up and stuff. So it was a lot of ups and downs, it was horror, it was like a roller coaster for a long time and, like I said, it's only been about 2 years now that it's really settled down and I just have this resolved now. It's like I did the best I could at the time and it seems like we are moving forward with this and working through it. I just want what's best.

At times Melissa questioned how this would have impacted her marriage had she known sooner. In her situation, her daughter revealed abuse by her step-father two years after it had ceased. Melissa said:

> There are some days I'm like, "What the hell happened?!" This is crazy and yet, I don't know, if I had known before I got married to him, that there was this problem, or if I would had suspected it, I wouldn't have married him. I feel like I didn't know him until years after we got married and at that point I really had given my life to him.

Christine's situation was a somewhat complicated story of abuse. As a child, she experienced sexual abuse by a family member who was never brought to the attention of law enforcement. Her husband's offense was sexual abuse of a family member that was revealed by the victim well over a decade after the offense occurred. When the incident was revealed, Christine's husband turned himself into the authorities and accepted a plea that resulted in a ten-year suspended sentence, five years on probation, and lifetime on the sex offense registry. So, Christine's marriage of more than three decades had been wrought with this long-hidden secret, for which the family now had to deal with very real legal ramifications. When asked if, in hindsight, she wished she had separated from her husband when she first found out about the offense, her response was:

> No. No, it would have been worse. Like I said, it felt like a death. It was a loss and … if I hadn't been molested as a child, I may have felt different. I may not have understood it like I do with regard to the drug use and pornography. I still don't … I trusted him with my entire soul and I don't anymore and I mourn for that. And it's not like I think he's going to hurt anybody, it's just that I never trusted anybody in my life like I trusted him and it's very sad. I wish I could trust him 100 percent, but I've got to protect myself. And that's sad.

When Christine was asked: "So, even now after all this time, you still haven't got the trust back?" She responded:

> No. 99.9 percent, but I can't say 100 percent. I can't. And alls I can say is that it's sad. I mean, I love him and can't see us ever being apart, but

for it to go that long and I didn't see anything … I don't know. I wish I could because I never trusted anybody and I trusted him with my life and thought I knew him.

Regardless of whether women were married to the individual when the offense occurred, or became involved with the person afterward, studies show that men do not typically recognize the burden placed on women from their involvement in such a relationship. Because he may view his partner in idealized terms, he may fail to see the stress the relationship and its demands place on her everyday life (Scheyett & Pettus-Davis, 2012). Rhonda married the man she dated as a teenager and who was charged with statutory rape for his involvement with her. She said: "I'm not gonna say it's always easy, it's not, it's not always easy being married to a sex offender, but we have a strong family and I think we can get through anything."

Discovery of the Offense

Honest Partners v. Hidden Offenses

Registered sex offenders experience a stigma that is a result of deviations from socially acceptable behaviors, termed a discreditable stigma. This is different from a discredited stigma, which is one that is visibly noticeable to others, such as a physical disability (Goffman, 1963). Not all RSOs experience and react to this labeling in the same way, and in order to manage or reduce stigma, modified labeling theory purports that coping mechanisms can be employed (Link, Cullen, Struening, Shrout, & Dohrenwend, 1989). Examples of coping mechanisms are the education of others to reduce stereotypes, and voluntary honesty about one's offense history. Because most RSOs are subject to public registries, the public can find out about their history with a quick online search. Voluntary disclosure puts the control back in the hands of the offender. An alternative method to manage stigma is secrecy, in which an RSO would seek to hide their status and attempt to pass as an individual who society does not stigmatize (Winnick & Bodkin, 2008). Of importance is that the processes of registration and notification have severely limited the privacy of RSOs and blurred the line between discredited and discreditable stigmas (Evans & Cubellis, 2015).

Of the 94 women in the study, 40 (43 percent) had partners who were upfront and admitted the offense voluntarily. Other ways in which women found out about the offense included law enforcement notification (e.g., when the police appeared with a search or arrest warrant), partner's not-so-voluntary admission (e.g., he called from jail), the victim revealed the incident, another individual revealed the offense (e.g., ex-husband found the RSOs listing on the registry), or she searched online and found the information (e.g., an online search for his name and the registry entry appeared).

80 Life With a Registered Sex Offender

TABLE 3.1 How Partner Found Out About Sex Offense

How Partner Found Out About Sex Offense	Frequency	Percent
Offender Admitted Offense Before/During Dating Voluntarily	40	42.6
Law Enforcement Informed Partner	17	18.1
Offender Admitted Offense Under Other Circumstances (e.g., Called from jail)	14	14.9
Victim Informed Partner	9	9.6
Another Person Informed Partner	7	7.4
Informational Source/Search (e.g., Online)	7	7.4
Total	94	100.0

Interestingly, 37 of the 40 partners who were voluntarily honest involved women whose partner had committed the offense prior to the relationship. So, if we look only at the 56 women who became involved with their partners after they became an RSO, 37 (66 percent) of these men voluntarily admitted the offense to their partners within the first two weeks of dating, versus 19 (34 percent) who hid the offense and let their partners find out another way, or divulged the material later than two weeks (often significantly later than two weeks).[2]

In intimate relationships, expectations are negotiated between partners regarding how each is to behave in order to reduce conflict and create predictability in the union (Roggensack & Sillars, 2013; Roloff & Miller, 2006). Rules may shift as the relationship changes and time progresses, but one prominent category that partners typically negotiate is that of honesty. In a romantic relationship, dishonesty is often viewed as manipulative and deceitful; however, ways to enact honesty in practical terms may vary between partners. One partner may deem unconditional honesty as important, while the other deems only a certain level of honesty as necessary. As such, they may both endorse the ideal of an honest relationship, but pragmatically the application is very different (Metts, 1989). For a relationship to be most successful, a couple should share an understanding of what is both ideal and practically acceptable in terms of honesty in their partnership.

Holly said her partner "was an open book and would tell me anything." He was found guilty at trial and sentenced to ten years plus five years on probation for what he alleged was a false allegation of molestation of a familial minor. The offense occurred prior to their relationship and he told her about the circumstances surrounding the offense before they started dating. Kelly's experience of honesty with her partner was similar:

> He just kind of told me his story from top to bottom sitting at a table at a little cute diner, so um, I'm somebody who, I really prize honesty

and compassion above all else and the fact that he was willing to discuss with me something, not only of a very personal nature, but also had to be humiliating, that really touched me. And he opened up and said he understood if it was too much and that he understood if I didn't want to continue seeing him and I told him that his honesty and openness was exactly why I wanted to keep seeing him.

His revelation came on their very first date. He revealed that he took a plea to two charges of statutory rape at the suggestion of his public defender and was sentenced to five years plus five years on parole. At the time of the interview, Kelly had married her partner and they had been together for approximately two years. The revelation by Sabrina's partner came approximately a week into dating. Her eventual husband had a juvenile sex offender record for a familial offense and an adult offense that he claimed was a false allegation of molestation of a family member. As both offenses involved minors, he will spend the rest of his life on the sex offense registry. Sabrina said:

My reaction was, to be completely honest, my reaction was, "Wow. You're telling me this now? Well, you're probably not going to lie to me about anything else." It's just, I don't know why that was my reaction. I guess I should have probably had a "oh my gosh" reaction to it, and I think I probably had for a little bit like, "Wow." But, I'm not one of those who would blame somebody for their past. I believe in second chances. It took me a while to process that and to be able to ask him questions and be comfortable with that. But it was a trust factor. He chose to tell me right away, and he probably wasn't going to lie about anything else. Because if you're going to lie, that's not something you're going to tell somebody right away.

More than half of the women in the study, however, did not find out in way that involved voluntary honesty from their partner. Deception is surprisingly commonplace in intimate relationships, despite most individual's desire for honesty (Metts, 1989). Deception, however, need not be outright lying. "Deception comes in a variety of guises, from flat-out lies, elaborate fabrications, misdirection and exaggerations, to evasions, equivocations, concealments, omissions, strategic ambiguity … to more subtle misdirection and camouflage" (Burgoon & Levine, 2010: 202). The ways in which RSOs kept offenses hidden were varied.

Cynthia had been with her partner for 14 years. He accepted a plea to molestation of a family member, served a term of probation and will spend his life on the registry. They were married at the time of the interview. Cynthia said:

I didn't find out until [we were married] and we were about to have our first child. He figured that, he was hoping that, it would just go away. And

82 Life With a Registered Sex Offender

> the only reason I found out was that he failed to register when we got married and he moved to another county and they came and arrested him for failure to register and he said he just wanted it to go away, but it didn't ... I couldn't understand why he didn't tell me. I think he thought that I wouldn't have anything to do with him. Which, I couldn't tell you if I would or wouldn't. By the time I found out, we were married and I loved the guy. I don't know what kind of an impact it would've had on me. Because now I wouldn't wish it on anybody. I have never been this exposed to so many ugly, hateful people.

Similarly, Pamela did not find out about her partner's history until after they were married. Her husband accepted a plea to a charge of kidnapping and attempted rape and had served more than two decades in prison before they became involved in their eight-year relationship. Pamela expressed her anger about not knowing before they got married:

> Well you know, he doesn't talk a whole lot about that, as a matter of fact, he didn't tell me about it before we got married, and I was always really mad about that. I think I should have had the choice and he thought I would leave him when I found out and I said, no. Because first of all, it was in [the 1970s], apparently, he was high on drugs, acid, maybe? And this whole thing happened, well he doesn't remember it. But he was convicted of it and put him in prison for it, well it was his second felony conviction so they gave him 43 years.... He doesn't really remember what happened, only what he was told in the courtroom.

Valerie was devastated by her partner's lies:

> Well, I was freaking out honestly (laughs). I don't mean to laugh, I just do that when I get nervous. But, anyway, I ... um ... was devastated and I was crying. I was honestly more upset because of the lying rather than what had happened because I had been in relationships before where there was a big age gap difference. When we went into the relationship, I had made decisions in the past that I wasn't very proud of and we had agreed, well, I said, "I don't want to discuss details of our past. I don't want to have any mental images of you, and I don't want you to hear about mine." So, that's how we went into our marriage. But the only problem I had was when our past became our present in his situation, and I thought, "Well, he lied about it instead of being truthful."

In Valerie's situation, she and her partner were engaged when he was arrested and charged with statutory rape. He initially lied to her about being involved with the female alleged in the statutory rape charge. He eventually accepted a plea

Relationship and Revelation **83**

and the accompanying sentence of was ten years on probation. Because statutory offenses involve a minor, he will spend his life on the registry. Valerie proceeded with the wedding and she and her partner were together three years at the time of the interview.

Janet had been dating her partner for 18 months at the time of the study. He served three years for sexual contact with a minor who he was dating prior to the start of his relationship with Janet.[3] He will spend his life on the registry. Janet said:

> He didn't tell me until a year into us dating. I was already in love with him. I was sick. Physically sick because my experience was from my neighbor and the stories that I had read about my neighbor were ugly. [The neighbor had been arrested for a third time for rape.] So, I knew exactly what I think most of the media knows. You hear those words and you think "monster," you know. And it's kind of weird, based on my neighbor, I read all that stuff, and that person that I saw playing with his daughter, who was so nice and loving, it messes with your mind because what you read doesn't match what you see. [When I found out], I was very, very, very angry. Extremely angry. I felt betrayed. But I had to come to terms with that too. Changing roles. How would I deal with that if I had to tell somebody what he had to tell me? You know, I think it's diffi-cult and I had to look at it from his point of view. I was still angry. Every now and then I think about it and I still get mad because he didn't tell me when I thought he should have. But I also can't hang onto it now because it's too far back and I made my decision to stay.

These are obvious examples of the RSOs trying to manage stigma with secrecy; however, in each of these cases, the men put their partners in extremely difficult positions. In some cases of deception, the women found out from someone other than their partner. Danielle found out the man she would eventually marry was an RSO from her ex-husband. She was not made aware of this until 4 months into the relationship.

> [After dating for 4 months and thinking her boyfriend had been in prison for counterfeiting, her ex-husband called her and told her otherwise.] I call [my boyfriend] and I say, "I'm going to give you one chance for you to be honest with me. Do you want to tell me what you really went to jail for?" And I figured that at that point he knew I knew considering that I was asking and the way that I was asking, and he told me. He didn't tell me the entire story … even to this day he hasn't told me everything. He talks about it more now … but it's not a subject that he shares. Most of the information that I have is from read-ing the actual court documents and the little bit that he shares every once in a while. But, really, what he shares, I already know because it's

84 Life With a Registered Sex Offender

> been in black and white. I think I found out the truth 1.5 to 2 years into our relationship.

Danielle had been with her husband for six years and said it's a subject that she wasn't fully aware of and that they did not discuss. Her husband accepted a plea of 18 months in prison and 1 year probation term to a charge of statutory rape. He will also serve ten years on the registry.

Cheryl was leisurely reading the newspaper when she came across her boyfriend's registry information:

> [I read about it in the newspaper. I saw the registry notification]. I called him right away when I saw the article and said [do] you have something to tell me? He was vague and he said it's true, it happened. And then we saw each other a couple days later but he still couldn't really explain what happened. And then it wasn't for like, I think it was two summers later he finally expressed what happened and it wasn't a huge concern for me because I knew what kind of person he was already and how he treated me. The more I got into learning about the laws and all the restrictions, I figured I should know. [It bothered me that he didn't tell me], but he explained that it was how do you tell someone that and it was prior to his conviction and I suffer from severe depression and I was going through a hard time, I was between medications on top of everything that summer. And he said he tried to tell me a couple times but that I wasn't handling anything very well. Part of me wishes he had told me, but the other part understands. You want to kind of know how somebody would react before you just throw that out there. He didn't want to lose me because of that.

At the time of the interview, Cheryl was still in a relationship of 3.5 years with her boyfriend who had taken a plea to a charge of possession of child pornography. Because the charge involved minors, he will spend a lifetime on the registry. Just fewer than half of the women in this study had partners who were honest with them about their offense. Though two-thirds of the women who became involved with their partner after he was designated an RSO experienced honesty from their partner very early in the relationship.

Reactions to the Offense

Reactions to finding out about the offense and its ramifications for the relationship and for the future depended, in part, on whether the offense occurred prior to the relationship or within the context of the relationship, and the partner's honesty. For women who were involved with men who were RSOs prior to

Relationship and Revelation **85**

their meeting, the reactions ranged from shock, to hurt, to nonchalance about the implications, to an understanding that individuals deserved a second chance. For some of the women, the men they were dating did not align with the stereotypes of an RSO that they had learned from the media. Sharon had been dating someone for 18 months who told her on the first date about his plea to a charge of possession of child pornography. She said:

> Well, it was shocking because when he told me was a registered sex offender, I was completely ignorant of what that was. When you were telling me 2 years ago about sex offenders, I thought about predators, guys raping little kids. I didn't understand that it's not just that. I do believe in second chances, so I let him talk and of course, I ask him, what was your charge, what did you do? And when he told me, I ask a lot of questions. Okay, this is not what I thought, I allow myself to know him and let him open up and see who he is and if it would work out. But at the beginning, I freaked.

Renee echoed similar sentiments about her partner not upholding stereotypes regarding sex offenders.

> I was pretty shocked because he didn't seem like what I thought a sex offender would be like. Shocked is a good word for it. And he told me the entire story and I processed it and I realized it didn't change the man that I knew and just moved on from there.

Renee did not find out about her eventual husband's offense until six months into their dating relationship. At that point, he told her that he had served two years in prison for solicitation of a minor and intent to distribute child pornography. He will spend 25 years on the registry. At that point, she felt quite involved in the relationship.

Melinda had been with a man for 18 months with a history of criminal justice system involvement, including multiple DUIs and varied sexual offenses, such as exhibitionism, public urination, failure to register an address change, and residing too close to a school. Two-months into dating:

> I found out he had a record and I said to him, is there anything else you wanna tell me because now would be a good time and he said, well, I'm a registered sex offender. And I mean my whole world just fell, because I thought, you're kidding right? I mean he's such a great guy, so fun and, you know, like I said, my idea of a sex offender is like what a lot of other people's is, unfortunately, so I thought, my god, he's into kids and what did he do. You know, I mean, I was out of my mind, because I thought, what did I get myself into?

86 Life With a Registered Sex Offender

Once Melinda realized her partner's offenses did not involve children, she decided to continue with the relationship. At the time of the interview, her boyfriend was serving a three-year prison sentence for a failure to register violation. Angela knew about her eventual husband's plea to possession and distribution of child pornography before they started dating. She said:

> I was really hurt that he had done something like that. Only because I had been sexually abused as a child so, it was kind of an off thought for me. I didn't want to think that other people, I knew, I already knew that the numbers are high from talking to people about my experience. That between one and four women will be sexually abused at one point in their life. I hate to think that people I know, that I like, are also into that kind of stuff, you know? It was really difficult on me. I had to really re-evaluate the way I looked at it. I had to judge him as a person and not what he did in the past and try to tell myself that he's trying to move past and trying to be a better person. I cried for a good day when I found out.

Kelly discussed similar themes of judging a person on their current actions and extending a person a second chance. Prior to meeting, her husband served five years in prison and a five-year parole term for two charges of statutory rape. At the time of the interview, her husband had not yet been assigned a tier level, so the future ramifications of his RSO status on their lives was unclear. Kelly stated:

> I guess because I've been through enough of life that things are not black and white. I make mistakes, I've been perceived for somebody I am not. You know, I feel that, for him, that time of shame and humiliation and come through it and continually working on healing and becoming a part of society again. I could relate to the situation where your judgment failed you and you are now perceived as something you are not. I believe everybody deserves, I believe that most people deserve (laughs) more than a second chance because everybody has screwed up royally at some point in their lives and everybody has had the grace to be given that second chance and forgiven by somebody. And that's why I didn't go running.

For Samantha, the same notions of forgiveness and change were what led her to pursue a relationship with and eventually marry her partner. Prior to their marriage, he pled guilty to what he said was a false allegation of sexual contact with a familial minor. He was sentenced to 15 years on probation and subsequently served five years on a drug violation. The alleged victim later recanted. Samantha, who found out about his history a couple of weeks into dating, stated:

I guess I just kind of thought, "The guy really seems to have turned his life around. And not just recently. He seems like he turned his life around years ago and has learned to become a normal human being that can follow society's rules and has learned from his mistakes," and all of that. I just kind of figured that's probably what happened and I just didn't really think much of it. I really didn't feel like, at that point in time, that there was any crime that, once you paid your dues, that you had to keep paying for it for the rest of your life. Even people who, like, murder people, once they do their sentence, they're out and I never knew the politics involved with sex offenders. That you're never out. Never. And you never stop paying and you never get out from under anyone's thumb. And these people who have done these other crimes, they end up walking away. Basically, the punishment that you have on you is "yeah, I was in prison before and it's kind of hard to get a job." And that's what I thought we would be up against if we moved through life together. So, I didn't think that I should bail at that point in time, but then it started to get more serious and I was thinking that I would probably marry this guy. And he was really open with that and was like, "You know, your life is probably not going to be that good because I can't ... I'm not a normal person according to the Federal Government. I'm not allowed to be normal, I'm not allowed to do anything without being constantly punished." And once I got deeper into understanding how that system works, that was hard, but I had already made a decision that this was the direction I wanted to move with my life ... I already loved him, so....

Samantha's husband will spend his life on the sex offense registry.

For women who were married to the men when the offense occurred, the reactions ranged from devastation, to anger, to shock, to fear, to disbelief, to suicide attempts. Yolanda's husband confessed to her immediately when the incident of familial molestation occurred. She described her reaction:

> And I'm not thinking ... but he brought me upstairs into the bedroom and told me what happened. And after that I was screaming. I was devastated. I was like, "Oh my God, what did you do?!" And I can't even describe ... it was like a blur at that point because I was so upset about ... just about ... I just couldn't believe it was happening. And he was crying and I was like, "Was this the first or has this been going on?" and he was like, "No, no, I can't even tell you ... this is the first time, I've never done ... I was abused by my father and I never, never thought this could happen...." It was just like, you couldn't believe it was happening. Well, I have to tell you that at that point I was like ... we were really ... I was in shock, he was in shock, the kids were like ... uh, okay, whatever. But we

88 Life With a Registered Sex Offender

> sat [our child] down and told [the child] that that was not a good thing that happened and that it would not happen again and that this was not right and not what you do. And [the child] was like okay, let's play video games and they were fine and dandy. But [my husband] was like, this is nuts. Our first inclination was … well our first inclination was not to call an attorney, which it should have been. And I'm going to say that loud and clear whether anybody understands that, I don't know. But it was, "Oh my God, we need help." I didn't know what to do. I didn't know if the kids should stay or if we should call somebody or what. We couldn't let that fester. It's at that point where something needs to be done and we called crisis because [my husband] was in a state where he didn't know if he was going to hurt himself. And neither of us could believe it was happening and you're feeling all kinds of feelings that you're just not even able … things are going so unbelievably fast through your head that you're not able to process it. You feel distrust and upset and sick to your stomach, and you're wondering, "How did I let this happen?" And you're wondering how you could not know … I don't know how other people deal with it if it's something that goes on over a period of time because I could not deal with it and it lasted less than 20 seconds.

This situation of abuse occurred in the context of a 30-year marriage between Yolanda and her husband. He accepted a plea of five years on probation. In Christine's situation, the familial abuse did not come to light until well over a decade after it occurred. Christine talked about her reaction to finding out what had occurred so many years prior:

> So, I came home and [my husband] came home and I asked him … he was upset and crying and I was crying and I said, "Is it true? Just tell me if it's true." And he said, "If she says so, then I guess it's true." And I remember screaming, "No! It either happened or it didn't!" And he said that it happened and he told me about it. I think we were awake for like 3 or 4 days, crying and holding each other. I can't explain that. It felt like mourning. Like someone had died. And the only thing that I could focus in on was he and I and our two daughters. And I can't explain that. You would think that I would be so angry … but it was like … I don't know how to explain it. It became so close … I mean … we, for like 3 or 4 days, we weren't out of each other's sight. And it was like a mourning period. Like when someone extremely close dies and you just feel shell-shocked. So, my [family member] had been emailing me back and forth and was like, "We don't want to cause any trouble, we just want [the husband] to get the help he needs." And, of course, [my husband] got into therapy right away … he went to AA and told me about drinking his cold syrup and things before he got home. And I still can't

Relationship and Revelation **89**

believe that I didn't have a clue. Then next came telling [our children] and making sure that they were okay. Of course, that's the first thing I did was question him about other kids and [our children] and he said no, never. And I asked him if he liked children or was attracted to children. And it was very painful, but I needed to know these things. I needed truth after all these years.

Shortly after the events came to light, Christine's long-time husband turned himself into the authorities. He quickly took a plea and received a ten-year suspended sentence and a term of five years on probation. Crystal and her partner of more than two decades had been experiencing some marital problems, issues with sexual intimacy, when one day the police appeared at the house with a search warrant. Crystal elaborated:

> I conveyed absolutely nothing. I just read it [the search warrant] and was stone silent. But what I was thinking was, "Oh, so this has been the problem all along." And the second thought I had was, "So, this is how this ends." [About 2 weeks prior] we had a huge fight about sex where I said, "We have to do something to fix this, we have to fix our marriage because this isn't normal." And he screamed at me, "If that's what you want, then you need to go find somebody else." And I told him to stop saying that because I didn't want somebody else, I wanted us to work. And he kind of had a breakdown in that moment. And he's not a screamer, but he had this shaking, frightening response where he said, "I am such a loser. I completely ruined my life. My life is completely worthless and if I knew where the gun was I would have used it by now." And I was horrified. Not only by his words, but the intensity behind them. And I stopped talking about sex and said, "Okay, obviously there's a bigger issue here than just sex. You are unhappy on a level that I didn't even know."

Two weeks later, the police showed up and arrested her husband for possession of child pornography. He was sentenced to 2.5 years in prison. Sarah's husband was also convicted for possession of child pornography and she described the terror of the police appearing at her home:

> I was terrified. There's no other way to explain the feeling, the emotions, no one will ever understand them unless you've had the police come into your home. You know, your first, your every emotion is like surprise, completely … no. Because in my head it's like it was inevitable. You're messing with fire when you're doing that, you know what I mean? I wasn't stupid to think that there wasn't stuff that – it's hard to explain everything that you're thinking at the time. I was scared for me,

90 Life With a Registered Sex Offender

> I was scared for my children, and I wanted to protect my children. I was mad as hell with him. At the same time, I was, I wanted to warn him, I wanted to talk to him, I wanted to know what he was thinking, what was going on. And I was afraid for him. So, every possible emotion you can think of.

At the time of the interview, Sarah's husband was serving a five-year prison term for one count of possession of child pornography. Of the 94 women interviewed for this research, 22 (23 percent) of their partners claimed the offense for which they were convicted or accepted a plea was a false allegation. In those cases, the reaction was most definitely shock, as in the case of Tracy:

> Stunned. Totally stunned, and we thought the justice system would work. I mean, we thought, "Nothing will come of this. She [the alleged victim] has to be interviewed, they'll have to interview [my husband], they'll have to interview me, and you know, she'll have to be able to say this or that happened." But they never interviewed [my husband], they never interviewed me. I was over there that evening; he was never alone with her. The [alleged victim's] mother was there. We knew it was a total lie.

Tracy's husband pled guilty to sexual misconduct with a minor at the advice of his paid attorney. The rationalization was that the potential sentence from a guilty finding at trial could be extremely long. He was sentenced to a term of ten years on probation and ten years on the registry.

Most women used words like "devastated" to describe their reaction to finding out about their husband's offense. Stephanie said: "Uh, yeah, I was devastated and angry and scared and I didn't know really what ... at that point and I was just devastated I guess." For women with existing mental health vulnerabilities, however, the impact could be extreme. Tina said:

> I ended up in a psych hospital when I found out, tried to kill myself and ended up in a psych hospital. And I had this dissociative episode that lasted about 7 months. I don't remember much of it. I don't remember losing the house, the psychiatrist made me sign power of attorney over to my [child] to deal with the house. I lost the house, I lost everything. And my family, my [children] deserted me and I had no support system set up. I'm bipolar.

For Erica it felt like the end of the world when her husband confessed to molestation of a family member two decades after the incident:

> [I felt] like it was the end of the world, I knew right away that he wouldn't be allowed to see our grandchildren. So, my first reaction, other than

knowing we couldn't have any more foster children, which was something I just loved. It felt like my children had died. It was intense grief.

Brandi said, "I was righteously pissed. I was angry at my husband. I was angry at a lot of things. I felt deceived." And Maria discussed the lasting impact on trust: "Trust was completely blown out of the water. I was devastated, I was in a fog for about 2 years, pretty much." The range of emotions women experienced was extensive and changed day-to-day as they dealt with the reality of their situation. Donna explained:

> Yeah, I was just kind of dumbfounded and upset and like, okay, well, you know, I guess we'll just get through this one step at a time. I guess at that point I didn't think it would turn out as it did, I guess. I didn't realize how much it would involve at that point.

Donna's husband of over a decade accepted a plea to molestation of a minor, after the minor told Donna about the incident and she confronted her husband with the details. He was sentenced to five years and served one year, and will spend his life on the registry. At the time of the interview, the family was still coming to terms with the ramifications of the registry and its collateral consequences.

Motives for beginning a relationship with an RSO or staying in a marriage with an RSO are varied and complex, and women in these relationships experience hesitations for moving forward with such relationships. Whether the partner kept the offense hidden or was voluntarily honest about the offense is very important to the success of the partnership and has ramifications for the women's reaction to the overall situation. Relationships bring many challenges and the stigma of a relationship with an individual reintegrating into society post-incarceration brings greater challenges. A relationship with an individual on the sex offense registry, stigmatized by society brings yet further challenges. Ninety-seven percent of the women in this study felt the relationship was worth the attempts to navigate these additional challenges.

Notes

1. Twenty-three men in the study (24 percent) had received probationary or community supervision sentences as a result of their conviction or plea, and one man had not yet been sentenced at the time of the interview with his partner.
-2. I elected to use a two-week dating timeline as the cutoff point between what was considered an "honest partner" and what was considered a "hidden offense." After much discussion with colleagues, I determined that several conversations/dates would have occurred by the two-week point. Additionally, many adults would have determined whether they were pursuing the relationship, and something of this magnitude should have been revealed to a potential partner by that point. The partners of the women in this study apparently agreed as there was a dramatic discrepancy in when they revealed their history. Most RSOs elected to tell potential partners very soon (often on the first

92 Life With a Registered Sex Offender

date and very often within the first two weeks), or they elected to wait a very long time (one year or more; and in several cases after the couple had been married), or did not tell their partner at all and she found out another way.

3. Because of the age difference involved in this offense, it was not considered statutory. There was well over a decade separating the RSO and the female in question.

References

Braman, D. (2004). *Doing time on the outside: Incarceration and family life in urban America.* Ann Arbor, MI: University of Michigan Press.

Burgoon, J. K., & Levine, T. R. (2010). Advances in deception detection. In S. W. Smith & S. R. Wilson (Eds.), *New directions in interpersonal communication research* (pp. 201–220). Thousand Oaks, CA: Sage Publications, Inc.

Christian, J. (2005). Riding the bus: Barriers to prison visitation and family management strategies. *Journal of Contemporary Criminal Justice*, 21(1), 31–48.

Comfort, M. (2007a). *Doing time together: Love and family in the shadow of the prison.* Chicago, IL: University of Chicago Press.

Comfort, M. (2007b). Punishment beyond the legal offender. *Annual Review of Law and Social Science*, 3, 271–296.

Evans, Douglas N., & Cubellis, Michelle A. (2015). Coping with stigma: How registered sex offenders manage their public identities. *American Journal of Criminal Justice*, 40, 593–619.

Farkas, Mary Ann, & Miller, Gale. (2007). Reentry and reintegration: Challenges faced by the families of convicted sex offenders. *Federal Sentencing Report*, 20(2), 88–92.

Goffman, Erving. (1963). *Stigma: Notes on the management of spoiled identity.* New York, NY: Simon Schuster, Inc.

Herman-Stahl, M., Kan, M. L., & McKay, T. E. (2008). *Incarceration and the family: A review of research and promising approaches for serving fathers and families.* Research Triangle Park, NC: Prepared for Department of Health and Human Services, Office of the Assistant Secretary of Planning and Evaluation and Office of Family Assistance.

Lindquist, Christine, Landwehr, Justin, McKay, Tasseli, Feinberg, Rose, Comfort, Megan, & Bir, Anupa. (2015). *Multisite family study on incarceration, parenting and partnering: Change in couple relationships before, during, and after incarceration.* ASPE Research Brief. Washington, DC: Office of the Assistant Secretary for Planning and Evaluation, U.S. Department of Health and Human Services.

Link, B. G., Cullen, F. T., Struening, E., Shrout, P. E., & Dohrenwend, B. P. (1989). A modified labeling theory approach to mental disorders: An empirical assessment. *American Sociological Review*, 54(3), 400–423.

Lopoo, L. M., & Western, B. (2005). Incarceration and the formation and stability of marital unions. *Journal of Marriage and Family*, 67(3), 721–734.

Martinez, Damian J. (2006). Informal helping mechanisms: Conceptual issues in family support of reentry of former prisoners. *Journal of Offender Rehabilitation*, 44(1), 23–37.

Martinez, Damian J., & Christian, Johnna. (2009). The familial relationships of former prisoners: Examining the link between residence and informal support mechanisms. *Journal of Contemporary Ethnography*, 38(2), 201–224.

McLaren, Helen Jaqueline. (2013). (Un)-blaming mothers whose partners sexually abuse children: In view of heteronormative myths, pressures and authorities. *Child & Family Social Work*, 18, 439–448.

Metts, S. (1989). An exploratory investigation of deception in close relationships. *Journal of Social and Personal Relationships, 6*, 159–179.

Petersilia, J. (2003). *When prisoners come home: Parole and prisoner reentry.* Oxford: Oxford University Press.

Patterson, J. M. (2002). Integrating family resilience and family stress theory. *Journal of Marriage and Family, 64*(2), 349–360.

Philpot, Terry. (2009). *Understanding child abuse: The partners of child sex offenders tell their stories.* New York, NY: Routledge.

Plummer, Malory, & Cossins, Annie. (2018). The cycle of abuse: When victims become offenders. *Trauma, Violence & Abuse, 19*(3), 286–304.

Roloff, M. E., & Miller, C.W. (2006). Social cognition approaches to understanding interpersonal conflict and communication. In J. G. Oetzel & S. Ting-Toomey (Eds.), *The Sage handbook of conflict communication: Integrating theory, research, and practice* (pp. 97–128). Thousand Oaks, CA: Sage.

Roggensack, Katlyn Elise & Sillars, Alan. (2013). Agreement and understanding about honesty and deception rules in romantic relationships. *Journal of Social and Personal Relationships, 31*(2), 178–199.

Scheyett, Anna M., & Pettus-Davis, Carrie. (2012). Let momma take 'em: Portrayals of women supporting male former prisoners: *International Journal of Offender Therapy and Comparative Criminology, 57*(5), 578–591.

Shapiro, C., & Schwartz, M. (2001). Coming home: Building on family connections. *Corrections Management Quarterly, 5*(3), 52–61.

Wildeman, C., Schnittker, J., & Turney, K. (2012). Despair by association? The mental health of mothers with children by recently incarcerated fathers. *American Sociological Review, 77*(2), 216–243.

Winnick, T., & Bodkin, M. (2008). Anticipated stigma and stigma management among those to be labeled "ex-con." *Deviant Behavior, 29*(4), 295–333.

4

UNDERSTANDING AND CONSEQUENCES

Techniques of Neutralization

Neutralization theory can be traced back to the 1940s, with roots in psychologists such as Fritz Redl, David Wineman, and Donald Cressey, and sociologists like Edwin Sutherland (though unacknowledged), C. Wright Mills, and Kenneth Burke (Maruna & Copes, 2005). Neutralization theorists suggest that individuals are generally committed to the social order and its social norms. As such, when they violate these norms, shame, or guilt typically occurs. For the most part, this shame and the resultant negative self-blame act to dissuade a person from engaging in future deviance. In order to continue to participate in deviance, neutralizations or rationalizations of the behavior must occur (Sykes & Matza, 1957). In studying offenders who do not offend further, and desist from sex offending specifically, researchers have found that optimistic future narratives and cognitive transformations which involve a positive self-image are important (Hulley, 2016; Maruna & Mann, 2006). Cognitive therapy for treatment, especially for sex offenders, centers on holding offenders accountable for their behaviors, and confronting excuses and justifications for deviance that insulate the offender from societal and self-blame (Blagden, Winder, Gregson, & Thorne, 2014; Sykes & Matza, 1957; Ware & Mann, 2012).

Neutralization theory is usually not viewed as a stand-alone theory, but instead understood as an enhancement to existing theoretical explanations.[1] It has influenced criminal justice applications such as restorative justice, cognitive therapy, situational crime prevention, and reintegrative shaming (Maruna & Copes, 2005). Many offenses are "based on what is essentially an unrecognized extension of defenses to crimes, in the form of justifications for deviance that are seen as valid by the [offender] but not by the legal system or society at large" (Sykes & Matza, 1957: 666). On a practical level, these psychological techniques include denial, minimization, excuses, justifications, cognitive distortions, and neutralization (Farmer, McAlinden, & Maruna, 2015; Maruna & Mann, 2006). These techniques help an offender maintain a personal positive narrative, and protect their identity from stigma, public labeling, guilt, and shame.

The techniques of neutralization according to Sykes and Matza (1957) are first, *denial of responsibility*. If an offender can define themselves as "lacking responsibility for his deviant actions, the disapproval of self or others is sharply reduced in effectiveness as a restraining influence" (Sykes & Matza, 1957: 667). Denial of responsibility extends beyond a simple lack of intention, however. An offender may deny responsibility if the cause of the offense was due to a factor beyond his control, such as abusive parents or addiction to drugs or alcohol. Second, *denial of injury*. This neutralization hinges on whether an individual was "harmed" during the offense. Defining harm, however, is subjective. Third, *denial of the victim*. This neutralization involves the offender's denial that a victim exists. Instead, the "victim" is transformed into one deserving of injury as rightful punishment or retribution. Fourth, *condemnation of the condemners*. In this neutralization, the offender transfers attention away from his own deviance and focuses it instead on the behaviors and motives of those who disapprove of his behaviors. This is a shift in the dialog from the offender's behaviors to the reactions of society. The goal in this neutralization is to mask the wrongfulness of the deviant behavior. Fifth, *appeal to higher loyalties*. This neutralization occurs when societal norms are rejected in favor of other norms, deemed to be more important (such as friend or family norms). As part of this neutralization, role conflict occurs when the offender believes in both sets of norms. Other techniques of neutralization have been developed in the literature since Sykes and Matza's work (1957), one of which is relevant for this study. *Justification by comparison* involves the belief that the crime committed is not serious in comparison to the crimes of others (Cromwell & Thurman, 2003).

Sykes and Matza argued that deviance "is based on what is essentially an unrecognized extension of defenses to crimes, in the form of justifications for deviance that are seen as valid by the [offender] but not by the legal system or society at large" (1957: 666). Research has demonstrated that both offenders and non-offenders make excuses for their behavior. Meta-analyses have revealed that most individuals make external attributions when we experience failures, and internal attributions when we experience successes (Zuckerman, 1979). This is normal blame deflection behavior. What this study found in interviews with partners of RSOs, was that they too used justifications for their partner's deviant behaviors. The four types of techniques of neutralization used by partners were: denial of responsibility, denial of injury, justification by comparison, and condemnation of the condemners.

Denial of Responsibility

Denial of responsibility occurs when a woman either denies responsibility for her partner's offense or shifts responsibility to a factor outside of her partner's control. Of the 94 women in the study, 20 (21 percent) denied her partner's offense happened, and two other women (2 percent) denied a portion of the charges. Michelle's husband served ten years in prison after pleading guilty to molestation of a male minor family member in what he alleged was a false accusation. This occurred prior to his involvement with Michelle, and while her husband was not forthcoming with her when they started dating, she maintained his innocence in the interview:

> [I believed from the outset that nothing happened] absolutely ... absolutely. Because when my girls were little, their father molested them. He went to court, he got a lawyer, he got 2-year probation and nothing else and he spent almost 10 years sodomizing and raping my little girls. So, I know what a child molester acts like. I know HOW they are. I was raised molested by my father from the time I was a toddler. I have something inside of me, it's like a sensor, I can tell when something's wrong, and it wasn't there with him.

Michelle's husband will remain on the sex offense registry for life. Seven of the 22 cases (32 percent) that were allegedly false allegations involved molestation of a child or step-child. Five of those seven cases occurred in the context of a separation or divorce proceeding.

Denial of responsibility that shifted liability to a factor outside of the partner's control revolved around two main issues: addiction and parenting. This technique of neutralization involved admission to the offense itself, but attribution of blame to another source: the idea that it was "not the offender's fault." In terms of addiction, while some women explained their partner's offense in terms of drug or alcohol addiction, most addictive behavior revolved around sex addiction or addiction to pornography. Andrea neutralized her husband's behavior with alcohol addiction and association with his military friends:

> So, he was around people he really shouldn't have been with, people who were basically alcoholics, partiers all the time. It's the military, they're just really into that in the culture and they're for it ... I think he was extremely drunk and I think he was a little bit out of his mind and I think he went in and I don't think he knew what he was doing. And I think he was rubbing himself on somebody and I don't know what he thought he was doing, but he has no prior history of doing anything like this, this was an isolated incident and I know he was drinking, that was

a lot of alcohol he was drinking and I have seen people do some crazy things, crazy, irrational, disgusting stuff, when they're under the influence of alcohol.

Andrea's husband pled guilty to attempted rape and received a ten-year suspended sentence. He later served 18 months for a GPS violation. At the time of our interview, he was on parole in a different state from where she resided, though they remained married and she remained committed to him.

Christine explained her husband's offense with a combination of addiction to substances and pornography:

> Oh my God, yes. I mean, this is the only thing he's done. I don't think he is a pedophile and I know that he was stoned out of his mind. I mean, it's like my dad. I mean he would have never, never done anything if he wasn't under the influence. I mean, I guess that's why I can live with it, because I know it wasn't him. And that's another thing, when VCRs first came out in 1981 we rented porn and we just thought it was hilarious. And I think that that along with the marijuana made his inhibitions low at that time. I think that the pornography had something to do with it. And we watched them together, so it's not like he hid it from me, but I think that pornography was part of the problem.

Her husband's offense was molestation of a family member which was not revealed until more than 15 years after its occurrence. Repeatedly, the women I spoke with revealed issues with intimacy and sex addiction as explanations for their husband's offenses. Stephanie's partner was in prison on a 16-year sentence at the time of the interview. He pled guilty to manufacture and distribution of child pornography. The offense involved taking pictures of a minor family member. Stephanie revealed knowing about the pornography addiction but not knowing how to address it with her partner:

> He's a sex addict … yeah, yeah. And I knew about the pornography, I didn't know what to do about it, it was one of those things where you know about it but you don't focus on it, I mean, I wanted, but, he wanted help for it, we had a couple talks about it, he didn't like that side of himself and didn't know how to stop it but didn't know where to get help for it. You can't just walk into a counseling place and say, I'm a sex offender or I'm addicted to child pornography, please help me. I mean, there's a part of you that, there was a part of him wanted help but there's a part of him that thought he'd never get caught too. And I didn't know what to do about it and it was quite a mess. And he got caught. And I mean, I'm glad he got caught. I wish we had a system set up that could actually help people.

98 Life With a Registered Sex Offender

Crystal, whose husband spent just over two years in prison for possession of child pornography, echoed similar themes:

> I guess he needed this other release, but he would never come to our marriage for it. So, why he wouldn't do that, I don't know because I know [my husband] loves me. I've always felt that [he] loved me, even today, but he's got internal struggles with intimacy and expressing himself sexually. So, to answer your question, did I know he looked at porn? Yes. Did I think it was to the extent that it was? Absolutely not. Did I think he was looking at it every day? Absolutely not. Was he looking at it every day? Yes. And we had some very severe problems with that because it was getting worse and worse for me. [And] I wasn't very brave about confronting [him]. I didn't confront him about the frequency or the intimacy and I didn't really confront him about the porn. Once I did, but ... and once he said that it helped him in our intimate life [which] was a crock of shit. If I had noticed it helping, I would have said, "By all means, have another run at it and I'll meet you in the bedroom," but it did not. And I think that was an excuse on his part. And the thing that I was going to say that I think is really important here, is that when I did confront [him] ... in regards to being more involved sexually, he said, "I can't do it. If that's what you want, go out and find somebody else." And I found that so threatening and horrifying that that would be my ... the possibility of losing him was what was on the table that I didn't push it any further. The idea of losing [him] and the idea of having to start dating again and the idea of never being able to find someone that I was this compatible with just put me into an apoplectic state. Just the idea that he and I wouldn't make it, and especially, and just, I always used the word "just" ... just over sex? I don't think I gave enough weight and I don't think [he] gave enough weight to the important role that sex plays in a marriage. I guess if both people don't care, then they're fine.... But, when you're unequally matched in that area ... I don't think either of us put enough weight on the fact that sex is the only activity that you don't do with other people. Sex is the only activity that separates marital activity from all other activities. So, I didn't give enough weight to it and he didn't give enough weight to it and thought he could get away with it on the side, on the sly, and it was a huge miscalculation on both of our parts.

The pornography addiction, and the imprisonment that followed the child pornography possession charge, had really taken a toll on their long-term relationship. At the time of the interview, Crystal's husband had not yet been assigned a tier level, so the extent and length of state control was unknown. Sarah mentioned similar recurrent themes with pornography in her relationship:

Going all the way back to the beginning, um, we had had issues on and off throughout our marriage with him, with pornography. You know, arguments, fights, different things, to the point that, at one point he went and got counseling, but it was kind of like, okay, I went once, now you've gotta go and it's an ongoing thing. Typical at times, to the point that what happened ultimately was inevitable I assume, in his search for pornography and the ease with which it was available on the internet. He started searching and spending a lot of non-family time on the computer. Like, literally getting up at 3 o'clock in the morning when the whole house is asleep to search the internet for pornography. And in the process, he obviously stumbled across some underage photos. But, in the end, they actually only found 15 photos, underage photos, on the computer. Which is reassuring for me, because that means that obviously that's not what his intent was and you know, it's something he probably stumbled across that he didn't actually dwell on, but it was enough to get him in trouble. Truthfully, and for my own purposes, I kept my head buried in the sand about a lot of the minute details. I did read from descriptions of some of the photos. My understanding is they were not like 6-, 7-, and 8-year-olds, they were just young teens. I mean, I don't know that there's really a difference. They were young females. They were not males or anything like that. Like I said, I don't know the details and it's one of those things I don't want to know. Certain things, I know a lot, and I've done research a lot, but then there's some of the details that you know, the less I know, the better off I am. But, like I said, the descriptions that I read, they actually, truthfully, some of the photos, they categorized as nature type photos. I'm guessing as to what that would mean and a couple conversations I've had with my husband, they were like, I want to say, like nude family photos.

Sarah justified her husband's offense as part of a pornography addiction, which from her perspective, removed some of his responsibility. She also did not see him as "intentionally" searching for child pornography, but something he "obviously stumbled across" in his larger pornography addiction. This helped her rationalize. At the time of the interview, Sarah's husband was serving a five-year prison sentence. Cindy justified her husband's offense as a larger part of addictive behavior as well:

Unbeknownst to me, he apparently had an internet addiction with adult women online, particularly exhibitionism. As stress in our lives escalated, he started getting back online and he, you know…. When he disclosed everything to me, he believed he had been a sex addict most of his life. He had gone from girlfriend to girlfriend before me … once we were married … I say girlfriend to girlfriend because he cheated on every

100 Life With a Registered Sex Offender

one of them, and when we were married, stopped. Then, as you know, relationships start to change, we had kids, the physical parts of our relationship dwindled, neither of us knew how to maintain a healthy long-term intimate relationship and so he started this internet addiction again. It also involved meeting women for lunch from craigslist and getting handjobs in the car as well. Sometimes going to massage parlors. And our sex life was almost non-existent.

Cindy's husband solicited an undercover law enforcement officer online for sex that he thought was a minor. He accepted a plea to a five-year term of probation and 10 years on the sex offense registry. The lack of intimacy Cindy spoke of in her marriage was common among many of the women, including Carolyn whose husband was incarcerated for rape with a weapon when we spoke for this study.

There was this lack of intimacy. Um … I had said to him on the trip, "Sometimes I feel like I'm with my brother." And I started thinking, "Is it me? Do I just want this romantic, hold my hand, things that a girl would want, but you settle into a marriage and things are different?" I started thinking that I needed to look at things that he did to me that were loving gestures. Like when we would have Christmas dinner, you know I would cook everything, but he would do all the dishes. And he would cook dinner and he would do other loving gestures like that, and so I started appreciating them more, I think. I thought maybe I just needed to change my thinking. So I thought that maybe when we were on vacation and we're standing on the boat watching the sunset and he doesn't hold my hand and it's not like a romance novel, maybe that's just not him and I need to look to other things that he does do. And things like that got better and I think it helped.

When women discussed lack of intimacy, it was typically linked to pornography addiction. Denial of responsibility in terms of pornography addiction was additionally applied to make a distinction between partners who "had a disease" and those who were deemed pedophiles. Carrie said about her husband:

Like I said, my husband is not a pedophile. He is not a threat to society. He just made some really bad decisions. And, like it or not, pornography is a disease that has trapped the majority of men in our country, and it's kind of like one of those unspoken sins. And he has, he will admit to you, even today, that it's a battle that he has to get over every day.

Carrie's husband was found guilty at trial of sexual contact with a minor and was sentenced to 11 months and a term of ten years on probation. Christine spoke in similar terms about her father:

Understanding and Consequences **101**

The way I explain my dad is that he craved affection and he never tried to get into our pants or make us touch him, it was almost like he just wanted to snuggle, but it didn't feel good, and it wasn't right. So … I look at him like it was his alcoholism and I don't see my father as a pedophile in the true description of the word…. Yeah, I would have to [see him as a sex offender]. He would have to be. But I believe there's a difference between a sex offender and a pedophile.

Shelly discussed her husband's attraction to children:

[I do view him as someone who is attracted to children]. It's a constant thing. He has no shut off with, um, you know everybody's got a shut off valve or switch where they will think that an adult is attractive, but not an 11-year-old, or well, an adolescent girl, maybe not a number age, but just um, a newly forming girl. I know that that will never go away. That's something that he acknowledges. Of course [it bothers me]. I wish it wasn't that way, but there isn't really anything he can do about that. It's just that he, because of something that happened in his childhood, and I know this is really common, they sexualize the person, the uh, people of the age when they got molested. And that's exactly the age that he, uh, thinks is cute, that he's attracted to. The difference is that he took action.

Prior to their engagement, Shelly's partner accepted a plea to a charge of molestation of a minor. The sentence was seven years, of which he served half, and he will spend his life on the sex offense registry. While many women may have neutralized their partner's past behavior through denial of responsibility as a result of addiction, other women, like Colleen, were unwilling to permit future digressions from the law. Colleen said:

Nope. It's choices, it's consequences of the choices that he made, so he'll have to live with them and he'll have to deal with them. Well, I mean, it's as honest as I can be. It's his decision to stay the way he wants to be and if he can't then he'll have to find somewhere else to go because I won't live with an addictive person. Like I said before, I think it's a one-time thing, but pornography and masturbation and sexual addiction … temptations are there in many, many forms and if he took it upon himself this way, there are many other temptations that can happen in other ways. And um, it's up to him to choose to do the right thing and not the wrong things. And to have accountability partners and, um, counselors and help in many different ways and he's going to have to be active in his recovery and healing just like I've had to be active in mine. I can't heal him.

102 Life With a Registered Sex Offender

Colleen's long-term husband was imprisoned at the time of the interview on a sentence of 15 years for molestation of his child and receipt of child pornography. She remained committed to their marriage, provided her husband was committed to his recovery.

The other factor outside of the partner's control that was typically implicated in denial of responsibility were the offender's parents. Poor parenting, absentee parenting, or sexual abuse by the parents served to shift responsibility for a sex offense from the partner to the parents. Carolyn attributed some of her husband's behavior to his parents and his childhood:

> I think with my husband there's some issue from his past that explain his behavior. Doesn't excuse it, but it explains it and I've always looked at my husband as somebody that deep down inside somewhere there was a hurt or something so deep that I could never figure out what it was and I don't think that he could either. And there was a lack of intimacy, not sexual intimacy, but intimacy that got worse over the years. I used to tell my girlfriends, "I'm married to a real, live dead person." So, I always felt closed off from what was deep inside him. It was always like there was something locked away very deep inside of him that I never knew what it was, but I knew that it hurt him. Does that make sense to you?

Carolyn continued her elaboration of the "closed" nature of her husband's personality that she saw as rooted in his past:

> His family never talks about anything and everything is a secret and they are always closed off. And, you know, my husband for whatever reason is making bad decisions that are destroying his children and destroying me and nobody can … it makes us all angry that nobody will open their mouths and at least say, "This is what I know." Even if they just say that they can't really talk about it, but to just let him know that something happened in their house just so he can get the therapy that he needs. Because I wish … I'm getting really emotional now … (crying) … but I wish that I could say that my husband beat the crap out of me and was a raging alcoholic … I wish he was like a worse person so I could leave, but there have been really good things with him. Really good things. I mean, this is a guy who can watch a movie like *Titanic* and cry. He has empathy and is always, even just in conversations, has always been an advocate for women. Like he thinks it's outrageous that women don't make the same amount of money as men, he doesn't like it if somebody disrespects a woman … I see really good things in him and I don't know where this other thing comes from or what motivates it. I wish I could say that he's a lousy, rotten bastard, but I can't say that. As hard as I try and

as much as my knowledge and training ... I want to be able to see him the way that parole sees him or other people see him, but I can't because I can still see the good side of him too.... He's always had difficulty with one on one, like having a close, intimate relationship with his girls, but as far as family things ... I mean we did so many wonderful family things. I wish that I could say it's all bad, but....

Carolyn suspected abuse of her husband as a child, but never had confirmation. Yolanda knew parts of her husband's family history, but much more was revealed after his offense:

There was a part of him that he hadn't shared with me. He started having flashbacks of his own victimization and he was having a hard time. He had been having a lot of nightmares and he didn't share that with me. I knew that his father was ... I knew that he had come from a difficult family and I knew that he had been in foster care and that his father was an abuser, to the extent that he had abused all of his siblings. And the thing is, they were such a fractured family; my husband came from a family of 13 children. There were really only three or four of the siblings that he even really had contact with. So, it was ... I think that there was a lot of craziness in that situation. And I knew that his father had been physically abusive. He wasn't open about his childhood. And he had been in different facilities and they knew that something was wrong because he had violent outbursts and things and they would ask if his parents had hurt him and he would always say, "No." And when I asked him why, he said because he felt like he had to protect his parents. When you are in that situation, that's how you are accepted or how you are loved. They didn't have normal things like going to the store to get a treat for good behavior, all they had were inappropriate ways of getting attention, but when that's the only way that you're loved, you don't see that. So, it took me a long time to realize ... it was not something that was going to ... I was never going to ... the way things happened were the way things were going to happen. I wish it hadn't happened, but in the long run, when it comes to how the boys are and how we are now, if we had ever kept [the abuse] as a secret, even if it was a small incident ... I don't think that we would still be living together as a family. I think that it would have broken us.

Much of her husband's past came to light when he touched their son inappropriately. He confessed the incident immediately to Yolanda and they went to the authorities, where he pled guilty and received a sentence of five years on probation. For Yolanda, her husband's behavior had much to do with his parent's behavior toward him as a child. For Yolanda, as for other women, denial of responsibility occurred when women either denied responsibility for their partner's offense or shifted responsibility to a factor outside of their partner's control, typically either addictive behavior or the influence of his own parents on him as a child.

Denial of Injury

The neutralization of denial of injury occurred when women denied that anyone was harmed during the offense. The definition of harm is subjective, and most frequently, women who employed the neutralization of denial of injury held that the offense was consensual. There were, however, a handful of women that employed this neutralization in other ways on their partner's behalf. Jenny's husband was in prison awaiting sentencing at the time of the interview after he pled guilty to molestation of a minor family member. Jenny found out about the offense in a phone call from her husband from the police station. She had no opportunity to speak with him unsupervised since his arrest many months prior:

> (sighs) Yeah, but he can't say anything. He just says, "I don't know what happened." One thing the detective told me was that my husband said that he thought that [the victim] liked it. And, also, that he had felt these urges for a long time. So, you know, I know pedophilia is a psychiatric diagnosis, but it's also a sexual orientation. And I, uh, I don't know. We won't really find anything out until he gets out of jail and we can really talk about it.

Jenny's neutralization was a small part of her attempt to understand the situation. Robin also employed the neutralization of denial of injury in her explanation of seven charges of sexual assault against her partner:

> He was sleeping on the couch, I was, you know, we were literally kind of trying to figure out if we wanted to continue our relationship. I had no idea anything had happened because I mean, he's been faithful, he's never, there's never been anything like this, but I know he was in a really difficult spot. I think he reached out to, you know, someone that he worked with and he did not know that it was breaking the law. To be completely honest, he had no idea … this woman was 24; she is high level cerebral palsy, she's graduated from high school, she can read, she can write, she had, let's see how can I say this, she, as far as her con- servatorship, she was able to live alone, she was able to make her own decisions and she was really attracted to [my husband]. She wanted a regular guy and I think that's actually when the, quote-unquote, incident happened. It wasn't like there was any, quote unquote, molestation that

happened. This is what's interesting for me and then because again, this was an adult [care] program for you know other people with disabilities, they have various level of cognitive process. Well basically, she said at one point that he tried to kiss her cheek and she turned away. Then she also said that at one point, I mean, she basically said that he hugged her and sadly enough to say, these hugs became breast fondling. He's a hugger, I mean, he hugged all of these clients, and that was basically it … I do think he got too close. I definitely think he got too close and I think he confused her and then when he realized that he got too close, I think he tried to pull away and actually even, in his own pulling away, I think that, um, that basically, that probably hurt her feelings and she got confused, she felt rejected in some way.

Robin's partner was imprisoned at the time of the interview. He pled guilty to multiple charges of sexual assault and was sentenced to more than six years in prison. Robin decided to remain in the relationship. The most frequent denial of injury neutralization, however, was that the offense was consensual, and therefore no harm had occurred.

Brenda's husband accepted a plea of seven years for a charge of statutory rape before they met. She stated:

In this society we allow girls at the age of 14 to have children. And they are allowed to give birth to these children and we recognize them as mothers. So, if we recognize a 14-year-old as a mother, she should be old enough to decide if she should have sexual intercourse. I think a 14-year-old who lies about her age needs to be held accountable for it as well. I just don't believe that everything should be … there should be consequences for a girl who lies about her age. It shouldn't always be, the guy that she lied to, his fault.

Brenda's husband served four years of his sentence, and three years on parole, and will spend his life on the sex offense registry. In another case that involved two charges of statutory rape, Kelly said:

I had not been aware how bad it was until I met my husband, but there's no consideration for the maturity of the "victim" and I dislike the term victim as well because it implies this person had no say whatsoever and is just there saying no, help me, no. And it also implies that young people can't make a decision on their own and it's true, some young people can't make these decisions on their own but I know 60-year-olds who would be classified as not being able to make their own decisions, and I know 11-year-olds who know exactly what they want. I mean, I know they're trying to protect people and it's a squirrelly situation no matter

106 Life With a Registered Sex Offender

how you slice it, and it's different from state-to-state. I mean, in Hawaii, this would not have been illegal because the age of consent is [younger]. And it's just a number, it's just insane.

In Kelly's situation, the statutory rape charges occurred prior to her marriage. Her husband accepted a plea and was sentenced to five years in prison and five years on parole. At the time of the interview, he had not been assigned a tier level by the state, therefore she was unaware of the length of time and levels of control that would impact their family.

Denial of injury in the form of consent was not just evident in cases of statutory rape. It was also evident in cases wherein the female was viewed as the "pursuer" and therefore consenting to the sexual behavior. Susan's husband was charged with molestation of his adopted daughter. When the adopted daughter reported the abuse to Susan, she turned her husband into law enforcement. Yet, she discussed her husband's behavior through the portrayal of the minor as the aggressor:

> The other thing I think about, in the instance with [my adopted daughter] who was 14 at the time, she was a victim legally. My husband is 100 percent responsible and I don't waver on that. But I did see that when you have a 14-year-old that is looking for that attention and aggressively seeking it, whether it be my husband or other guys, I was aware of that…. She had a role too.

Sandra employed denial of injury in her explanation as well:

> She went around doing things, and I know they tell you it's never the teenager's fault, at least in a court of law, but give me a break. There's a lot of teenagers that know full well what they're doing, and she was one of them…. He was, he made a mistake common to many men. And some women, but especially men. Looking at a younger woman and thinking she was old enough. And especially how some women act, and society thinks you can't blame them because they're so innocent, no they aren't. There are some teenage girls out there that aren't girls. But there are some that know full well what they're doing. And I know society doesn't think that's a cool thing to say, but yes they do. And to most of the world, you're at the age of accountability at the age of 13, when you start going into puberty. When you start becoming a woman. I know teenagers can't always make smart decisions, as many adults can't make smart decisions at times. But throughout most of history, they've got an age of accountability being age 13 or so. And now they're trying to treat kids even into their 20s as little kids. He's not a sex offender.

Sandra's husband had sexual contact with a minor, though the offense was not reported for more than a decade. Stacey neutralized her husband's sexual contact with a minor student through the depiction of the female as the aggressor:

> She pretty much pursued and seduced my husband until he caved. And it happened for a couple months before he said you know, this can't happen, I love my family and I can't do this and so she went and told one of her friends what had happened. They never had intercourse, it was pretty much just touching, and then of course, he was put on leave from his job … I mean, I consider, most of society considers it a sex offense so that's kind of a hard question, I feel like he did offend, but a 17-year-old who can drive a car and put people's lives at risk with a car, I feel can make decisions and she even told the prosecutor that it was consensual, that she had pursued him. So, in a sense, I consider it a sex offense, but not in the way that, it's been totally blown out of the water in our society. I don't know if that makes sense.

Many of the neutralizations that invoked denial of injury were child pornography offenses, and as such, non-contact offenses. Crystal talked of her husband, who pled guilty to possession of child pornography:

> What's interesting is that in the beginning he called them "models" for a few days after this happened, and I finally looked at him and said, "These aren't models. This wasn't a career choice. They didn't answer an ad and go interview like you do for Playboy or something. They had to be coerced." Though I'm sure there are many girls who have pictures on the internet that they took themselves. I mean, they're 15, 16, 17 … they're interested in sex and now we have this technology that instead of kissing behind the gym, they're doing this. I mean it seems logical to me that there are probably a lot of girls who have taken pictures of themselves and texted them or something and now they've ended up on these sites, but the rest of these girls had to be coerced by some parent or guardian or sex trafficker or something. But I think that because of the way these photos we taken, artistically and set up like that and only involving nudity, that coercion never even crossed his mind. Don't ask me why somehow that he missed that.

Crystal's explanation of her husband's offense demonstrated that he neutralized his behavior much more than she did. While she recognized that some of the explicit images of youths found online may have ended up there accidentally, she was aware of the role of sex traffickers and coercion in the production and

108 Life With a Registered Sex Offender

distribution of child pornography. Sykes and Matza's (1957) denial of injury neutralization occurred when women denied the existence of harm to a victim during the offense. Most frequently this neutralization was used to suggest that the offense was consensual.

Justification by Comparison

Justification by comparison is not one of Sykes and Matza's original techniques of neutralization, but one developed since their theorizing. It involves the belief that the crime committed is not serious in comparison to the crimes of others (Cromwell & Thurman, 2003). As applied to this study, justification by comparison was most frequently seen by the partners of those who had committed non-contact offenses (specifically child pornography offenses), though was utilized by a handful of other women to minimize their partner's offenses. Melissa used justification by comparison when she discussed the molestation of her step-daughter by her husband: "the abuse was pretty much just him touching her, he didn't make her do anything disgusting to him there was no penetration, it wasn't rape or anything … it happened when she was 8, 9, 10, maybe those years." And Renee used this justification when she explained the offenses her husband served time for prior to them meeting. These charges included solicitation of a minor prostitute overseas and intent to distribute child pornography:

> At the time he committed the crime, he was 20 years old. And that had a bearing on how I thought about it as well, it seemed different to me someone who was 19 or 20 looking to have sex with a 13-year-old than a 60-year-old looking to have sex with a 16-year-old. I don't think of my husband as a sex offender, I think he's someone who made a mistake when he was young and stupid. I know I made a lot of mistakes when I was 19 and 20.

Overwhelmingly, however, the women who employed justification by comparison were involved with partners who had committed non-contact offenses, and the women saw a clear distinction between those types of offenses and contact offenses. Angela's husband accepted a five-year plea for possession and distribution of child pornography before they met, and she discussed the lack of seriousness of this type of offense:

> I'm not worried [about him reoffending] because I know he never actually hurt a child physically. He was really young when he saw these videos. He always thought the children were happy in the videos because they're always smiling. He justified it that that was something they wanted. He didn't realize that they were being hurt. He can't watch horror movies

Understanding and Consequences **109**

or torture movies, he's a very compassionate individual, he's a vegetarian since the age of 12. He didn't like to see suffering.

Crystal's husband was found in possession of over 1000 images of child pornography. She said:

> There is such a big difference between looking at pictures and contact. There's nothing that shows that looking at images leads to contact and because of that I feel that I have very firm ground to stand on for arguing and fighting the laws that have to do with child pornography. But, when it comes to contact … I don't know, it's just really hard for me to understand how someone could be so asleep at the wheel that they couldn't know that that's really wrong and exploiting and harmful to somebody else. And if [my husband] had any sort of contact I would have been divorced and moved on a long time ago. Believe it or not, he's really respectful around women.

Crystal saw a clear distinction between her husband's behavior and contact behavior which disrespected and harmed women and children. She further elaborated her beliefs on child pornography offenses:

> I don't believe that a child pornography offense actually touches that child that's in the photographs. And this is probably the major difference in my philosophy. The child has probably been equally scarred by the act of the pornography, but the fact that people are looking at it later is embarrassing for that child and humiliating as that child grows up, but I don't think we should be arresting and incarcerating people for embarrassing or humiliating someone. And that's ultimately what she's experiencing from the thousands of fans who have looked at that child's picture. And the reason I don't think that looking at the photos damages that child as much as they say, the reason I don't think it's revictimization, is because if you … and I might have said this analogy before … but if you have a picture in your hand of a kid who has cancer or who is impoverished or something, and you wish really good thoughts for that child, it is not going to put food on their table or cure them of cancer. They don't know it, they can't feel it, and nothing happens in real-time. The same thing if you hold a picture of a child in your hands and you think disgusting things about them. In the same manner, that's not affecting that child in real-time. What's affecting that child is the crime at the point of conception. So, do I think possession of child pornography should be illegal? Of course, but only because it promotes production. If you decrease the market, you decrease the production. So, what I think should be is a huge public awareness campaign about what the consequences are.

110 Life With a Registered Sex Offender

Crystal also employed justification by comparison when she discussed the age of the girls portrayed in the pornography viewed by her husband:

> I knew he looked at porn, but I didn't realize how much and I didn't realize it was an addiction.... Okay, so there were no pre-pubescent persons and it was females only. So, there was none of that in his material. If there had been I would feel differently. Certainly, if there had been like actual children ... any child that is under 12. I mean 13, 14, 15 ... they're not children. They are very young and they shouldn't be having sex and I don't think they should be exposed to the sexuality that they are exposed to in our current world, but those aren't children. I mean, 100 years ago the age of consent was 12, so, you know ... they're not children. But they are teenagers. Which isn't to say that I think it's appropriate for a grown man to look at teenagers, but I don't think it's criminal. And I don't think it's biologically or evolutionarily bizarre. It's only inappropriate because our culture says that teenagers are inappropriate for grown men. Lots of other cultures in lots of other times didn't say that and no one would have gotten the creeps by it. I'm only creeped out because I'm a product of my culture. You know, 100 years ago lots of men were married to 13-year-old girls and now they're called sex offenders. So, the fact that it was all teenagers, the fact that there were no men involved, the fact that there were no sexual acts beyond masturbation involved ... in other words, the girls involved in [my husband's] particular stash were not involved with doing anything they wouldn't normally be doing. He said it was a short-term thing and that he got interested in.... He didn't think it was a felony even though he thought it was morally questionable and that it was wrong and didn't feel right, which is why he stopped, but he certainly didn't think it could get him in trouble.

Some of what may have provoked the justification by comparison were the sentences that were incurred for child pornography offenses versus contact offenses. Of the 12 women (13 percent of the participants) who had partners that committed child pornography offenses, four partners (33 percent of the child pornography offenders) received probationary sentences, the other eight partners (66 percent of the child pornography offenders) received prison sentences. These sentences ranged from 21 months to 16 years in prison. Stephanie whose partner was serving a 16-year sentence at the time of our interview for manufacture and distribution of child pornography spoke to this point:

> You know, he didn't deserve a 16-year sentence, he never touched anybody, you know, it's like the crack cocaine laws of the 1980s, it's so backwards. I mean you can physically rape somebody and get a couple years

but if you download a digital image, you get 15–20 and it doesn't make sense and there's no treatment until 3 years before release … so they just throw you away for 15 years and you know, you can't do anything, there's no hope.

While state laws vary, federal law dictates that possession of child pornography (which could be a single image), triggers a mandatory minimum sentence of five years in a federal prison. The maximum sentence is 20 years of imprisonment. This is the same penalty for distribution of child pornography. What this means practically is that the sentence for a non-contact child pornography offense can be as long, or longer, than for contact offenses.

Condemnation of the Condemners

In the last technique of neutralization, condemnation of the condemners, the offender transfers attention from his own deviance to the behaviors and motives of those who disapprove of the deviant behaviors. The partners in this study engaged in condemnation of the condemners to transfer attention from their partner's behavior primarily to society and the ways in which society sexualizes young girls. Angela stated:

> I also believe that there are many people who have this similar attraction [to young people as my husband]. I also blame society a lot for sexualizing children. Constantly I see little kids, 5- and 6-year-olds, wearing high heeled boots, Juicy shorts and tank tops and you know…. So, I blame society a lot for it.

Crystal echoed similar sentiments:

> I think it's really bizarre how we punish men for stepping outside the lines about what they're allowed to look at. We throw sex at them and we readily say that men are visual and then we supply them with tons of eye candy in the media and girls at the mall and it's just everywhere, but if you want to see one naked you are a sick fuck. It just makes no sense.

In a study of teen's, women's, and men's lifestyle magazines, research revealed that girls were commonly "adultified" through clothing, hairstyle, and makeup, with an adult sexuality imposed upon them. As part of the "adultifying" process, young girls were dressed provocatively, in attire such as high heels, cleavage, and in outfits similar to lingerie, sending a clear sexual message (Speno & Aubrey, 2018). The mainstream media is littered with "sexy little girl[s] and baby faced nymphet[s] with preternaturally voluptuous curves … whose scantily clad bod[ies]

112 Life With a Registered Sex Offender

gyrate … in music videos, pose … provocatively on teen magazine covers, and populate … cinema and television screens around the globe" (Durham, 2008: 24). This has a societal and interpersonal impact (Egan & Hawkes, 2008).

While the partners of offenders provided neutralizations, it is important not to pathologize these justifications.

> The criminal justice community's seemingly deep-seated desire to make offenders take "full responsibility" for their behavior may result from cognitive dissonance involved in criminal justice work. If we are to punish … a person as an "offender," the individual needs to be responsible for the offense. In the face of a body of social science work that exculpates offending behavior by shifting blame to parents, schools, communities, [etc.], there is no small comfort in having the individual him- or herself take full responsibility for the crime.
>
> *(Tidmarsh, 1999: 50)*

Recall that neutralizing behavior is natural. It is problematic, however, when we attribute "our" bad behavior to circumstances outside of our control, but the bad behavior of others to personal traits (Maruna & Copes, 2005).

How Life Changes When Friends and Family Find Out

Explanations and justifications aside, the labeling of sex offenders creates significant obstacles to community integration for both the offender and his family. Partners and family members report a "courtesy stigma" as a result of their association with an RSO, the result being social marginalization, ostracization, disrespect, and judgment (Farkas & Miller, 2007). The partners in this study had a lot to say regarding reactions from family and friends to their involvement with a registered sex offender.

Responses From Family Members

When the offender reunifies with their partner, or a woman starts a relationship with an RSO, they often find they are left out of family celebrations. Alternatively, the female partner may be asked to attend family functions without her partner. Many women experienced negative reactions from family members. Melissa, whose husband served a six-year sentence for molestation of his stepdaughter, said:

> It's really, I just never thought after all this time that the biggest battle I would be fighting is my own family. Especially when they have been tolerant for several years. And they say, "Keep him away from the kids because he's a sexual predator or he's a pedophile" and I'm like, "God,

Understanding and Consequences **113**

he's been through so much therapy. Which one, which therapist do you want to talk to? They can tell you that he's not."

Susan experienced similar animosity with her parents after her husband served a six-month sentence for molestation of his adopted daughter. She conveyed their disapproval of her parental skills:

> Um, after about a year-and-a-half, and, like I said, I was living above my parents' apartment ... and to just give you a ... they are very strict religious people and there's no room for forgiveness once you fail. And it takes a lot to get back in their good graces. So, there was no room for my husband anymore, nor his family. And it bothered them that I would allow my children [who are 17 and 9] ... to see their dad under supervision. And I allowed them to see their other grandparents, and that really bothered them. So, they asked me to move out.

Angela married a man who spent time in prison for possession and distribution of child pornography. She knew about his offense prior to dating him. She discussed the irony of her parent's disapproval:

> Oh no, they're not happy at all. I can't blame them. I would be very unhappy if my daughter married someone with a criminal record, especially one like this. I mean, I completely understand. But they don't know the insides and outsides of our relationship and that's the difference, I guess, and it's not their life. I figure they haven't been very much more successful. My dad's been married three times and spent jail time for, not for a sex offense, but served jail time. My mom's been married twice, and she's married to a sex offender as well and won't admit it.

For Erin, her mother was able to deal with her partner's offense of solicitation of a minor online, but the rest of the family was not:

> The only one that's here is my mom. So, actually, I am the youngest of five, the four older siblings blew a gasket and will not, well, they don't even acknowledge that he even exists, but they won't, you know, he was no longer invited to anything with my side of the family, he was just a monster. But my mom is still part of our lives, but as far as anyone else, his family is still supportive, but mine is not.

Anita remained hopeful that her mother would accept her partner eventually:

> [My mother and I] were extremely close, she was my best friend. Um, I have not given up on her, I still send cards, I still email her, I still try

114 Life With a Registered Sex Offender

to contact her and she just ignores and when she does, I say okay, she's dead to me and then a couple months later, I try again. I just keep wading in.

Prior to their engagement, Anita's partner was convicted of molestation of a minor. He was sentenced to one year in jail and two years on probation. Anita and her partner were friends prior to their relationship, so she was aware of his history. He will spend a lifetime on the sex offense registry. Some women had parents who were supportive, but the rest of the family was not due to the nature of the partner's offense. Victoria's husband was sentenced to eight years, seven years suspended, plus five years on probation, for two counts of molestation of a minor. She said:

> I think that once [my parents] realized that I wasn't going to change my mind, they re-evaluated how they were going to deal with the situation. And my parents trusted me enough to make this decision. But it definitely strained the other relationships. My sister has children and her husband is extremely willful about what they think sexual offenders are. So, essentially, he wouldn't allow my husband, and by extension me, to be around the family. And that was hard on me because my sister and I were very close. And, uh ... so that relationship was extremely strained. Anytime you've got kids in the picture, it gets complicated. [And we're still not around my sister's children]. And that was really hard because we only lived about a mile away from them and I didn't really get to see my nieces and nephews grow up. And that's something that I always thought I would be a part of.

In some scenarios, it was not the parents concerned about their daughters in relationships with RSOs, but it was the children concerned for their mother in a relationship with a registered sex offender. In Carolyn's case, she was in a very long-term marriage with her husband, who had a history of both non-sexual and sexual offenses both prior to the marriage and during the marriage. At the time of the interview, Carolyn's husband was in prison for ten years on a charge of rape with a weapon for which he accepted a plea. Upon his release, he would also have to serve five years of supervised probation. Carolyn spoke about the concerns of her eldest daughter and son-in-law:

> My oldest daughter, she doesn't hate her father, she's seen him a few times ... but she really thinks that I should have left him. And the reason that she thinks that is because if it happened to her and her husband, she could not forgive him. And she's angry because she's seen what it's done to me and her sisters, and her husband is the same way. I had a good chat with him last night. He said, "The first time? Eh. But this? For 8 years

I've seen your heart break and you deserve a nice man and a nice life and I'm mad that [he] did this to you."

Melinda's husband also had a history of offenses over his lifetime, though their relationship was significantly shorter. Melinda and her partner were together about 18 months and at the time of the interview her partner was incarcerated on a three-year term for a failure to register violation. He had a history of offenses throughout his life, sexual and non-sexual, which ranged from exhibitionism, public urination, residing too close to a school, a number of DUI offenses, and culminated in the failure to register offense for which he accepted a plea. She discussed her son's anxieties about the relationship:

> [My son] is definitely worried about it for the same reasons, I lost my job and my apartment, so how can I go on and trust him? But it's not like he set out to do that, but because it happened, [my family] all think I should give him up, my son included. But I don't, that's not what I feel. My son doesn't think he can ever let him be a part, he can't let him into his home, and I told him about it, that he was a sex offender, but once he got arrested in my county and I lost everything, then his mind changed, everybody's mind changed. So, you know, I don't know, I feel bad because I would like my son to be close to him but he's a grown man so I can't change his mind. And I know he just worries about me, I was a single mom and we were very close, I was single when I had him. But if he can't be part of it, then he can't be and that's too bad.

For Laurie, the animosity toward her partner extended throughout her family and was fueled by her ex-husband:

> So, my ex-husband is kind of psychotic. [He] told my kids that I abandoned them for a sex predator who goes out and molests little kids. And so, there's some work that needs to be done with my children first before we can really even begin to become a family unit. The rest of my family is pissed to high heaven. I know it's probably not the most appropriate term, but that's probably the best way to describe it. Um, my mother looked at me and said how could I feed my kids to a sex predator. And this is from the same woman who, when I told her I was being molested by her brother said, "He would never do that." And then allowed him to sleep with me in my bedroom and molest me that night. So, there's been some animosity that's built up in the past.

Laurie was in a relationship for six months with an RSO who had served 30 months for possession of child pornography prior to them meeting. He told her about his past on their first date and she chose to move forward with their

116 Life With a Registered Sex Offender

relationship knowing that he would serve the rest of his life on the sex offense registry.

For Angela,

> the only people who have really made it difficult for me is my family. So, that's really difficult on me because I love them and I seek their approval. My kin can just run off and go to hell because they shouldn't be judging people. I'm sure they have just as many skeletons in their closet.

Cindy also experienced very significant familial consequences after she remained in her marriage following her husband's offense. She said: "I have no relationship with anybody in my family anymore. I lost everyone." To avoid the potential loss of family, some women chose not to tell either their entire family or part of their family about their partner's offense. Janet was involved with a man who spent three years in prison for sexual contact with a minor. Both her and her family grew to love this man. In fact, he failed to reveal his past to her until a year into their relationship. Janet decided not to tell her family:

> Well, my dad passed away, so it's just my mom and my mom loves him. My whole family loves him absolutely and I don't really know to tell you the truth. I think my mom eventually would be [supportive], when I explained things to her, but I think it might be hard, so I don't say a word.

Tara decided not to tell her mother about her husband's offense of receiving child pornography because of her judgmental nature:

> And the other thing is, my parents, my mom doesn't know. My dad does, but my mom doesn't know because she has a very cynical outlook on people in general, so if I were to tell her, that would be, just by me telling her because of the subject matter, she would make an immediate judgment and say, "Okay, it's time for you to leave." She would come up and try to pack me up and move me out or she would disown me, one of the two. So, she does not know.

Natasha's husband pled guilty to a statutory offense prior to their marriage and was sentenced to 16 years in prison. She reflected on her decision to only reveal his history to her immediate family:

> Outside of my parents and my sisters, my family doesn't know. My grandparents and my cousins, that sort of thing, but I just don't feel that

it's necessarily fair to him for them to know all about his dirty laundry and for other people to not have to reciprocate that. So, if we're going to sit down and talk about the worst things we've ever done, we can do that, but I don't feel that his is any more of their business just because the state feels that it's everybody's business.

Recall that RSOs experience a stigma that is a result of deviations from socially acceptable behaviors, termed a discreditable stigma (Goffman, 1963). Most offenders choose to manage or reduce stigma through coping mechanisms. While for some offenders, voluntary disclosure can give them back control, Natasha and her husband chose secrecy, wherein they hide his status (Winnick & Bodkin, 2008). While many women were not able to find support among their family, other women found some support at home. Overwhelmingly, however, the women in this study had at least some difficulties with their families as a result of their involvement with a registered sex offender.

Colleen's only support was from her father. At the time of the interview, Colleen's husband was serving a 15-year sentence for molestation of his daughter and receipt of child pornography. They had been in a relationship for more than 15 years. Colleen said:

> My dad is fully supportive of me and my husband and fully believes that change can happen because he's seen the change in his own life through sobriety and help and recovery. My mom feels that I need to throw him away, never look back, and pretend he doesn't exist. And she curses the ground that he walks on.

Felicia found both her parents to be supportive of her decision to remain with her husband, who admitted to molestation of their children, but her siblings were not supportive at all.

> Oh gosh, [my family] thought I was out of my mind. My parents are the only ones that supported us from the start. It was kind of like whatever decision I made they were supportive. And they really see him as a son, so that's really helped through the years that they've been there for us. And my brother and my sisters…my brother stayed involved with the kids through their growing up years. But my sisters were always at a distance. So, I've never really been that close to them and I thought that as time went on it would get better, but really as time has gone on, it's gotten worse. They've gotten more angry with me. My brother too. I used to feel like he was the closest one to me, but he kind of blames everything that's bad that's happened in our family he blames it on me and my decision. And I don't think I'm ready to take all that blame, you know?

118 Life With a Registered Sex Offender

Heidi was intimate with an RSO who accepted a plea to a statutory rape charge before they met. While her family got along with him, they still held some stereotypes about sex offenders:

> My mom said she was definitely, well, she doesn't want her daughter to be with a sex offender but she's like me, she knows [my partner] and knows that he's not a "weirdo" as she puts it (laughs). And then, you know, my dad really gets along well with him and all he really cares about is that he makes his daughter happy. My sister loves him; everybody really just loves him.

In Samantha's situation, the fact that her husband maintained the allegation was false and the individual later recanted likely influenced her family's support. She said:

> And I really thought that the men in my family would be the most against him because they were protecting me, but it was actually the men that were the most welcoming. Because everything you hear, you just don't know until you start hearing these stories, but all the men in my family know somebody who was falsely accused about different crimes like this. And they either had to struggle with the court system or they got it resolved before it went to the court system, but it was still a scary situation. So, immediately, when I would tell them this story, they would say, "Oh yeah, I believe that happens all the time because one of my friends had the same thing happen to him." So, that was a real surprise to me that instead of them being automatically skeptical of him, they were automatically skeptical of the charge.

Prior to Samantha meeting her husband, he pled guilty at the suggestion of a public defender to a charge of sexual contact with a familial minor. He was sentenced to 15 years on probation. During his probationary period he served five years in prison on a drug violation. On multiple occasions during the probationary period, the alleged victim recanted. Samantha's husband will serve his life on the sex offense registry as a result of the plea. Alison's familial history also prepared her family to be more accepting of her husband:

> I have been very blessed that my family has been so accepting but, there again, because they had a brother in prison and saw what he went through, I think that kind of prepared them to be more accepting than say, a lot of other people would.

Alison's husband was sentenced to almost four decades in prison for a charge of sexual contact with a minor (likely due in part to a prior non-sexual, but violent, felony). He served 19 years in prison, and Alison started writing to him while he was incarcerated. While there was mixed support in terms of family, overwhelmingly the women in the study received negative reactions from friends.

Responses From Friends

Stacey was in the extreme minority in that her friends were supportive of her and her husband through his plea to sexual contact with a minor. She said:

> We have not actually lost any friends at all. We have an amazing group of friends, church friends, colleagues, and we really have not had any negative, we've had most everyone say, we know who you are, we know people make mistakes so as far as friends go, we've actually had, it feels like we've made more friends because we've been so open and sharing with people, you know, that not every mistake you make has to be the worst thing it could possibly be.

Linda also experienced support from her friends, though that may be attributed to the fact that she was less open about her partner's past. Linda's partner served 11 years in prison after being found guilty at trial for rape. Linda said:

> I suppose I've been selective about the friends that I've told. And I've told people I've trusted, which means I've told people I thought would support me. Yeah, the people I've told have been supportive. Yeah, the people I've told have been very glad for me that after so many years of a difficult marriage that I've found love and passion in my life and they think that's great.

For the most part, however, the women spoke of abandonment and stigma from their former friends. And several women spoke of this stigma extending to their children as well.

Amber was in a relationship with an RSO who was found guilty at trial for rape. He was finished his sentence before meeting Amber and was honest with her about his past. Amber spoke about the impacts on her daughter when friends found out her partner was an RSO:

> My daughter was completely ostracized by these people. I mean, before all of this she would be invited to sleepovers and parties and playdates … it was actually too much because it was all the time. Then this happened and all of that came to screeching halt. I thought these people were friends. I would call them up and ask if [my daughter] could have a play date and they'd be like, "Oh we don't do play dates anymore." And then the next week I would see them going on a play date.

120 Life With a Registered Sex Offender

Diana discussed the loss of a very good friend, whose son was also no longer friends with her son:

> I still have one friend that's totally against it. I don't talk to her about my husband at all. She'll never come over to my house, um, her older son and my oldest son were best friends, but now they're not friends at all. We just talk to each other in passing, like "Hey how's it going?" at church and stuff like that. So, I lost a great friend over it because she could never see why I would do something like this or put myself in this situation and her exact words were that I was "settling for less." So, it was really hard at first, but there are lots of things that people in this world do that we don't agree with and sometimes we just have to be by their sides and be there if they need them.

Prior to meeting Diana, her husband was found guilty at trial for rape and attempted rape. He was sentenced to 15 years in prison, of which he served 13 years and two years on probation. He received a probation violation for solicitation of a prostitute and the state filed an unsuccessful civil commitment application.[2] At the time of the interview, Diana and her husband were married and had been together for just over two years. Melissa also had a very close friend turn her back on her. After Melissa's husband was charged with molesting his step-daughter, Melissa's best friend couldn't accept her decision to remain in the marriage:

> I mean, you talk about your best friend walking away from you at a time when you really, really need them to be there for you. And she wasn't, she wasn't supportive. She disagreed with the decisions that I was making.

In search of emotional support, Maria and her family picked up and left their neighborhood. Married over three decades, Maria's husband was found guilty at trial of sexual misconduct with a minor. He served eight years in prison and six years on parole and will spend his life on the sex offense registry. They relocated to be closer to family:

> Well, we ended up moving ... from where it happened, just to leave the area and start anew to live next to relatives ... to be a support system and that was a great decision, they ended up being a huge help during those first difficult years. Yeah, when we moved, you always lose friends when you move away, but I guess I lost a lot of friends emotionally long before that, because I just, I guess, they just didn't know how to deal, or what, but it was very painful because people didn't know what to do with the situation.

As with family, some of the women attempted to keep offense information private in an attempt to avoid stigma. Tara chose not to disclose to many people, but lost friends from community notification of her husband's child pornography offense:

> Some [friends] know. It depends on, you know, we kind of don't tell people right away. We've lost friends, a couple that we were very close with, and they read in the paper twice and because they read it in the paper twice, they think it happened twice. They didn't bother to ask us about it, they just took on the assumption that he was guilty.

Victoria had a situation with a friend who was seemingly supportive of her decision to remain with her husband after his plea to a charge of molestation of a minor ... until several years later when the friend had a child:

> [My friend] was supportive, so to speak, until she had her own child, and 7 years after the fact she wrote a letter to me essentially breaking off the relationship and saying that she wouldn't see me again until I had left my husband. So, she got this misperceived perception of what a sex offender is and recidivism rates and all of that. And once she had her own child, I think this weighed on her more and more. And more of our conversations turned to my husband and I felt like I was under a microscope. So, she came out with this in a letter. She didn't even have the courage to face me, but she said I had so much potential for my career, but then didn't have a head on my shoulders when it came to this. And she blamed the church for allowing these "pedophiles" into the church system and, you know, a lot of sensationalist perceptions based on the media. I was devastated.

Angela and her husband thought they were close friends with a couple until his plea to molestation of a family member: "Uh, we have one couple that used we used to be friends with. [They] have been harassing us on Facebook and posted my husband's registry information on Facebook for all the world to see."

Because of these types of incidents, many of the women in the study (and their partners) had elected seclusion, to the extent possible. Brandi, whose husband served one-year probation for possession of child pornography said:

> I keep very much to myself now. I don't have but one friend at work, I don't want them to know my address. Because people at work will even look it up on the internet. They want to see where your house is, what it looks like ... my house carries a scarlet letter.

To avoid further rejection, Cynthia kept to herself since her husband's probationary sentence for molestation of a family member: "I've become pretty much

122 Life With a Registered Sex Offender

a recluse. It's kind of hard to explain when somebody has been so mean that you just don't want to put yourself out there and take the chance that somebody is going to reject you again." Women discussed the hurt experienced in what they thought were valued friendships and the impact of this on their trust level in future relationships. Katherine said: "I don't trust. I don't trust. I just don't trust. There's too much negative in the media and I don't want to take that chance." Misty spent a decade with a man who had been convicted of a statutory rape offense. She dated him during his court proceedings, and during the six months he spent in jail, and the five years he spent on probation, though the offense occurred prior to their relationship. Unrelated to his RSO status, they were no longer together at the time of the interview but had remained friends. Misty's relationship with him left her with scars:

> I don't really have any friends anymore. Mostly because of this, yes. I'm really slow to trust people and giving people chances but once I'm convinced that that person is just being really ignorant, then I just give up on it.

Martha discussed a similar impact that trust violations had taken on future relationships:

> Umm no, like I said, I don't have a lot of friends so it's, it is something that makes it hard for me to feel like I can make new friends. You know, because it's such a big part of our life and I feel like if somebody doesn't know about that then it would be hard for them to really get to know me. I definitely have to be careful about who I talk to, you know, who I open up to and I think that's prevented me.

Martha's partner had a juvenile sex offense record for molestation of a minor family member and will spend his life on the sex offense registry. April echoed similar themes of distance from potential friends, but elaborated potential reasons:

> I'll be honest with you, I don't really have friends. You don't want to get close to people. Especially people who aren't family. When you walk in these shoes and you're split with many different feelings. One is, give up. What I know is that, in today's society that anybody can accuse anybody of anything. And just the mere accusation is enough to lose your freedom. I don't need it. I don't want it. Having gone through this and making that choice, that decision, I see things different. I'm not mean to people, but I'm certainly distant.

The "courtesy stigma" of female partners as a result of their association with an RSO was well-elaborated among the women in interviews. They provided examples of social marginalization, ostracization, disrespect, and judgment from both close family and friends. Unfortunately, they provided few examples of support networks. While some women had marginal support from family members, overwhelmingly the women were left to fend emotionally for themselves. For many relationships, this abandonment by family and friends brought the couple closer. Nicole said: "It's made [our relationship] stronger because it's me and him against the world."

Notes

1. In the theoretical literature, techniques of neutralization have been integrated into theories such as rational choice theory, subculture theory, control theory, reintegrative shaming theory, psychological theories, strain theory, and learning theory (Bohm, 2001; Braithwaite, 1989; Cornish & Clarke, 1986; Hirschi, 1969; Lanier & Henry, 1998; Maruna & Copes, 2005; Williams & McShane, 2004; Winfree & Abadinsky, 2003).
2. In *Kansas* v. *Hendricks* (1997) the Supreme Court allowed the original offense (even if it was a decade or more prior) to be a justification for continued confinement. This law is constitutional as it is considered a civil proceeding and not a second punishment. It allows the state to indefinitely confine a sexual offender that is believed to have "serious difficulty controlling [their] behavior" if their behavior is "dangerous," they have a history of sexual offending, and a "serious mental disorder" as recognized by the psychiatric community (*Kansas* v. *Crane*, 2002). That said, standards vary widely as to commitments in each state. As of 2019, there were 20 states with such statutes: Arizona, California, Florida, Illinois, Iowa, Kansas, Massachusetts, Minnesota, Missouri, Nebraska, New Hampshire, New Jersey, New York, North Dakota, Pennsylvania, South Carolina, Texas, Virginia, Washington, and Wisconsin.

References

Blagden, N., Winder, B., Gregson, M., & Thorne, K. (2014). Making sense of denial in sexual offenders: A qualitative phenomenological and repertory grid analysis. *Journal of Interpersonal Violence, 29,* 1698–1731.

Bohm, Robert M. (2001). *A primer on crime and delinquency theory* (2d ed.). Belmont, CA: Wadsworth.

Braithwaite, John. (1989). *Crime, shame and reintegration.* Cambridge: Cambridge University Press.

Cornish, Derek, & Clarke, Ronald. (1986). *The reasoning criminal.* New York, NY: Springer.

Cromwell, Paul & Thurman, Quint. (2003). The devil made me do it: Use of neutralization by shoplifters. *Deviant Behavior, 24,* 535–550.

Durham, Mimi. G. (2008). *The Lolita effect: The media sexualization of girls and what we can do about it.* Woodstock, NY: Overlook Press.

Egan, R. Danielle, & Hawkes, Gail. (2008). Girls, sexuality and the strange carnalities of advertisements: Deconstructing the discourse of corporate paedophilia. *Australian Feminist Studies* 23(57), 307–322.

Farkas, Mary Ann, & Miller, Gale. (2007). Reentry and reintegration: Challenges faced by the families of convicted sex offenders. *Federal Sentencing Report,* 20(2), 88–92.

Farmer, M., McAlinden, A.M., & Maruna, S. (2015). Understanding desistance from sexual offending: A thematic review of research findings. *Probation Journal,* 62, 320–335.

124 Life With a Registered Sex Offender

Goffman, Erving. (1963). *Stigma: Notes on the management of spoiled identity*. New York, NY: Simon Schuster, Inc.

Hirschi, Travis. (1969). *Causes of delinquency*. Berkeley, CA: University of California Press.

Hulley, Joanne L. (2016). "While this does not in any way excuse my conduct ...": The role of treatment and neutralizations in desistance from sexual offending. *International Journal of Offender Therapy and Comparative Criminology*, 60(15), 1776–1790.

Kansas v. Hendricks, 521 U.S. 346 (1997)

Kansas v. Crane, 534 U.S. 407 (2002)

Lanier, Mark & Henry, Stuart. (1998). *Essential criminology*. Boulder, CO: Westview.

Maruna, Shadd, & Copes, Heith. (2005). What have we learned from five decades of neutralization research? *Crime and Justice*, 32, 221–320.

Maruna, S., & Mann, R. E. (2006). A fundamental attribution error? Rethinking cognitive distortions. *Legal and Criminological Psychology*, 11, 155–177.

Speno, Ashton Gerding & Aubrey, Jennifer Stevens. (2018). Sexualization, youthification, and adultification: A content analysis of images of girls and women in popular magazines. *Journal of Mass Communication Quarterly*, 95(3), 625–646.

Sykes, C. M., & Matza, D. (1957). Techniques of neutralization: A theory of delinquency. *American Sociological Review*, 22(6), 664–670.

Tidmarsh, David. (1999). Necessary but not sufficient: The personal view of a psychiatric member of the parole board. In Murray Cox (Ed.). *Remorse and Reparation* (pp. 49–62). Philadelphia, PA: Jessica Kingsley.

Ware, J., & Mann, R. (2012). How should "acceptance of responsibility" be addressed in sexual offending treatment programs? *Aggression and Violent Behavior*, 17, 279–288.

Williams, Frank P., III & McShane, Marilyn D. (2004). *Criminological theory* (4th Ed.). Upper Saddle River, NJ: Prentice-Hall.

Winfree, L. Thomas & Abadinsky, Howard. (2003). *Understanding crime: Theory and practice* (2nd Ed.). Belmont, CA: Wadsworth/Thompson Learning.

Winnick, T., & Bodkin, M. (2008). Anticipated stigma and stigma management among those to be labeled "ex-con." *Deviant Behavior*, 29(4), 295–333.

Zuckerman, Miron. (1979). Attribution of success and failure revisited, or: The motivation bias is alive and well in attribution theory. *Journal of Personality*, 47, 245–287.

PART III

Collateral Consequences for Partners of Registered Sex Offenders

5

REGISTRATION AND COMMUNITY NOTIFICATION

Registered sex offenders experience a stigma that is a result of deviations from socially acceptable behaviors, termed a discreditable stigma (Goffman, 1963). RSOs are labeled and stigmatized by society, and while not all RSOs react to this experience in the same way, most individuals employ coping mechanisms to reduce and manage stigma (Link, Cullen, Struening, Shrout, & Dohrenwend, 1989). Some offenders try to educate the public and reduce stereotypes about the sex offender population, and in doing so they are honest about their status. Voluntary disclosure can be empowering for offenders as it puts them in a position of control. After all, the overwhelming majority of RSOs are subject to public registries, which means a quick search online and their identity can be revealed. Alternatively, some offenders attempt to manage stigma through secrecy and try to pass in society as a non-offender. The difficulty with this approach is that registration and the community notification that often accompanies it has severely limited the privacy of RSOs.

The stigmatization of SOs is frequently explained through social reaction theory, commonly known as labeling theory. Lemert (1951) developed the idea that some perpetrators and their behaviors are labeled negatively by both society and by the criminal justice system, and the stigma and negative societal response may fuel the behavior underlying the initial label. He further made the distinction between primary deviance (the action leading to the label) and secondary deviance (actions occurring after the individual accepts and acts on the label). As applied to sexual offending, social reaction theorists would suggest registration and community notification places a public label on an offender. This may decrease the ability of an individual to reintegrate into the community or increase an individual's propensity to commit another offense. Of relevance here are the ideas of Braithwaite (1989) who discussed how reintegrative and disintegrative shaming are used by society and the criminal justice system as methods of control. Reintegrative shaming is temporary and occurs when an offender is being punished: once punishment has ended, the offender is again integrated into society as a full member. Disintegrative shaming involves continued shaming and stigma even after the offender's punishment is complete. The offender is not welcome back as a full member of society but is instead treated as a social outcast; this stigma has a significant and detrimental negative impact on their self-worth (Braithwaite, 1989). The floodgates of sex offender labeling began in 1994 with the passage of the Jacob Wetterling Crimes Against Children and Sexually Violent Offender Registration Act.

Brief Legal History of Registration and Community Notification

> Policymakers are affected by the horrible acts committed against young victims, especially those covered in the national news media.... Policy makers were able to speak with great specificity about the details associated with these victimizations. It is interesting that the crimes the policy makers referenced, in response to a general question regarding how the legislative process works in their state, were often not related to sex crimes in their own jurisdiction or even in their own state.
>
> *(Meloy, Curtis, & Boatwright, 2012: 443)*

It is in this climate that policies like registration and notification laws are created. While you would think the level of social controls that impact an individual sex offender would correlate to his individual risk level and likelihood of recidivating, that is not how many states assign tier levels for sex offenders. A brief legal history of registration and community notification is necessary to understand the significance of current legislation. Recall from Chapter 1, the Jacob Wetterling Crimes Against Children and Sexually Violent Offender Registration Act became effective in 1993 and was amended in 1996 with Megan's Law. Though many states had community notification guidelines in the 1990s as part of the Wetterling Act, revised laws involved public disclosure of sex offense registry information (under the rubric of public safety), mandatory registration of an RSO's residence with law enforcement, access to an RSO's personal information via a publicly accessible website, and the creation of a class of offenders deemed Sexually Violent Predators (SVPs).

At this time, states decided how Sex Offender Registration Notification (SORN) laws were implemented and selected policies that best fit their needs. As a result, there was broad discrepancy from state-to-state. States such as Minnesota used evidence-based policies and risk assessment tools and placed only high-risk offenders on the public registry and only notified the community regarding high-risk offenders. New York state placed both medium-risk and high-risk offenders on the registry. States such as Florida included all sex offenders, regardless of risk, on the registry. Everything changed in 2006 with the Adam Walsh Child Protection and Safety Act which completely rewrote the federal standards for registration and notification into the Sex Offender Registration and Notification Act (SORNA). SORNA resulted in increased registration and notification requirements and eliminated individualized risk assessment in favor of tier assignment by offense type designated by statute. As states signed SORNA into law, similar get-tough rhetoric was uttered across the nation. For example, in 2011 Governor Tom Corbett, as he brought Pennsylvania into compliance with the Adam Walsh Act (AWA), said:

> Children are irreplaceable. But we can hope that by making our laws tougher, we can spare others the pain and grief that has visited too many families in the many years since we named laws in memory of these lost youngsters.
>
> *(Megan Kanka and Adam Walsh, www.governor.state.pa.us/)*

The goal of SORNA was a streamlined system in which all states would have identical information posted online about RSOs and would also track offenders with a requirement that they register with law enforcement at time intervals depending on their tier level.

Victoria talked about the importance of using a risk assessment protocol instead of a tier assessment protocol, and the influence of plea bargaining in the process of tier assignment. Her husband accepted a plea to two counts of child molestation and will be on the registry for life.

> And when I talk to the few people that I talk to about this, what I tell them is that a lot of people are not going to have any sympathy for us and they are going to say, "Well, it's better to be safe than sorry." But, what they don't understand is that people who are high-risk when they are going through their legal proceeding, there's so much fear about the registry and what it means for having a normal life or the chance of a normal life, they are pleading their cases down for a lesser charge. So, what can happen is that you have a person who is clinically a higher risk offender that pleads their case down to a lower tier on the registry. So, this is what I try to explain to people about SORNA … that it's not about a person's clinical risk assessment, it's based on the title of the crime, which is absolutely not reflective of a person's risk to reoffend.

Generally, a Tier 1 offender is deemed to be the lowest risk to the public and has committed a non-violent offense against a victim who is an adult. Tier 1 offenses usually include possession of child pornography; voyeurism offenses; public indecency offenses; or non-penetrative sexual contact offenses without consent of an adult victim. These offenders register annually with law enforcement for 15 years. A Tier 2 offender is deemed to be a higher risk to the public and is an individual who commits a second Tier 1 offense or an individual who commits a non-violent sexual offense against a minor. Examples include sexual contact with a minor aged 12 to 15; a sexual crime against an individual in the offender's custody (such as a foster child); distribution or production of child pornography; sex trafficking of a minor; transporting a minor with the intent of sexual activity; or sexual coercion of a minor. Offenders at this tier register semi-annually for 25 years. A Tier 3 sexual offender is deemed to be the highest risk to the public. This is an individual who is a repeat Tier 2 offender or an individual who commits a sexually penetrative act (as opposed to a contact crime) or a crime involving violence. Tier 3 offenses include sexual acts that involve threats, force, drugs, or intoxication, or involve the victim's mental or physical inability to consent; sexual acts or contact with a victim under the age of 12; or kidnapping or false imprisonment of a minor. Offenders at this tier must register quarterly for life. It is possible for a Tier 1 RSO to have his time on the registry reduced from 15 years to ten years if their record is clean for that ten-year period. It is also possible for RSOs who register as a result of a juvenile conviction to have their registration removed after a 25-year clean record (SMART, 2019a). Under the SORNA guidelines, reduction of a registration period or removal from the registry is not an option for either a Tier 2 or Tier 3 offender.

Failure to adhere to the registration protocol is a felony punishable by fines and/or imprisonment of a maximum of ten years. In fact, failure to register can result in a longer sentence than the original offense. If any change is going to be made to an offender's personal information (name, address, address of employer, license plate, description of vehicle, etc.), it must be done within three days or it is considered a failure to adhere to the registration protocol. Fourteen states impose an initial registration fee, and 28 states impose an ongoing registration fee, with some states allowing county fees as well. This does not include other fees that may be required by an RSO, such as fees for DNA samples, community treatment, or GPS devices. Fees vary dramatically by state (Makin, Walker, & Campbell, 2018). For example: a lifetime registrant in Wyoming would pay approximately $3,000, in Tennessee $6,000, and in Georgia more than $10,000 just in registration fees. Further, many states consider a failure to pay registration fees the same as a failure to register which is a felony in most states and subjects the RSO to imprisonment (Makin et al., 2018). According to Catherine, some RSOs may not have the financial means to register, especially if registration is required every three months:

> [The county we're in] did this new thing and this was the final thing, they raised the amount the sex offenders have to pay to register. It was $60, it's now gonna be $600 ... every time! And you know what, I work all the time and I just can't afford that. No way!

Registration and Community Notification **131**

For Catherine's husband, this was going to be a $600 fee four times a year. The first registration laws required RSOs to provide law enforcement with their name, address, photo, and fingerprints. Under SORNA, offenders may also be required to supply driver's license information, birth records, a conviction history, employment information (including employment address for inclusion on the public registry), social networking passwords and identifiers, email address(es), instant message address(es) or other internet identifier(s), and several states require DNA samples.

SORNA's passage expanded the number of sexual offenses that required registration,[1] changed the tier assignment for many offenses, strengthened residency restrictions, added foreign convictions to the registration requirement, and added registration for offenses that occurred pre-SORNA.[2] All states were required to comply with the provisions SORNA by July 2011 or risk a reduction in federal funds. As of June 2019, only 18 states were in substantial compliance with SORNA's requirements.[3] States not in compliance cite cost as the main reason for failure to comply.[4] The initial costs to implement SORNA across the U.S. were estimated at $481million (Justice Policy Institute, n.d.).

There are many inconsistencies by state in the registration and notification policies for sex offenders even after the passage of SORNA. While some states do implement the tier system of classification, other states have all RSOs, regardless of the seriousness of the offense, register for life. For example, Florida continues to have offenders register for the duration of their life. They may petition for relief from registration after 25 years for less serious offenses if there has been no subsequent arrest for either a felony or misdemeanor. Only a full pardon relieves registration obligations in Florida (Fla. Stat. §943.0435).[5] Catherine's situation was an example of state-to-state incongruity:

> [My husband] pled guilty to a Level 1 sex offense that he didn't even know what it was. He spent 18 weekends in jail and 5 years on probation in 1997. And when he was released, he was assigned a Level 1 status in New York. We then moved to Louisiana where he's a Level 3. They've given him no justification for the Level 3 status, they just sent him a letter. And we sent a letter back of course, but we've heard nothing back from it. So, we are moving, there's no getting around it, we are moving. We're going back to New York, he's a Level 1 in New York and yeah, that's a pain because he was supposed to be done with [registration] 5 years ago, but they extended the time he has to register to 20 years. But he's a Level 1 there. In New York there's not gonna be any newspaper ad, and I think you only have to go down there once a year. Go down once a year to fill out paperwork, every 3 years get your picture taken. We can handle that, I mean I hate the cold weather, I hate it and I have rheumatoid arthritis and the cold will really bother me, but it's worth it. I have a chance of having some kind of life instead of this thing in hiding we're doing in Louisiana.

132 Collateral Consequences for Partners

Jackie's situation also demonstrated state-by-state dissimilarity. Prior to getting married, her husband pled guilty to molestation of a minor in Florida which is a Tier 3 offense and life on the registry. She explained their decision to relocate to Tennessee:

> [We moved to Tennessee] because at the time, they had the least strict sex offender registry and with Tennessee we had a chance. In Tennessee, if after 10 years on the registry, you got nothing, absolutely nothing, I mean not even a speeding ticket, there's a chance they can take you off the sex offender registry. And that's what we've been able to do. And within a year of being here, he wrote the state attorney and asked to be removed and he was. But he's still on the sex offender list in Florida which we don't understand.[6] But we knew that with Tennessee, once you get the request letter in for him to be taken off the registry, you know, he met all the requirements, there was no reason for him not to be taken off and so they took him off immediately and that was such a huge relief for him mentally, you know, because we had a hard time moving from our family, you know, you left your world back there in Florida. So, it was hard, a lot of people don't even know about it, but it was such a relief. I got home from work when he got the letter and he was just bawling and I thought something was wrong, but it was just because it was such a huge relief.

The federal authority of SORNA brought concern to some states: the notion that the system could not adequately separate offenders who were high-risk from those who were low-risk offenders. Since its implementation, research has demonstrated a net-widening effect, with a significant number of RSOs classified as high-tier offenders versus pre-SORNA (Freeman & Sandler, 2009; Harris, Lobanov-Rostovsky, & Levenson, 2010)

Perhaps the most controversial aspect of SORN laws is not the registration element, but the requirement that community members be put on notice when a sex offender moves into the neighborhood. There are no national standards regarding type and method of community notification, so it varies by state and the offender's tier status, with wide variation in the type of information that is available to the public and the method(s) of dissemination. Notification may be via a flyer (either hand-delivered or via mail), website notification, newspaper advertisement, a police station flyer, door-to-door announcements from law enforcement, phone calls from law enforcement, media releases, and/or community meetings. Several states also have a recognizable stamp, "SEX OFFENDER" in bright red letters on the driver's license of an RSO. New apps now assist in notifying and tracking sex offenders. As of October 2019, Louisiana has an app that community members can download called Safe Virtual Neighborhood. According to the OffenderWatch website:

It is the only app that directly partners with law enforcement to analyze sex offender data. Safe Virtual Neighborhood cross-references sex offender data pulled directly from participating law enforcement departments with people contacting your child's smartphone or device. If a registered sex offender in our network contacts your child using Snapchat, text messages, email, or phone calls – or if your child is near an offender's home – you'll be alerted. Once you sign up for Safe Virtual Neighborhood, you'll also receive email and postal OffenderWatch alerts if a registered sex offender moves into your neighborhood.

(https://offenderwatch.com/safe-virtual-neighborhood/)

OffenderWatch has plans to launch similar apps in other states by the end of 2019.

Such policies raise questions of privacy: Why are communities notified when sex offenders move in, but not drug dealers, or gang members, or murderers? Sarah, whose husband was incarcerated for five years on one count of possession of child pornography at the time of the interview, reflected on the registry:

> I'm not sure it really serves a benefit. Especially when you learn on this end that most kids, if you're talking about kid's safety, are affected or harmed by someone they know. So, I don't know that there's any public benefit to a public registry. And if that would be the case, if it was strictly limited to law enforcement, then I would say, if you're going to require sex offenders to register, then murderers, especially drunk drivers, then they all need to be registered too. Because if you're gonna do it for one, you should do it for all. I don't know how you can sit and say this one particular group is the worst of all of them. No, I mean, I know a friend of mine, he was charged with DUI 4 times before they finally they put him in jail and he lost his license and he realized he needed to change his life. The fourth time was cause he had his kids in the car. So, you tell me who's the worse offender. So, I would do it for everyone. If you're gonna do it for one, then everyone should be on a list. Would I want to know that the guy next door to me murdered somebody when he was 14? Yes, I would. Is that information available to me? No, it's not. To me, that's more scary. That's worse.

Brandi, whose husband will spend ten years on the registry for two counts of possession of child pornography, had similar thoughts:

> Nobody gets tough on gang members very much. Why don't they put gang members' address and photos on a website so people can know who to look for that might shoot them while they're walking down the street? [The area] I live in we have a lot of gang shootings around.

134 Collateral Consequences for Partners

Variance exists from state-to-state regarding notification of the public. States that use a tier classification (versus a risk classification) of offenders frequently have a narrower system of notification for Tier 1 and 2 offenders, forcing the public to seek information regarding RSOs instead of having the government bring the information unsolicited to the public. States with broad notification policies make privacy and community reintegration for the offender more difficult as law enforcement often uses media releases, door-to-door notification, and flyers to residents to inform of an RSO's arrival to the community. Minnesota uses a tier system and has a reasonably narrow system of community notification. Notification of Tier 1 offenders is to crime victims, witnesses, law enforcement personnel, and those the prosecutor's office deems necessary; notification of Tier 2 offenders includes all those for Tier 1 offenders, plus schools, daycares, and any location there may be a victim of the specific offender; notification of Tier 3 offenders is public, involves a media release and/or town meeting, and posting of the RSO's information on the website for public access (Zevitz & Farkas, 2000a). It becomes confusing, however, when an offense is considered Tier 1 in one state and Tier 3 in another state. Catherine's husband pled guilty to molestation of a familial minor in New York and was designated a Tier 1 offender. When they moved to Louisiana, his tier status was changed to a Tier 3. His offense did not change, but the ramifications of his offense changed dramatically. In Louisiana, his tier status means life on the registry and broad community notification. Catherine explained:

> They sent out mailers on his level once a year to everyone within 3/10 of a mile of us. In addition, he has to go down to the newspaper to get his picture taken and have his picture and a description of his offense put in the newspaper. He has to go and put a full-page ad, he has to pay for it, with his picture, in the paper. Every year or every time he moves. At the minimum once a year. [It says] my name is X, I am a registered sex offender, I was convicted of sexual assault of a 5-year-old child. They type it up right at the paper, he just has to pay for it and go down and get his picture taken. It even lists who the landlord is and his place of work.

Catherine's situation is an excellent example of inconsistency by state. Additionally, some states give discretion of notification to whomever probation and parole officers deem appropriate; and still other states provide information about the registered sex offender only to those who submit a written request to law enforcement.

In the past several years, released sex offenders have questioned the constitutionality of SORN laws and challenged legislation in two significant U.S. Supreme Court cases. *Smith* v. *Doe* (2003) ruled the law is not in violation of the *ex post facto* clause of the constitution which means that sex offenders who were convicted prior to SORN laws can still be required to register and comply with notification guidelines that were not in existence when they were sentenced. Additionally, the regulatory nature of SORN legislation was underscored, and the court reiterated that registration and notification were not additional punishments. In *Connecticut Department of Public Safety* v. *John Doe* (2003), the U.S. Supreme Court examined whether SORN laws constituted excessive punishment or punishment that was cruel and unusual, and the court ruled online posting of sex offender's pictures in a registry was not a barrier to personal freedom. This ruling has been upheld at the state level and the U.S. Supreme Court has not heard further cases dealing with the constitutionality of RSO legislation.

Since the *Doe* decision, subsequent legislation occurred due to increased registration and notification requirements. The U.S. Supreme Court, however, declined to examine any *ex post facto* implications since 2003. On the federal level, from the time of *Smith* v. *Doe* in 2003 until 2016, there was agreement that SORN requirements were not in violation of the *ex post facto* clause. Then, the Sixth Circuit Court of Appeals in *Doe* v. *Snyder* (2016) determined that Michigan's SORN law was punitive and could not be retroactively applied. At about the same time, an Alabama federal court ruled that certain provisions violated the *ex post facto* clause in *McGuire* v. *Strange* (2015). These rulings stood in stark contrast to the judgments of previous courts which had rejected constitutional challenges to sex offender laws. While the courts are at least beginning to entertain challenges to sex offender policies, the outcomes remain mostly in favor of the state. For example: in *Doe* v. *Harris* (2013) a California court held that a defendant whose plea agreement was in 1991 (pre-SORN guidelines) was lawfully required to register in 2004. At the end of 2019 and into 2020, the Pennsylvania Supreme Court was hearing five separate cases addressing issues of constitutionality in SORNA. The court's rulings have the potential to dramatically alter the sex offense registry.[7]

These legal decisions primarily rest on the distinction that registration and notification are civil penalties (which fall outside of the scope of constitutional protections), not additional criminal penalties. Taking this one step further, Louisiana has a supervised release statute (LA. Rev. Stat. §15:561.5 2012) that outlines additional provisions sex offenders must follow for a specified time after completion of their sentence. Conditions include:

> subjecting the offender to random visits from supervising officers and monthly meetings, the imposition of curfews, the requirement that the offender report to an officer whenever ordered, forbidding the offender from possessing firearms, and subjecting the offender to website and e-mail monitoring.
>
> *(Eagan, 2013: 277)*

In 2008, the timeframe of supervised release for sex offenders whose victim was 13 years or younger was extended from five years to a lifetime and was done so

136 Collateral Consequences for Partners

retroactively. This decision was upheld as constitutional and not in violation of the *ex post facto* clause at the level of the Supreme Court of Louisiana in *State* v. *Trosclair* (2012).

When the courts upheld the constitutionality of the first notification laws, two elements were emphasized: "First, courts found that the information was no greater than that discerned from the public record of a conviction, and second, that the amount of personal information disseminated was specifically tied to the risk level of the offender" (Carpenter & Beverlin, 2012: 121). As such, a lower risk level meant that fewer members of the community found out less personal information about the offender. This is not the case with SORNA, however: regardless of the offense committed, everyone in the community is "entitled" to large amounts of information about the offender. This has dramatic negative implications on the lives of sex offenders and their families.

Attitudes of the Public, Law Enforcement, and Treatment Professionals

Recall from Chapter 2 how sex offenders are counted in the United States. One method is the publicly available national registry, drawn from a phone survey conducted twice per year by the National Center for Missing and Exploited Children (NCMEC). This provides a jurisdictional distribution of offenders by state however does not provide any information regarding demographics, offense type, residence of the offender, etc. As of year-end 2018, NCMEC (2018) reported a total of 917,771 RSOs in the United States and its territories. Recall again, however, the obvious limitations to NCMEC reporting. One limitation is the aggregate nature of the data which advances the media's homogenized view of the sex offender as a repetitive and dangerous criminal. The second limitation is that most reporting jurisdictions (38 of 57) include some variation of RSOs who are incarcerated, deported, or residing in another state (Harris, Levenson, & Ackerman, 2014). Research reveals that as many as 8 percent of RSOs live out of state and could therefore theoretically be counted twice on registries, thus falsely increasing the count of sex offenders in the NCMEC data (Harris et. at., 2014). A significant percentage of the public view SORN laws as integral to the reduction of sexual victimization.

> Sex offender laws are intended to prevent sexual violence, identify potential perpetrators, and punish convicted perpetrators. The public process of creating knowledge about people who commit sexual crimes effectively institutionalizes a new kind of criminal: the sex offender. The behavior of the new sex offender is largely the same as the historical rapist, but his actions are now solidified for life in a social identity that trumps all other statuses.
>
> *(Small, 2015: 113)*

Many researchers, over a span of years, have found widespread knowledge and support among the public for SORN laws (Anderson & Sample, 2008; Kernsmith, Craun, & Foster, 2009; Levenson, Brannon, Fortney, & Baker, 2007; Phillips, 1998). A study in Washington revealed that more than three-quarters of the public were familiar with notification laws and felt safer with these laws in place, despite widespread acknowledgment (84 percent) of the increased difficulty such laws pose for reintegration for RSOs (Lieb & Nunlist, 2008). A study conducted in 2005 in Florida, (six short months after Sarah Lunde and Jessica Lunsford were murdered) revealed 95 percent of those surveyed supported notification laws; three-quarters supported SORN laws for offenders of all tiers, and over 70 percent at least partially agreed they would support SORN laws without scientific proof that such policies reduced sexual victimization (Levenson, D'Amora, & Hern, 2007). Those individuals more likely to access registry information were women, younger individuals, those with children, and those residing in an urban environment (Anderson, Evans, & Sample, 2009). Among the public then, SORN policies have widespread appeal even with the recognition that reintegration of RSOs may prove difficult and even with the absence of proof that these policies reduce sexual victimization. Expanding attitudes one step beyond SORN policies, a recent national poll revealed that almost 75 percent of the public believed that sex offenders could not be rehabilitated (Mancini, 2014), and most of the public attributed individual deficits such as selfishness, immorality, and moral depravity to sex offenders, as opposed to situational or environmental causes of offending (Spencer, 2009). "As knowledge about sexual victimization grows more sophisticated, understandings of sexual perpetrators becomes ever narrower" (Small, 2015: 111).

These attitudes extend beyond the general public. In a study of 61 policymakers responsible for sex offender laws, researchers found the main rationales for SORN laws were public safety (two-thirds of respondents), a desire to push sex offenders into treatment (about 20 percent of respondents), and to assist in tracking offenders (less than 10 percent of respondents). Only half of policymakers responded that SORN laws in their state were working as intended, but about 65 percent asserted these laws were necessary to deter potential sex offenders (Meloy et al., 2012). In studies of professionals that manage sex offenders, law enforcement officials demonstrated much support for SORN laws. Law enforcement asserted that community notification deterred sex offenders from reoffending and provided greater community surveillance (Farkas & Zevitz, 2000; Gaines, 2006; Redlich, 2001). The negatives for law enforcement personnel, however, were increases to labor and capital expenses to execute notification, costs associated with harassment of sex offenders, and overreactions by the public when a sex offender moved into the community (Gaines, 2006; Zgoba, Witt, Dalessandro, & Veysey, 2008).

Perhaps the most skeptical about the alleged benefits of SORN policies were mental health professionals. A study of almost 500 sex offender treatment

138 Collateral Consequences for Partners

professionals revealed one-third believed that neighborhood safety was increased by community notification, whereas another one-quarter of participants believed community notification served to reduce neighborhood safety (McGrath, Cumming, Burchard, Zeoli, & Ellerby, 2010). Other studies of sex offender treatment professionals found upwards of 70 percent believed notifying the community of an offender's arrival gave a false sense of security (Levenson, Fortney, & Baker, 2010; Malesky & Keim, 2001). Sex crimes are perceived as impacting a vulnerable population, in a way that other offenses are not, and having an impact that extends beyond the occurrence of the individual crime. The incomprehensibility of sex crimes by the public fuels strong anti-sex offender attitudes, "get-tough" policies and knee-jerk reactions (Mancini & Pickett, 2014).

Effects on Recidivism and Community Integration

Registration and notification laws may impact the offender's likelihood of successful reintegration into the community by widely labeling him a sex offender, thereby making it more difficult to find housing, employment, and other opportunities, and additionally undermining his rehabilitative efforts. For most of the public, however, these effects are "collateral damage" if SORN laws work to reduce sexual violence and recidivism. The United States has expanded sex offender legislation each year: Are these laws working?

Jacob Wetterling's parents became activists for children as a result of the kidnap and murder of their son. Jacob's mother, Patty, has mixed views of broad-based community notification laws:

> I based my support of broad-based community notification laws on my assumption that sex offenders have the highest recidivism rates of any criminal. But the high recidivism rates I assumed to be true do not exist. It has made me rethink the value of broad-based community notification laws, which operate on the assumption that most sex offenders are high-risk dangers to the community they are released into.
>
> *(Human Rights Watch, 2007: 4)*

Recall the recidivism statistics from Chapter 2: While findings vary dramatically in studies of recidivism of sex offenders for a variety of reasons, regardless of the type of methodology used, what is clear is that the public believes SOs have a significantly higher recidivism rate than they do. SORN laws were created under the assumption that sex offenders were high recidivists and greater public knowledge about their whereabouts and identity was going to mean greater public safety. Megan Kanka's mother said herself: "We knew nothing about him. If we had been aware … my daughter would be alive today" (Human Rights Watch, 2007: 47). So now we have a lot of information about even low-tier offenders.

Are we safer? Or have we just created policies "to enforce the need of police and the criminal justice system to deal with such offenders harshly and for the public to be more scared than informed" (Ferrandino, 2012: 394).

In a meta-analysis of nine rigorous studies to examine the correlation between SORN laws and crime rates, Drake and Aos (2009) found no specific deterrent effect. That is, registration and community notification was not a deterrent for convicted sex offenders. Researchers found a small decrease in the overall rate of sexual offending, pointing to a minor general deterrent effect in the general public (Drake & Aos, 2009). Other researchers found similar results (Letourneau, Levenson, Brandyptadhyay, Armstrong, & Sinha, 2010; Socia & Stamatel, 2010). A Minnesota study examined broad community notification for Tier 3 offenders and determined this policy was effective over an eight-year period in reducing sexual recidivism. The offenders in this study, however, were Tier 3 offenders also on intensive supervision, so it is unclear which variable impacted the lowered recidivism rate (Duwe & Donnay, 2008). Research has demonstrated no clear substantiation of a specific deterrent effect of community notification policies for Tier 1 and Tier 2 offenders.

Research examining the relationship between SORN legislation and changes in the yearly frequency of sexual offenses by state found little evidence of any impact of notification laws according to Uniform Crime Report data (Vasquez, Maddan, & Walker, 2008). Other research distinguished between registration laws and notification laws. This research found registration of offenders was correlated with a decrease in sex-related offenses, likely a result of increased monitoring by law enforcement. No link between notification laws and reduced crime via recidivism among RSOs was evidenced (Prescott & Rockoff, 2011). Another study used a time-series design to examine rates of forcible rape prior to and after the implementation of SORN laws in all 50 states from 1960 to 2008. In 17 states there was a significant decrease in rape reports after SORNA; in 32 states there was no significant decrease. This study determined there was no significant correlation between type of notification and reduction in forcible rape rates (Maurelli & Ronan, 2013).

One unforeseen consequence of SORN laws is that an individual, as part of a plea negotiation, may plead guilty to a non-sexual offense and therefore avoid registering as a sex offender. One offender indicated:

> For me, the most important thing, even more important than doing time in jail was avoiding the sex offender label. They are seen as the scum of the earth and I wanted nothing to do with that label. I don't want people seeing me that way.
>
> *(Meloy, 2006: 81)*

This example is also illustrative of the incomplete nature of sexual offender registration lists. This individual committed a sexual offense. But due to his plea

140 Collateral Consequences for Partners

agreement and his desire to avoid the stigma associated with a sexual offense, he will never be classified with similar offenders. Conversely, another offender may strike a plea agreement that involves a short amount of probation time, provided he agrees to placement on the sex offense registry. In such situations, the state may be interested in lengthy or lifetime monitoring of the individual, rather than a jail or prison sentence. The latter was the case for Suzanne's husband who pled guilty at the suggestion of his hired attorney to sexual contact with a minor:

> [The lawyer] made it seem like in order to keep it quiet, because he knew we wanted to keep it quiet because of [my husband's] kids and everything, he made it seem like this would be the easiest way. Three years on probation and don't break any laws or anything, if you do, you go to jail, but I'm not worried about you doing that, it's just 3 years probation and it's all over with. Nobody knows anything about it, it's just done and you can go on with your life is basically what he said. And everything was a lie. We had no idea what we were in for.

From Suzanne's perspective, the attorney did not clearly articulate the consequences of spending a lifetime on the sex offense registry and the many restrictions that would entail. Plea agreements create situations in which two offenders with the same offense may experience extraordinarily different outcomes.

What impacts do SORN laws have on the lives of offenders? Criminological literature is clear that desistance from offending is encouraged by reintegration into the community, stress management, and a stable lifestyle through supportive friends and/or family, employment, and residential stability. Broad notification policies can disrupt all these elements of reintegration. Offenders worry about vigilantism and harassment (Bedarf, 1995; Meloy, 2006). In interviews with RSOs, they report stress, avoidance of activities, feelings of isolation, and loss of employment as a direct result of community notification (Levenson et al., 2007). Several studies of RSOs and their families across various states confirm collateral consequences of SORN laws that include difficulty or inability finding employment, inability to locate housing, loss of friends, and community isolation (Ackerman, Sacks, & Osier, 2013; Beck & Travis, 2006; Burchfield & Mingus, 2008; Levenson & Cotter, 2005; Levenson & D'Amora, 2007; Mustaine, Tewksbury, & Stengel, 2006; Zevitz & Farkas, 2000b). If there is no correlation between community notification laws and reduction in recidivism by RSOs, and labeling and stigmatizing RSOs serves to disrupt reintegration with documented negative impacts, policies should be redesigned accordingly. For both the safety of the public and to avoid stigma of offenders, SORN policies should be geared toward Tier 3 offenders only. For Tier 1 and Tier 2 offenders, registration and notification has become a greater burden on the offender than the value of public knowledge obtained (Levenson & Cotter, 2005; Tewksbury, 2005).

Collateral Consequences on the Partners of Registered Sex Offenders

There is a conflict between reality and the media construction around sex offenders and "the current culture of fear is significantly disproportionate to the actual probabilities of threat" (Kenny, 2005: 51). It is in this risk society, that sex offender registries are encouraged. The public fears the violent pedophile in search of his next victim, but that is not the typical offender on the registry.

> Unfortunately, that singular perception ignores the reality that sex offender statutes stigmatize wide-ranging actions and apply to broad segments of the population. Although the cast of characters may change, countless cases relay stories of offenders, no longer dangerous, struggling to maintain stability in lives governed by ever-evolving and increasingly stringent legislation.
>
> *(Carpenter & Beverlin, 2012:110)*

From the perspective of policymakers and law enforcement, the purposes of the registry are informational and tracking of offenders. From the perspective of criminologists and other researchers who have analyzed the ineffectiveness of registration and community notification policies, the purposes are to shame, label, ostracize, and deter offenders.

The most comprehensive studies of the impacts of SORN laws examined almost 600 family members of RSOs (partners and children). Children of RSOs reported feeling overwhelming anger and depression, 65 percent indicated other children in the community sidelined them from activities, and almost half were harassed (Levenson & Tewksbury, 2009; Tewksbury & Levenson, 2009). Financial hardships were reported by more than 80 percent of partners, harassment by almost one-half, and 7 percent experienced physical injury or assault. Partners experienced emotional consequences they attributed to SORN which included isolation, stress, shame, and loss of friends (Levenson & Tewksbury, 2009; Tewksbury & Levenson, 2009). For the women in this study, SORN brought many negative impacts: the reclassification of tier assignment which dramatically increases the length of time on the registry; the community stigma that results from notification; and fear and harassment in the community.

Reclassification of Tiers

SORNA implementation expanded the number of offenses that require registration and community notification, and perhaps most profoundly changed the tier assignment of many offenses. This increase in tier level for many offenses meant that many offenders arbitrarily became perceived by the public as a greater risk, despite no actual risk assessment of their dangerousness to the community.

142 Collateral Consequences for Partners

> When a crime is reclassified as more dangerous, so, too, is the individual convicted of that crime. Upward reclassification increases registration and notification burdens, and reclassification affects both future offenders and those previously convicted and classified as less dangerous. Consequently, burdens associated with the reclassification are being applied retroactively to convicted offenders who were deemed a lower risk under previous registration schemes.... Particularly disconcerting is the fact that revised classifications are often made without individualized assessment of the convicted offender's level of dangerousness.
>
> *(Carpenter & Beverlin, 2012:113)*

This reclassification scheme and its retroactive nature made many families feel hopeless. Rhonda's partner pled guilty to statutory rape with Rhonda as the alleged victim. They later married. He will be on the sex offense registry for life. Rhonda said: "Every time they make a new law it's retroactive and we can never get ahead. We can never get over it." Christine also discussed her husband's tier reclassification:

> Nearing 5 years, they made it retroactive for 10 years. And still we were like, "Okay, we can do this." And then he had to register twice a year. But, before that 10 years was up, they changed to Tiers 1, 2, and 3 and because it was a Tier 3 sex offense which is supposed to be the worst of the worst, and now he has to register for life and he has to register every 3 months. So, now he has to go in and get his picture taken every 3 months. And I'm a secretary at an elementary school and I'm constantly worried ... I don't think that I'm going to lose my job. I'm sure people probably already know ... it's not something that people are going to come up and ask you about. But, with the teachers, if the subject of child molesters comes up I'm just like frozen and try to act normal, but not join the conversation. Just terribly uncomfortable.

Nothing about Christine's husband had changed. The offense was molestation of a minor family member that was revealed more than 15 years after its occurrence. He pled guilty and accepted a suspended sentence and a term of probation. His risk level was assessed at very low. The only element that changed was reclassification by the state and the public's *perception* of him as more dangerous.

Tara's husband pled guilty to one count of accepting child pornography and served a probationary sentence. His registry term was to be ten years.

> At first they said that he was only going to be on it for 10 years, then they extended it to 15 years, and we don't even know from what date because he finished his probation 3 or 4 years before they ever

registered him. So, do they take it from the date of probation? Do they take it from the date of registering? And that wasn't even his fault. That was the court's fault because they never notified him as far as the hearing goes, and as far as leveling goes, that didn't happen until almost 6 years later.

Renee's husband also experienced a reclassification for his offense of solicitation of a minor prostitute overseas and intent to distribute child pornography:

[The state we're in] does use the three-tier system, in fact, since we've moved here they've changed their system a bit. When we moved here, he was supposed to be dropped from the registry after 10 years. I don't know if it would have been this summer or next summer. And just last October, everything changed and now he'll be on it for 25 years!

Tracy was passionate about the flaws inherent in SORN laws in Virginia and the inadequacies of the criminal justice system in general. Her husband accepted a plea to what he asserted was a false allegation of sexual misconduct of a minor. He served 10 years on probation. Tracy elaborated:

Only 2 percent of charges make it to trial here in Virginia. The other 98 percent are plea bargains, so it's a business for them. This is what they do. They know that the way the laws are written allows them to just use an accusation to convict. They don't need a witness, they don't need proof, they didn't even interview the girl 5 months after the accusation was made and we showed up to the first preliminary hearing. He took the plea deal and he was put on the registry. And it was supposed to only be for 10 years. Ten-year minimum in Virginia for a non-violent offender because we don't have a three-tier system here. And we thought, "Okay, we'll do the 10 years, you'll keep your head down and in 10 years we can move on with our lives." And then within 2 months, the General Assembly met and increased it from 10 years to 15 years retroactively. And no one ever told us this. We just happened to find it while we were looking for why they asked for his DNA later that summer. And we realized that they were going to continue to do this every year. Every year they're going to increase the penalties or it's going to be retroactive or they're just going to keep adding on more years. They're going to keep bringing in more people on the registry to keep filling it up because it's a business, and you know, you pay every time you register. If no one else is going to stand up and say, "Hold on. Let's look at some research and some reports. Is it actually making society safer? Is it actually reducing crime and victimization? No, it's not." So, why do you want to keep passing more severe restrictions

144 Collateral Consequences for Partners

and regulations? We don't even call it a tier. It's a classification. But, it's violent and non-violent, and twice now they've reclassified thousands of people from non-violent to violent in one broad swoop. So, what they've done, they took charges that were misdemeanors when they were convicted and now they're felonies, and because everything with sex offenders is retroactive, it's made them from non-violent to violent. So, that changed, instead of them being on the registry for 15 years, they're now lifers and instead of registering once a year, they have to register every 90 days. And the neighbors and co-workers who looked on the registry saw that it went from non-violent to violent and their first thought is going to be that that person reoffended. And they didn't. They didn't even have a chance to petition the court, they found out after the governor signed it in whichever year that those people were reclassified. So, they had no due process, it's a done deal. From what I understand only two or three people get off a year. Um, and you're usually denied the first time. And I think you only get three tries. I think if you apply, if I remember correctly because we're not quite there with [my husband], but if you apply and you get denied then you have to wait 2 years, and then the second time if you're denied you have to wait 2 or 5 years, and then if you're denied the third time, you can never get off.

Reclassification is never accompanied by less registration time: it always means increased registration time and usually broader community notification. Both the offender and the family are impacted by these policies. Yolanda, whose husband accepted a plea to touching their son inappropriately, explained:

And that's where I get upset with the laws that remind us every time we turn around that we are bad people and that we have no rights and that we're scum of the earth. Because I've seen how much work we've done to try to get on with our life and put the pieces back together and we did that very well, but now we're always reminded of ... when it comes to the annual registry ... because we're not on the registry for 10 years anymore, we're on for life. And I say "we" because, really, it's all of us. It's him, but it's also me and our children, and when people say, "Well, you're not on the registry, you didn't do anything wrong," and I say, "No, I didn't, but this is how you're made to feel by law enforcement and the government and everything." God bless Adam Walsh and I understand he lost his son to a terrible man, but it wasn't my husband. And my husband is not a terrible man, and there are a lot of people on the registry that aren't terrible people. You know, you shouldn't be restricted as to where you can live and I don't think that there should be restrictions to your employment. I'm not saying that there aren't individuals out there, men and women, who cannot be around children because they have a sexual attraction, and I understand that maybe they need to be in that situation. But, when you lump everybody together, it's not going to work. And I think it's wrong, and that's where I get angry because my husband hasn't been able to work in 2 years now and he worked and was self-employed since this happened, and we were doing well until [a few years ago] when one of his, a fellow that he worked for, got mad at him and told people [he was a sex offender] and he got blackballed. Now he can't even get a job picking beans and it's frustrating to me to see him not being able to provide for his kids and not be able to help pay our mortgage. And it kills me because most people don't even give a shit. And I'm sorry, I know I shouldn't swear, but when you talk to people, they don't really care because they feel … you're a sex offender! They'd rather have you dead. They won't even look at that you are rehabilitated, you're just a bad person and they don't care. And that's the tough part for me. Terrible. Because at times I've said to people that I wish we hadn't said anything [about the offense], and that's a terrible, terrible thing to say. And I've had friends say, "Oh, you don't mean that," and I say, "You know, sometimes I do mean it." Because there's no sense to it all and after almost 15 years we're not going forward (crying) … we're going backwards and that's what bothers me the most. I'm sorry, but that's what just kills me and breaks my heart. (crying) I'm sorry.

Like other sex offenders who were reclassified, the risk assessment and level of dangerousness did not change; the state changed the classification of their offense and that meant an increase in the amount of time the offender was required to register, and therefore a change in how the public *perceived* their level of dangerousness. That also means increased community notification, increased frequency of registration, increased visits from law enforcement, increased difficulty finding employment and housing, and overall significant difficulty reintegrating into society when the *offense did not change*. Carrie, who married her husband after his conviction, said:

So, every year we just hope that they won't pass another law that's going to turn our lives upside down. People look at the registry and his charges look pretty scary on paper, I won't deny that, but he's not a pedophile who is going to steal the neighbor's 7-year-old and rape her and kill her and leave her in the woods. You know, he made some really bad, stupid decisions when he was a young, arrogant prick and he's going to have to pay for them for the rest of his … our … lives. And I don't regret marrying him at all. But I never knew how hard life would be as the years went by. It just never gets any easier.

Stigma in the Community

The stigma that comes from being a sex offender and the wife/partner of a sex offender is the direct result of community notification. Not many members of the public proactively search the registry for RSOs in their neighborhood, so those that are aware of the presence of an RSO in the community, are made aware because of community notification policies. As mentioned earlier, some states have very broad notification policies, and this makes for a greater level of stigma for the offender and his family. Melissa found out a couple of years after the abuse ended that her husband was sexually touching her daughter. Her daughter revealed the abuse to Melissa, and Melissa reported it immediately to the child welfare agency in her state. After accepting a plea, the husband (daughter's step-father) served six years in prison and 18 months on probation. The family decided to reunify upon his release from prison. He will be on the registry for life. Melissa discussed the very broad community notification that applied to her husband:

> Well, I'll tell ya. When they started registering, they did it every year and I used to call it sex offenders on parade in the local paper. I looked at that paper for years and I still do, twice a week to see. So, I knew when that edition was coming out and I could prepare myself because it was a just huge blow to me. His mug shot in the paper, these are the most hated people in our communities and stuff. I kinda, I laid low. I actually left a pretty decent job and took a job working from home 'cause I was afraid of the backlash. That somebody would recognize him as my husband. So that, there was a lot of shame there because for a long time it, I felt the guilt by association. I lived in the past a lot, I didn't know it was happening, but it happened and what kind of, I got labeled as the sex offender's wife. And, "How can I still be married to somebody that molested my child?" I still, even my sisters call me a bad mother, because I stayed with him. I just, you know, like I tell him and I tell the family, nobody knows him like I do.

Amber's community had a method of notification that she was unaware of prior to her boyfriend moving into her residence:

> The day he moved in with me, we didn't know this, but in our state people can sign up to receive email notifications when any sex offender moves within a mile of whatever address they put in. And I live in an upper-middle-class community with a lot of stay-at-home moms, well-educated people, but a lot of people had signed up for these email alerts. So, the day my boyfriend moved in with me, these email alerts went viral, and created a pretty big scandal within my community. So, everybody in

Registration and Community Notification **147**

my community now knows. I got notes on my door, I got death threats, and I got horrible, horrible emails from people who I thought were my friends. The police got involved because they were getting so many calls … they were doing anything to get him removed from the neighborhood. After this happened people wouldn't even walk in front of my house. They would cross the street where there was no crossing guard, on a dangerous street, just so they wouldn't have to walk in front of my house. It was horrible!

Her partner was found guilty at trial of rape in what he claimed was a false allegation. He served three years of a four-year sentence prior to meeting Amber. He will spend 15 years on the registry.

In an attempt to reduce familial stigma, Tracy's husband suggested divorce and that she return to her maiden name:

When this all happened [my husband] said, "If you want to go back to your maiden name, I have no problem with that." He actually said, "If you want to divorce me and we still live together, we can do that." And I immediately said no to all of that. I mean, they weren't even thoughts that entered my mind. And it actually made me angry that he suggested them. But he knew with the stigma and all that, and that being related to the person that's on the registry with the last name and that address… he knew what it meant. But I immediately said no. This is my thing too and we're not going to hide in shame.

Margaret's husband served 14 years in prison for rape prior to their marriage and will spend a lifetime on the registry. They live in a state with broad community notification and one way she reduced stigma was to distinguish his offense from a child sex offense.

They send cards to our neighbors with my husband's picture on it every 3 months. This will be for the rest of his life. I would definitely change the public notification because I believe it takes a toll not just on the sex offender's life in finding employment and finding housing, but their families too. It could be their wife or their children, it affects their parents, their siblings. I would say, people see those cards and they see sexual predator, people automatically assume, oh my gosh, child molester. And that is wrong, people get the wrong outlook immediately. So, if they're gonna keep those cards, they should change them. Put NOT CHILD CASE. Because all these cards say the same thing, you know: "If you see this victim around children, notify the police immediately, identify what he/she is wearing and tattoos and marks on their body, description of the vehicle." And I think they should change

148 Collateral Consequences for Partners

> the cards, so that maybe it's bright orange or bright yellow if it is not a
> child case to make people understand that hey, this person had nothing
> to do with a child.

She further explained how she tried to mitigate stigma among her neighbors:

> We've had our car windows busted out, we've had our tires slashed,
> it could be a random person, but it seems like when it's that, there's a
> pattern, you know, down the street or the next street over too. I used
> to decorate my house for holidays, you know, Easter, Christmas. I had
> lights laying on the ground, I'm trying to explain, but anyways, the lights
> was destroyed and someone had tried to string the lights where it said
> molester on my yard. There's been a couple times, the neighbors told
> neighbors, hey, he's a child molester, watch him. And when we first
> moved in here, I sent out letters, giving them a heads up, hey my hus-
> band's a sexual offender, he was convicted of rape, it was not on a child,
> it was on an adult. I want our neighborhood to be safe too, please don't
> react, um, we have children too, we're a family, please do your research
> before you judge him pretty much is what I put.

For women like Sarah, whose husband was incarcerated for possession of child
pornography, her community shunned her family. "There's nobody other than
my immediate neighbor who speaks to me on my street anymore. A majority of
people shunned us out." For many women, the community stigma and evasion
remained true at community centers, churches, and in the neighborhood generally. Donna spoke of her experience in a religious group:

> I had actually been involved with a Bible study and I had confided in
> my Bible study group about some of the stuff that had been going on,
> not all of it, but when it hit the newspaper all of them were like, "Well,
> we can't be involved with you." And I was like, "What?" And they just
> said, "Well, that's bad, that's really bad." And granted the newspaper
> never makes it sound good, especially if they don't like it, which I don't
> know how it could ever really sound good, but it definitely made it
> sound worse than I thought it was at the time and they just … This
> one couple, you know a good Christian couple, said "We can't forgive
> you, we can't be around you people." And I was like, "Oh that's good
> Christian of you."

Donna's husband pled guilty to molestation of a minor during their marriage
and he served one year of a five-year sentence. He will serve life on the registry. Erica shared a similar experience that she and her husband had at a senior
citizen center:

At the time we moved in here, [my husband] and I started going to the senior citizen things, it was a small community and we thought well, before everybody finds out about it, we'll get to know people and be a part of the community. And at the time, that was when Jessica's Law was going on and it passed and so they put the newsletter out with all the headlines, "Men, protect your wives and children! All of these men are dangerous, none of them are safe to be around." And it became quickly obvious that we were not welcome there. Now we stay away from the community affairs.

Erica's husband also pled guilty to a charge of molestation of a minor and will be on the registry for life.

In a community, especially one with broad notification policies, people gossip to each other about sex offenders and the partners of sex offenders. Amber said:

I remember this one spring I was at the local Farmer's Market and somebody came up to me and said, "It's so amazing that you keep showing up to things. If it were me I'd just run and hide. I mean, I think that's so great that there are all these people talking about you, but you just hold your head up high." And I was like, "Well, why shouldn't I come to the Farmer's Market? I need to buy lettuce." But, apparently everywhere I went people were talking.

Amber had another experience at her son's soccer game:

There was a time really early on where I would go see my son play soccer and nobody would stand next to me or talk to me. It was like the Red Sea parted and I would just stand there alone. I mean, people would move their chairs over and it was pretty tense and pretty ugly. It caused a lot of tears in my family. I mean, I would keep my head up high, but then I'd go home and cry. And I kept [my husband] away from all of that. He didn't need that added stress.

Some signs of stigma demonstrated by community members are obvious, whereas others are more subtle. Victoria said:

The neighbors across the street had a girl that was about 12 and they obviously knew because every time we would pull in the driveway the girl would get up and run inside the house. So, we've had all sorts of responses. From people just kind of ignoring us and not saying anything, to the little girl who would run inside the house every time she saw us.

150 Collateral Consequences for Partners

The response of Tanya's neighbor was much different:

> [Our neighbor has children and] the littlest girl, she's 4 and she came up to me and said, "Has your husband ever killed anybody?" And I said, no (laughs) and she said, "Oh, my mom said we can't come over anymore because your husband kills people." That's not true, but okay, I understand, I can't explain a sex offender to a 4-year-old, I understand.

For women whose partners have lifetime registration (and under SORNA this is an increasingly larger group of offenders), their dilemma is do you withdraw from community activities entirely, or do you attempt to integrate into the community and face the potential backlash and stigma that comes with the community knowing your association with a sexual offender? Sabrina married a man with a juvenile sex offense conviction and an adult familial sex offense conviction that he claimed was a false allegation. As a result of these two offenses, Sabrina's husband must serve his life on probation and on the registry: that is, a lifetime of law enforcement monitoring. Sabrina and her husband had a child and she decided to join a Moms Offering Moms Support group in her community to provide activities for herself and her child. Her experience was not a positive one.

> The MOMS Club (Moms Offering Moms Support) confronted me about his offense. This is a social club for stay-at-home moms and their kids. Well, at the beginning the Board confronted me. I was on the Board as Vice President of the Chapter. And they confronted me about it. Somebody anonymously told the head of the organization, and then they said to me, "Your husband is a registered sex offender." And I was like, "Yeah, and?" And they just said, "Well, we didn't know if you knew." And they started to ridicule me about what I was doing and why I didn't tell them and this and that. So, they told me that they were going to have to have an emergency meeting and I was going to have to tell all of the members about his history and they were going to have to vote about whether I could stay or not. Ultimately they cast their vote and three people said, "yes, I could stay" and ten people said, "no." And I wrote an email later that day and stated to them that I was very disappointed and if I knew that the results were going to be that one-sided that I would have never stood up there and told them my private business. I felt ridiculed and my counselor called it a public lynching. And my mom said that it reminded her of an old Western where all of the angry people gathered in the street for a hanging. It was bad and I was humiliated.

Such situations make integration into a community extraordinarily difficult. The stigma, and fear of being stigmatized, extends to the children as well.

Most of Susan's concern was for her children:

> I worry, not so much for myself or my husband, but for our kids. Because I know that once people see his name on the registry, especially with the word "predator" there, they'll treat our kids differently. And I know that it's affected our son. He's 17, and he's been very strong through this and he loves our family to death, we have such a good time with him, but I can tell. He has friends at school and he doesn't bring anybody to the house, which is fine. We don't want people finding out and claiming that something happened, so we've just told the kids, that if they want to have something, it has to be at the other person's house. And I know that my son is much more private about his family. He worries that once he starts dating and if he gets close to someone, they're eventually going to find out and they'll make their decisions or judgments based on who [my husband] is at that time. So, we don't get close to anybody in the community.

Jill, whose husband was incarcerated on a violation for attending a school function, spoke about some of the things her daughter was told at school about her father:

> [My daughter] came home and said that [her friend] told me that Dad kills kids. And I looked at her and I said, "Honey are you a kid?" and she says, "Yeah." And I said, "Has your Daddy ever hurt you?" She said, "No." "Then you're Daddy's not a kid killer, otherwise you wouldn't have made it." And she just kind of blew it off, but I'm scared, what's going to happen when they're in middle school and high school and they understand what this is and they're being teased for it. How is it fair to them? They had nothing to do with it. At all. At the same time, what do I do? Give up on him? Leave him? For something he didn't do? It's not fair.

Prior to meeting, Jill's husband pled guilty at the suggestion of a public defender for familial molestation of a minor for a situation he claimed was a false allegation. He was sentenced to ten years in prison and lifetime on the registry. Undoubtedly, the stress of community notification impacts the male/female intimate relationship. Catherine's husband will spend his life on the registry for what he alleged was a false charge. During the interview with Catherine, her husband was at the point where he was no longer leaving the house ... for any reason other than registering:

> He doesn't stay home because of his disability. He does not leave the house, he doesn't go out, period. We have a dog, thank god she's a

> wonderful dog, because I take her out when I leave for work and I let her out when I come home from work and she's fine. I go home on my dinner break and let her out and then I go back to work. She's fine. He will not even take her outside, he does not leave the house unless he absolutely has to. Every 3 months, he has to go to the police station, so he does that. Every month or so he has to go to the doctor, so he does that. But that's it. He won't even go to a grocery store with me. We do nothing together. Absolutely nothing.

The answer for many couples was isolation, in order to avoid (or at least minimize) community stigma that resulted from notification. Jill described how the public viewed not just her husband negatively, but her as well:

> Because they think of me like that. It's not just him. I'm the whore. I'm the sleazebag that's sleeping with a child molester. And, you know, they don't want to hear that I don't have a criminal record, that my father and my brother are police officers. They don't want to hear that it's not true. I've never done anything wrong in my life that's a criminal offense. All I've done is worked hard. But they don't want to hear that. They want me to be that villain. They want me to be that woman who doesn't give a crap about her kids and is more worried about him than my children and villainize me because that's what makes them feel better. Because they don't understand that there are people that are out there in my situation, it's easier for them to understand the bad side because that makes more sense. And so that's the way I'm treated. So, we just tried to find a place that was out in the middle of nowhere, away from everybody, and unfortunately there are still 18 other houses out here, so there are 18 people that hate us. So, I try not to care about what they think about me.

Anita conveyed her hope that people could one day see beyond the label of sex offender:

> There's people who've known him for a couple of years and then they find out he's on the list and don't want anything to do with him. But to me, it's like you meet somebody and they're really a good person and they're a friend of yours and then you find out something they did years ago and your opinion of them all of a sudden changes, it just makes no sense to me. It's something you did, not something you are.

Community stigma also occurs from the inability of offenders to participate in holidays, such as Halloween, due to law enforcement restrictions. Recall from Chapter 1 that many states have Halloween-specific laws that target sexual offenders who are either on the registry, on parole, or conditional release. The false assumption behind these policies is that children are less safe on Halloween than at other times of the year. Restrictions vary by state and by the offender's status, but may include required attendance at an education program, prohibition from leaving the house, opening the door, or giving out candy, prohibition from attending Halloween parties, prohibition from decorating, or a requirement to meet with law enforcement (Chaffin, Levenson, Letourneau, & Stern, 2009).

Sandra spoke about Halloween restrictions for her husband:

> He has to stay home [on Halloween]. A couple years he had to go to the probation officer's office during certain hours on Halloween. Last year he was allowed to stay home, but he had to turn out the lights, no decorations and pass out no candy. Furthermore, he's not allowed to participate in anything Halloween. He can't go to a Halloween party or dress up for Halloween or anything like that. No hayrides or anything like that either.

Cindy's husband had similar restrictions:

> Oh my gosh, oh my gosh, that's the other thing that just frickin' pisses me off. We live in this cool, historic neighborhood, we get an average of 1,200 to 1,500 trick-or-treaters a year. It was our biggest holiday, we have more Halloween decorations than anything else, than Christmas. We always had this huge party where everybody brings their kids over … and we'll never have trick-or-treaters again. It's a probation violation and he'll go to jail. We can't have any decorations and the porch light has to be off all night.

Sometimes the rules are clear, but for Patricia and her husband, not always:

> We also weren't allowed decorations, outside or inside the house. Which could be a little hairy because at one point I had a basket of apples on the kitchen counter and one of these rotating probation officers told me it constituted a holiday decoration. A wooden basket of apples was a holiday decoration! She told me that it was a fall fruit and could be considered a Halloween decoration. It was a pretty interesting interpretation of Halloween decorations.

None of the women in this study had husbands who were forced to spend time in jail for Halloween. Valerie was thankful she and her husband did not reside in a county that required jail attendance on Halloween.

> There are some counties in [our state] where you have to spend the night in jail. Thankfully we don't live in one. As long as the lights are

off and he's in the back of the house and he doesn't answer the door, then he's allowed to stay at the house. We can't have any light on outside or any decorations on the house, even if it's just visible through the window.

At Catherine's house, there had to be a sign on the lawn that said, "no Halloween candy at this address, registered sex offender on the premises." That was an obvious way to stigmatize the family in the eyes of the community. Her husband was on the registry for life, so will be subject to labeling at Halloween forever unless the laws in his jurisdiction are tempered. Research, however, reveals no greater harm to children from sex offenders on Halloween than at other times of the year (Chaffin, Levenson, Letourneau, & Stern, 2009), yet states continue to increase law enforcement attention to the imaginary problem of increased risk to children on this one night. In fact, law enforcement has acknowledged that there is no greater risk on Halloween. San Antonio has Project S.A.F.E. which requires sex offenders to be under law enforcement supervision for four hours on Halloween. Bexar County Supervising Officer Shannon Jones said:

> It is a win–win situation. The community gets that extra level of protection. The sex offenders are no more dangerous on Halloween than they are on November 1, but it makes the community feel better to have that extra layer of protection.
>
> *(Lustbader, 2019: online)*

Judgments based on a person's inclusion on the registry are quick and severe and while the courts believe the public is entitled to much information about an offender, sometimes the public misuses that information and instills fear in an offender and his family, or outright harasses the family.

Fear and Harassment in the Community

Many of the women in this study discussed examples of harassment from members of the community or by law enforcement personnel. Those who had not experienced harassment personally, lived in fear of being harassed based on stories of harassment they heard from the families of other sex offenders. Susan's husband will spend his life on the sex offense registry and she was against the registry due to the fear it instilled in families.

> I personally would never have a public registry because it puts families in fear. It doesn't just affect the person on the registry, it affects their whole family. You know, I live in fear of people looking, just randomly looking up sex offenders and "let's go do something nasty to them." So, I live in fear of that. It's paralyzing.

Mary's boyfriend will be on the sex offense registry for life for a statutory rape that occurred prior to them meeting. She struggled with the decision to have him move in with her because of the potential ramifications for herself and her daughter. They had been together for nine years.

> I have not wanted to have him registered to our address and I'm afraid of the impact that will have on my daughter, because of her friends' parents finding out, something like that. I guess I didn't understand the laws very well and he didn't either, and we thought there was some way to get him off the list. And we've hired attorneys and we've been waiting, I've been waiting. The plan has been that when he gets off the list, we'll get married, move in together and I think I've decided, that maybe that's never gonna happen. So, I don't know, we decided that in the long run, it's better to have a strong family and deal with what might come than to live like this. But I'm still scared.

Jill described harassment that she reported to law enforcement. Her concerns however were not taken seriously:

> It specifically says ... that people are not allowed to harass you. Well, when they're sending an anonymous letter with no return address on it, how can I say that I'm being harassed? And when we do call the police because one of these letters said that [my husband] was going to be "watched" on Halloween night and if he so much as set a foot on the porch they were going to call the police, and we call the police and they look at him like he's a filthy dirtbag anyway and they tell him, "You're not being harassed, they're just letting you know that they're watching you." Really? So, it's like a catch-22. I mean, it's a scarlet letter, and it's not fair. I mean, also, somebody told my daughter on the school bus that her dad kills kids. How is that not harassment?

Catherine also experienced various forms of harassment in her community:

> I had a dirty word that I will not say carved with a knife into the hood of my car. I had windows broken in my house four times, I had other things that are stupid done, I mean, people would egg my house wherever I was living. Just dumb stuff. Vandalism, that's the best way to put it. Also, physical threats, physical confrontations. I almost got fired when his picture went into the paper. I had to agree that he would never drop me off or pick me up from work [so I could keep my job].

For life, Catherine's community will be notified of her husband's status as a sexual offender for what he alleged was a false charge prior to their marriage.

156 Collateral Consequences for Partners

They had been together for 11 years. Sabrina said: "One of the neighbors who lives around the corner was reposting the flyer, running me off the road, flipping me off, giving me dirty looks, and various other things." For Michelle, one of her "friends" found out about her husband's offense and posted the information on Facebook. "[The next day] we had a car go by [our house] and there were people leaned out the window screaming, 'we're gonna burn your house down, you pedophile fag!'" These incidents of harassment frequently occur *years* after the offense happened for which the sex offender is listed on the registry. However, because community notifications occur in some states each time an offender registers (every 3 months for lifetime registrants), and in other states notification occurs yearly, the community is reminded repeatedly of an offender's past. So, while an offense may have occurred five, ten, even 20 years prior, the community views the offender as a *new* threat to their safety.

It is not only community harassment that families deal with, but also harassment from law enforcement personnel. April discussed the frequent visits law enforcement made to her home and the resultant perception of her neighbors:

> Our local police, they say they come to verify your residence. It is supposed to be *up to* four times a year. Well last year it was seven times. They come in a marked car, not an unmarked car and come to your door in broad daylight, usually between 10 am and 3 pm. To me, I don't get it. I just don't get it. I know what I would be thinking if I was the neighbor. It would not be good.

Brandi talked about the constant pressure from police to relocate:

> And every time the police come to the door to check my husband's residency, they say, "So, you ready to move?" My husband is a Vietnam veteran; he fought for his country, something a lot of men never did. He never harmed a child. He never touched a child.

Brandi's husband will serve 10 years on the registry for two counts of possession of child pornography. Catherine felt like the sheriffs in her neighborhood were doing a little extra community notification: "We live on a street with a few sheriffs and they feel that anytime they see [my husband] talking to anybody that it's their call of duty to inform that person that he's a sex offender." Some women felt like the police were too quick to question their partner and too heavy-handed in their response, and that was a direct result of their partner's status as an RSO. Jessica believed she was constantly patrolled by law enforcement in her community to the point where she and her husband eventually relocated.

> The people we rented from knew [my husband was a sex offender] of course. They said, yeah, you can rent the house and 2 days after we

moved in, cops came and parked outside of our house and camped there. Two days after that, there were letters on everybody's doors about us. I think it was the neighbors, but I think the police started it. They kept coming and parking outside our house. So anyway, I felt like a prisoner of my own house, we lived there a year, until the lease was up and it felt like a prison. I didn't wanna go outside, it was just, I felt like a prisoner, like I was in jail. Like people were talking and I don't know, I had nightmares that whole year. We even went on vacation on Halloween because you know, big sex offender time. Halloween, we went on a cruise over Halloween, and we got back and the police were all over us. It's a smaller town, and it discourages sex offenders from moving there by harassing them. You know, they just make it so uncomfortable so you have to move. We did.

Tammy described a series of events over a period of about a year where her husband was arrested multiple times on a series of charges that were all dismissed. These events, however, left a significant impact on their family.

> At first my neighbors were all fine with it, but people began to change. And in my state, in my county that I lived in we had a murder that occurred on Christmas which kind of pushed all these bills through and everything changed from there. When October came and then with the death of this girl, people start searching online. My husband had been arrested in the last year, I think seven times, every time on a false charge. We've had the SWAT team in our house, I mean, it's just been a nightmare. And my mother because of all the charges said she didn't want him around the kids anymore. My parents have called social services on me and so I haven't been seeing the kids anymore. We went from having this beautiful house that my husband got for us to having absolutely nothing. We had cars, I had a job making $100,000 a year and I lost my job. We lost our home. I mean it's just, I spent all of my savings, I've gone through two 401k's just for attorney's fees and bonds just so every case could be dismissed, every single case was dismissed.

Sabrina experienced harassment from community members, but when she attempted to remedy it through the courts, she experienced prejudice:

> I went in front of the judge to get an injunction against this girl so she will stop telling everybody that [my husband's] a sex offender when he's not even around. But the judge told me that she can say whatever she wants whenever she wants. And he said, "You took on the Scarlet A when you married him, so you need to put up with it, and if you don't want to put up with it, you can get a divorce."

158 Collateral Consequences for Partners

The conflict between reality and the media construction surrounding sex offenders where fear is disproportionate to the likelihood of risk permeates the general public and individuals in the law enforcement field as well. Registries and notifications are encouraged in this society of risk in order to quell the public's fear. SORN policies brought many negative impacts to the women in this study, including the reclassification of tier assignment which dramatically increased the length of time their partners spent on the registry; the community stigma of notification; and fear and harassment in the community. Given the negative impacts of SORN laws and the questionable effectiveness of these laws, how can this legislation be improved?

Improvements to Registration and Community Notification

Given that labeling and stigmatization is a major impetus in the reintegration of offenders into society and prevents a sex offender's family from functioning effectively, any SORN law should be reasonably narrow in scope. Narrow in terms of not applying to an overly broad range of offenses, and narrow in terms of notifying the community of only the most serious offenders. Research demonstrates no clear specific deterrent effect of community notification policies for Tier 1 and Tier 2 offenders (Duwe & Donnay, 2008). With that, there is no reason to notify the public of sex offenders at these tiers but restrict this information to law enforcement personnel. The public should be provided with notification of Tier 3 offenders, as research has demonstrated this is effective in reducing sexual recidivism (Duwe & Donnay, 2008).

In line with this, the net-widening of SORNA and reclassification of tiers has meant more offenders are considered Tier 3 and are required to register for life. Tara discussed her views on the registry as a catch-all:

> I feel like no matter what the crime is, if it has a sexual connotation, they make you be on the registry. No matter what it is. I think a lot of it is propaganda. I think the laws are made to have the politicians look good. I don't think it helps anybody. I think it needs to be reorganized and revamped. I think it needs to be stripped down and to start all over again. Something just doesn't make sense in the law. I don't understand why they feel the need to put people on a list. I don't know what purpose it serves. I would probably have a list for the most serious offenders, but they have to be the most serious offenders. I don't think the list was originally meant to be a catch-all. I think it was meant to monitor the most serious offenders. I don't think it was intended to be misused for misdemeanors and low-end criminals ... you know, but just for the most serious offenders.

Criminological research indicates that the longer an individual remains offense-free, the less likely they are to commit another offense. As such, for an overwhelming number of offenders, lifetime registration is unnecessary and merely serves to undermine community reintegration. A significant number of offenders assigned a Tier 3 also serves to undermine what the public and law enforcement consider a "serious" offense and thereby negates the public safety factor of the registry. Not every sex offender can be considered "dangerous." There are inherently some sex offenses that are more serious than others; some offenders that are at a higher risk of reoffending than others. This aspect of SORNA needs to be reevaluated. Victoria discussed the changes she would make to the registry:

> Because the Adam Walsh Act is so prevalent right now in the public's eye and in law enforcement's eye, I would definitely make the change to the way they approach the tier system. The way in which they put people into the tiers has got to be reconsidered. There has to be independent, clinical assessments as to where to place these people. And I specifically mention independent. It can't come from the prosecuting side, it can't come from the defense. It has to be an independent risk assessment by people whose business does not have a vested interest in making money off of this.

When states used a system of risk assessment it was a much more developed concept. At that point an offender's level of "risk" much more accurately represented their level of "potential dangerousness" to the community than today's tiers system which most often is based on the categorization of the offense to which an offender has accepted a plea. Jill suggested that only the most serious offenders be on the registry:

> I don't believe that you should get rid of the registry, but that it needs to be reserved for people that the community really needs to be aware of that could potentially be a danger. There's people out there that people need to be aware of. There are dangerous people out there. There are legitimate dangerous people. And there are people that the community needs to be aware of, I don't want to get rid of the registry. But it needs to be reserved for those people who have a serious potential to reoffend. Those are the ones that people need to be aware of. Right now it's so convoluted with people who don't need to be monitored.

To remedy some of the issues with SORNA, the government could allow states to keep risk assessment based classification systems, used by about half of the states to classify sex offenders as opposed to the three-tier system. The current tiered system of classification is a barrier to SORNA compliance for many states, as lawmakers must reclassify crimes and alter notification procedures (Wang, 2014/2015). Perhaps of more relevance is that research has demonstrated tier systems are less effective at predicting sexual recidivism than they are for actuarial risk assessment scores. In a study of 500 randomly selected RSOs who were formerly incarcerated in New Jersey, Minnesota, Florida, or South Carolina, researchers found that "actuarial risk assessment scores consistently outperformed Adam Walsh Act tiers. More important from a policy standpoint is that the tiering systems already in use by the states outperformed Adam Walsh Act tiers in predicting sexual reoffending" (Zgoba, Miner, Knight, Letourneau, Levenson, & Thornton, David, 2012:4). SORNA did not improve upon the system that existed prior: on many levels it made it worse.

Sex offenders need to be given the opportunity to challenge their inclusion on the sex offense registry. Some states permit this; other states do not. Instead of working against barriers put up by SORN, individuals should have a goal to move toward. Carolyn elaborated the difficulties of abiding by the social controls of law enforcement:

> You know, when I was an "innocent" as I call it, I used to see that someone had violated parole I thought, "Oh the idiots had a chance to be out and now they're back in. How stupid!" But, now I've seen that some of these laws are so crazy that you don't even know what [law enforcement] mean. Like, for instance, what is considered a toy? For the first time I bought a garden gnome and I have to ask the parole officer, "Is this a toy?" I mean, I don't see a garden gnome as a toy, but it might be something kids like. It's ridiculous. And then one of the restrictions of his parole is that he can't be around alcohol and I had to ask, "Well, does that mean that we can't go to lunch at Olive Garden?" And he was like, "Well, if you've got to ask, you probably shouldn't do it." And I just feel like I've been thrown in a room of insane people and I'm the only level-headed one.

With a minimum registration period of 15 years under SORNA, there should be some positive goals for individuals to work toward. Heidi discussed her perception of SORN laws as a death sentence:

> I would reform the laws so they're not such a death sentence for people, because I think it is, especially for a lot of first-time offenders who really, who can't, I can't think of the word, show people that they're doing right now, that they messed up once but that doesn't define who they are.

Evidence of treatment, evaluation (or re-evaluation) of risk assessment, and/or time without a sexual offense should allow for an individual to be able to petition to end the requirements of registration and community notification.

Finally, when community notification does occur it should be used as an opportunity to educate the public regarding the realities of sexual victimization

Registration and Community Notification **161**

and ways in which to prevent sexual abuse. It is important to dispel myths about sex offenders and aid the public in recognizing that protecting oneself from sexual violence means more than identifying those on the sex offense registry. Stephanie discussed the importance of educating children:

> The public is kind of brainwashed to think it's the stranger with the candy in the van who's gonna attack your child when it's really the uncle who's gonna do it. So, it gives them a false sense of security, I mean, now there's an app for your iPhone with a sex offender registry on it and it will alert you when you go near a sex offender's house from the registry. Now that's creating unneeded fear and a false sense of security. And ostracism for these people who can't get any jobs because it's common knowledge that they committed a sex offense. So, you know, the best they can be is a dishwasher, so you know what kind of life they're gonna have, what is the future gonna look like? You know everyone needs social support and we're taking away all their social support and like saying where they can live and making some of them homeless and you can't get a job because it's public knowledge they're a sex offender. And you know, I'd like to see the evidence this registry has helped save one child, seriously. And you know I just don't think we have. I think we need to spend that money on education of children. You know when is the uncle's touch not appropriate? Let's spend more on education and let children know that it's okay to tell. I think the list just continues to ruin their lives. And they're never done serving their sentence, they never get a chance to prove they can be productive members of society and that hopelessness is much more detrimental than anything else you can do to a person. I mean, you take away their hope and their chance at having a good, normal, productive life and what are they gonna do?

Education means conveying to the public that sexual violence often comes from within the home, and it means teaching children the difference between good and bad touch and to tell a trusted adult when an inappropriate act occurs. Tricia spoke about educating the public regarding myths surrounding sex offenders and ways to avoid stigmatizing offenders:

> I don't think that the public can handle a registry. That's proven. How many sex offenders have been beaten or killed because somebody found them on a registry? They just can't handle it. How many children have been yanked out of school and are now being homeschooled because of the registry, because their dad is on it? Because of the registry. It does more harm than good. What good does it do me to know that there's a sex offender next door? It's my job as a parent to supervise

162 Collateral Consequences for Partners

my child. It's our job as parents, not society's. I think the registry gives people a false sense of safety. The majority of sex offenses happen with somebody you trust. So, really, the registry is just another waste of time and money.

Education means moving beyond the easy vilification of the registered sex offender.

Sex offenses and offenders are safe political targets, no doubt. The sex crimes that are covered in the media are tragic and linger in the minds of the public. In the climate of public fear, registration and notification laws were passed, and enhanced, and continue to be expanded, with little regard for empirical studies that demonstrate their ineffectiveness. Brandi said: "So, I think to me, a lot of it is a fabrication. It's a politician who wants to stand up and say, 'Look, I fixed this for you.' But, you didn't." Amber echoed a similar sentiment:

People don't even know what to do with this information. I really feel like it's law enforcement and the legislators saying, "We don't know what to do with this and we don't know how to deal with sex crimes, so here, public, you deal with this. We'll let you handle it. Here's the information, good luck with that."

The registry and the negative community impact of sex offender notification is something that society does not care about until it impacts them personally. No one is "sympathetic" about the collateral impacts of sex offender legislation until your father, or brother, or uncle, or husband, or boyfriend is the one impacted by these laws ... and you are negatively impacted by them as well, and this impact lasts a lifetime. Janet explored this idea:

Nobody ever expected to be on this registry and nobody gives a shit until it's their loved one. Then they pay attention and get the same back-lash that everybody else has been getting. And the people in charge that could actually do good, don't do anything. Problem is that everybody wants everybody punished forever, regardless of what the crime is. And even before all of this I never thought that way. I don't believe that you have to punish somebody for life for everything, but that's what society wants. Eye for an eye. You know, you committed a crime 20 years ago, and you watch the story or you watch the news, I mean 20 years ago is 20 years ago and has nothing to do with the person now. I'm not the same as I was 20 years ago. Are you the same person as 20 years ago?

Changing sex-related laws is an uphill battle when sex crimes are viewed as having an incomprehensibility that other crimes do not have, and an impact on the victim that lasts long beyond the occurrence of the crime. The result is policymakers and a public that just react, instead of evaluating existing best practices evidence.

Notes

1. In Indiana in 1994, for example, there were eight crimes that required sex offender registration: Indiana's current registration law (Zachary's Law) lists 40 offenses that require registration. Other states indicate a similar upward trajectory.
2. Other changes of SORNA included: elimination of the statute of limitations for prosecution of felony child sexual offense cases and child abduction, establishment of a federal DNA database, funding for electronic monitoring (GPS) of offenders, the requirement that offenders as young as 14 years of age register, lengthening of minimum prison terms for offenders crossing state lines with minors, and permitting victims of child abuse to civilly sue the offender for damages. SORNA also created mandatory minimum sentences for select offenses: 30 years for child rape and 10 years for child sex trafficking or coerced child prostitution.
3. The 18 states in substantial compliance as of June 2019 were: Alabama, Colorado, Delaware, Florida, Kansas, Louisiana, Maryland, Michigan, Mississippi, Missouri, Nevada, Ohio, Oklahoma, South Carolina, South Dakota, Tennessee, Virginia, and Wyoming.
4. For example, it was estimated that SORNA compliance in Texas would cost approximately $38.7 million for the first year; however, the reduction in federal funds for failure to comply was only $1.4 million (Wang, 2014/2015).
5. Certain juvenile sex offenders provide the exception to Florida's registration requirement. If a juvenile offender is not more than four years older than the victim who was at least 13 (but still a minor), the juvenile may petition for registration relief immediately.
6. This is an example of the over-counting of sex offenders on the registry that was mentioned in Chapter 2 as a drawback of the National Center for Missing and Exploited Children data (NCMEC, 2018). Prior to his removal from the registry in Tennessee, Jackie's husband would have been "counted" on the registry in both Tennessee and Florida. Currently, though residing in Tennessee permanently, he is still listed on the sex offense registry in Florida and will for life.
7. *Commonwealth v. Moore* (2019) found that the provisions of SORNA which required internet dissemination of SO registration, when applied retroactively, violated the *ex post facto* clause of the Constitution and were punitive in nature. The Court ruled:

> The adverse impact to a sex offender's reputation, imposed purposefully as a consequence of conduct deemed criminal, is widespread. It is not limited to those individuals who would benefit from this information because they might reside or work in close proximity to the offender. Rather, the effect of this affirmative restraint extends to any person who has access to the Internet and who may obtain the registration information solely for gratuitous purposes. Thus, such harm is not merely collateral or incidental, but rather consequential and far-reaching.

References

Ackerman, Alissa R., Sacks, Meghan, & Osier, Lindsay N. (2013). The experiences of registered sex offenders with internet offender registries in three states. *Journal of Offender Rehabilitation, 52*, 29–45.

Anderson, A. L., Evans, M. K., & Sample, L. L. (2009). Who accesses the sex offender registries? A look at legislative intent and citizen action in Nebraska. *Criminal Justice Studies: A Critical Journal of Crime, Law, and Society, 22*, 313–329.

164 Collateral Consequences for Partners

Anderson, A. L., & Sample, L. L. (2008). Public awareness and action resulting from sex offender community notification laws. *Criminal Justice Policy Review*, 19, 371–396.

Beck, V. S., & Travis, L. F. (2006). Sex offender notification: An exploratory assessment of state variation in notification processes. *Journal of Criminal Justice*, 34, 51–55.

Bedarf, A. (1995). Examining sex offender community notification laws. *California Law Review*, 83, 885–939.

Braithwaite, John. (1989). *Crime, shame and reintegration*. Cambridge: Cambridge University Press.

Burchfield, K. B., & Mingus, W. (2008). Not in my neighborhood: Assessing registered sex offenders' experiences with local social capital and social control. *Criminal Justice and Behavior*, 35, 356–374.

Carpenter, Catherine L., & Beverlin, Amy E. (2012). The evolution of unconstitutionality in sex offender registration laws. *Hastings Law Journal*, 63, 101–163.

Chaffin, Mark, Levenson, Jill, Letourneau, Elizabeth, & Stern, Paul. (2009). How safe are trick-or-treaters? An analysis of child sex crime rates on Halloween. *Sexual Abuse: A Journal of Research and Treatment*, 21(3), 363–374.

Commonwealth v. Moore, No. 1556 WDA 2018 (Pa. Super. 2019)

Conditions of Supervised Release, 2012, LA. Rev. Stat. §15:561.5

Connecticut Dept. of Public Safety v. Doe, 538 U.S. 1 (2003)

Doe v. Harris, 302 P.3d 598 (Cal. 2013)

Doe v. Snyder, 834 F.3d 696 (6th Cir. 2016)

Drake, E. K., & Aos, S. (2009). *Does sex offender registration and notification reduce crime? A systematic review of the research literature*. Olympia, WA: Washington State Institute for Public Policy.

Duwe, Grant, & Donnay, William. (2008). The impact of Megan's Law on sex offender recidivism: The Minnesota experience. *Criminology*, 46(2), 411–446.

Eagan, Kelsey. (2013). Forfeiting sex offenders' constitutional rights due to the stigma of their crimes?: *State v. Trosclair*. *Loyola Law Review*, 59(1), 267–288.

Farkas, M. A., & Zevitz, R. (2000). Sex offender community notification: Assessing the impact on law enforcement: A research note. *Journal of Crime and Justice*, 23, 125–139.

Ferrandino, Joseph. (2012). Beyond the perception and the obvious: What sex offender registries really tell us and why. *Social Work in Public Health*, 27, 392–407.

Freeman, N. J., & Sandler, J. C. (2009). The Adam Walsh Act: A false sense of security or an effective public policy initiative? *Criminal Justice Policy Review*, 21(1), 31–49.

Gaines, J. (2006). Law enforcement reactions to sex offender registration and community notification. *Police Practice and Research*, 7, 249–267.

Goffman, Erving. (1963). *Stigma: Notes on the management of spoiled identity*. New York, NY: Simon Schuster, Inc.

Harris, Andrew J., Levenson, Jill S., & Ackerman, Alissa R. (2014). Registered sex offenders in the United States: Behind the numbers: *Crime and Delinquency*, 60(1), 3–33.

Harris, A. J., Lobanov-Rostovsky, C., & Levenson, J. S. (2010). Widening the net: The effects of transitioning to the Adam Walsh Act classification system. *Criminal Justice and Behavior*, 37, 503–519.

Human Rights Watch. (2007). *No easy answers: Sex offender laws in the U.S*. New York, NY: Human Rights Watch.

Justice Policy Institute. (n.d.). *What will it cost states to comply with the Sex Offender Registration and Notification Act?* Retrieved from www.justicepolicy.org/images/upload/08-08_FAC_SORNACosts_JJ.pdf

Kenny, S. (2005). Terrify and control: The politics of risk society. *Social Alternatives*, 24(3), 50–54.

Kernsmith, P. D., Craun, S. W., & Foster, J. (2009). Public attitudes toward sexual offenders and sex offender registration. *Journal of Child Sexual Abuse*, 18, 290–301.

Lemert, E. (1951). Social pathology. New York, NY: McGraw-Hill.

Letourneau, E. J., Levenson, J. S., Brandyptadhyay, D., Armstrong, K. S., & Sinha, D. (2010). Effects of South Carolina's sex offender registration and notification policy on deterrence of adult sex crimes. *Criminal Justice and Behavior*, 37, 357–552.

Levenson, Jill S., Brannon, Yolanda N., Fortney, Timothy, & Baker, Juanita. (2007). Public perceptions about sex offenders and community protection policies. *Analysis of Social Issues and Public Policy*, 7(1), 1–25.

Levenson, Jill S., & Cotter, Leo P. (2005). The effect of Megan's Law on sex offender reintegration. *Journal of Contemporary Criminal Justice*, 21, 49–66.

Levenson, Jill S., & D'Amora, D. (2007). Social policies designed to prevent sexual violence: The emperor's new clothes. *Criminal Justice Policy Review*, 18, 168–199.

Levenson, Jill S., D'Amora, David A., & Hern, Andrea L. (2007). Megan's Law and its impact on community re-entry for sex offenders. *Behavioural Sciences and the Law*, 25, 587–602.

Levenson, J. S., Fortney, T., & Baker, J. N. (2010). Views of sexual abuse professionals about sex offender notification policies. *International Journal of Offender Therapy and Comparative Criminology*, 54, 150–168.

Levenson, J. S., & Tewksbury, R. (2009). Collateral damage: Family members of registered sex offenders. *American Journal of Criminal Justice*. www.opd.ohio.gov/AWA_Information/AW_levenson_family_impact_study.pdf

Lieb, Roxanne, & Nunlist, Corey. (2008). *Community notification as viewed by Washington's citizens: A 10-year follow-up* (Document No. 08–03–1101). Olympia, WA: Washington State Institute for Public Policy.

Link, B. G., Cullen, F. T., Struening, E., Shrout, P. E., & Dohrenwend, B. P. (1989). A modified labeling theory approach to mental disorders: An empirical assessment. *American Sociological Review*, 54(3), 400–423.

Lustbader, Sarah. (October 31, 2019). In leaked audio, prosecutor admits locking people up is not about public safety. *The Appeal*. https://theappeal.org

Makin, David A., Walker, Andrew M., & Campbell, Christopher M. (2018). Paying to be punished: A statutory analysis of sex offender registration fees. *Criminal Justice Ethics*, 37(3), 215–237.

Malesky, A., & Keim, J. (2001). Mental health professional's perspectives on sex offender registry web sites. *Sexual Abuse: A Journal of Research and Treatment*, 13, 53–63.

Mancini, C. (2014). Examining factors that predict public concern about the collateral consequences of sex crime policy. *Criminal Justice Policy Review*, 25, 450–475.

Mancini, Christina, & Pickett, Justin T. (2014). The good, the bad, and the incomprehensible: Typifications of victims and offenders as antecedents of beliefs about sex crime. *Journal of Interpersonal Violence*, 31(2), 257–281.

Maurelli, Kimberly, & Ronan, George. (2013). A time-series analysis of the effectiveness of sex offender notification laws in the USA. *The Journal of Forensic Psychiatry and Psychology*, 24(1), 128–143.

McGrath, R. J., Cumming, G. F., Burchard, B. L., Zeoli, S., & Ellerby, L. (2010). *Current practices and trends in sexual abuser management: The Safer Society 2009 North American Survey*. Brandon, VT: Safer Society Press.

McGuire v. Strange, 83 F. Supp. 3d 1231 (M.D. Ala. 2015)

Meloy, Michelle, Curtis, Kristin, & Boatwright, Jessica. (2012). The sponsors of sex offender bills speak up: Policy makers' perceptions of sex offenders, sex crimes, and sex offender legislation. *Criminal Justice and Behavior*, 40(4), 438–452.

Meloy, Michelle L. (2006). *Sex offenses and the men who commit them: An assessment of sex offenders on probation*. Boston, MA: Northeastern University Press.

Mustaine, E. E., Tewksbury, R., & Stengel, K. M. (2006). Residential location and mobility of registered sex offenders. *American Journal of Criminal Justice*, 30, 177–192.

National Center for Missing and Exploited Children (NCMEC). (2018). Registered sex offenders in the United States. www.missingkids.org

Office of Sex Offender Sentencing, Monitoring, Apprehending, Registering, and Tracking (SMART). (2019a). *Sex Offender Registration and Notification Act (SORNA) State and Territory Implementation Progress Check*. Washington, DC: U.S. Department of Justice. www.smart.gov/pdfs/SORNA-progress-check.pdf

Phillips, D. M. (1998). *Community notification as viewed by Washington's citizens*. Olympia, WA: Washington State Institute for Public Policy.

Prescott, J. J., & Rockoff, Johah E. (2011). Do sex offender registration and notification laws affect criminal behavior? *Journal of Law and Economics*, 54, 161–206.

Redlich, A. D. (2001). Community notification: Perceptions of its effectiveness in preventing child sexual abuse. *Journal of Child Sexual Abuse*, 10, 91–116.

Small, Jamie L. (2015). Classing sex offenders: How prosecutors and defense attorneys differentiate men accused of sexual assault. *Law & Society Review*, 49(1), 109–141.

Smith v. *Doe*, 538 U.S. 1009 (2003)

Socia, K. M., & Stamatel, J. P. (2010). Assumption and evidence behind sex offender laws: Registration, community notification, and residence restrictions. *Sociology Compass*, 4, 1–20.

Spencer, D. (2009). Sex offender as *homo sacer*. *Punishment & Society*, 11, 219–240.

State v. *Trosclair*, 89 So. 3d 340 (La. 2012)

Tewksbury, Richard. (2005). Sex offender registries as a tool for public safety: Views from registered sex offenders. *Western Criminology Review*, 7: 1–8.

Tewksbury, R., & Levenson, J. (2009). Stress experiences of family members of registered sex offenders. *Behavioral Sciences and the Law*, 27, 611–626.

Vasquez, Bob Edward, Maddan, Sean, & Walker, Jeffery T. (2008). The influence of sex offender registration and notification laws in the United States: A time-series analysis. *Crime & Delinquency*, 54, 175–192.

Wang, Jennifer N. (2014/2015). Paying the piper: The cost of compliance with the Federal Sex Offender Registration and Notification Act. *New York Law School Law Review*, 59, 681–705.

Zevitz, Richard G., & Farkas, Mary Ann. (2000a). *Sex offender community notification: Assessing the impact in Wisconsin*. Washington, DC: U.S. Department of Justice, National Institute of Justice.

Zevitz, Richard G., & Farkas, Mary Ann. (2000b). Sex offender community notification: Managing high risk criminals or exacting further vengeance? *Behavioural Sciences and the Law*, 18, 375–391.

Zgoba, Kristen M., Miner, Michael, Knight, Raymond, Letourneau, Elizabeth, Levenson, Jill, & Thornton, David. (2012). *A multi-state recidivism study using Static-99R and Static-2002 risk scores and tier guidelines from the Adam Walsh Act*. Washington, DC: U.S. Department of Justice, National Institute of Justice.

Zgoba, K., Witt, P., Dalessandro, M., & Veysey, B. (2008). *Megan's Law: Assessing the practical and monetary efficacy*. Trenton, NJ: New Jersey Department of Corrections.

6

EMPLOYMENT, HOUSING, AND PARENTING CHALLENGES

Upon release from formal criminal justice control or during a community sentence, a registered sexual offender has significant challenges to address. Three of these major demands involve finding employment, locating suitable housing, and abiding by any restrictions on contact with minors.

Employment Challenges and Consequences

A significant part of reintegration following a term of imprisonment or during a community sentence is securing stable employment. Research demonstrates that employment facilitates economic independence and security for an offender and his family, reduces the likelihood of recidivism, and thereby increases community safety (Couloute & Kopf, 2018). In a 5-year longitudinal study of the relationship between post-release employment and recidivism among more than 6,500 offenders of various types, researchers found a significant relationship between unemployment and recidivism. Researchers also noted the tremendous hurdles encountered by ex-offenders to secure employment, and the persistence of these hurdles for a considerable length of time following release from incarceration (Nally, Lockwood, Ho, & Knutson, 2014).

Using 2008 data from the National Former Prisoner Survey, the Prison Policy Initiative analyzed unemployment in an ex-incarcerated population. The study revealed that there were approximately five million formerly incarcerated individuals across the United States with an unemployment rate of more than 27 percent: this was almost five times greater than the unemployment rate in the general population, and a clear demonstration of the structural barriers this population faced in attempts to secure a job (Couloute & Kopf 2018). In the white male population (represented primarily in the current study), the general population

168 Collateral Consequences for Partners

unemployment rate was just over 4 percent, whereas unemployment for white men formerly incarcerated was about 18.5 percent (Couloute & Kopf, 2018). This highlighted the imperative need for services after release from prison as joblessness was highest in the first two years following incarceration (Couloute & Kopf, 2018).

When those who were incarcerated found employment, the jobs were often temporary and frequently earned an income below the poverty line (Looney & Turner, 2018). Alison's husband found employment, though it was typical post-incarceration, low-paying employment:

> The main other thing, I guess, is the problem of getting a job. He went back to college, to a truck driving school, at a local college here, got his CDL license and he has a job now but, it's like bottom of the totem pole type stuff. He's in woods all day long driving a truck, logging truck, no regular pay, no regular benefits, it's only by the load he carries so, if anybody's equipment on any of the three sites breaks down, he may sit there all day and not earn a cent. So, he's always out more than 12 hours a lot of times, 14 hours. He has to get up before 4 in the morning and like last night, he didn't get home 'til 10:30 pm. But every time we put in an application somewhere it gets turned down and we don't have to ask why, we know why. A good portion of the jobs state right upfront, if you've had a felony of any kind they won't hire you. Then the ones that will, tell you to turn in an application they come up with "no we hired somebody else," and you know why, they don't wanna hire somebody who's both been in jail and is a sex offender. It gets really frustrating for him because he has turned his life around but nobody wants to give him a chance.

Additionally, many states have policies that limit access to financial and social needs-based resources if an individual has been convicted of a sexual offense.

Yet, studies have demonstrated that job stability can significantly reduce the probability of recidivating among sexual offenders (Kruttschnitt, Uggen, & Schelton, 2000). This remained true even in populations of juvenile sex offenders who experienced frequent changes in jobs and short durations at each place of employment (van den Berg, Bijleveld, Hendriks, & Mooi-Reci, 2013). Employment is important in that it acts as an informal social control, a way to meet role models outside of a criminal lifestyle, provides pro-social opportunities, as well as social capital. Employment brings meaning to a person's life, vests them in the community, and is a hallmark of both personal satisfaction and financial success (McAlinden, Farmer, & Maruna, 2017). Without stable employment, there is a sense of being unoccupied and without purpose. An important element of desistance from future crime is the fulfillment and personal satisfaction that comes from stable and rewarding employment (Kruttschnitt et al., 2000). Overwhelmingly,

Employment, Housing, and Parenting **169**

those who have been incarcerated find employment after prison an important goal and use multiple strategies to find a job (Visher, Debus, & Yahner, 2008).

Looking specifically at registered sex offenders, there are many barriers to employment: educational and/or skill deficits may be a factor; employer discrimination certainly is an issue, especially because in 35 percent of states the name and address of the employer is included on the sex offense registry; lack of familial support may be a factor; and residential restrictions may keep offenders away from places of suitable employment (Brewster, DeLong, & Moloney, 2012; Brown, Spencer, & Deakin, 2007). A study of employers in several major cities revealed that approximately two-thirds of employers would not hire a known ex-offender of any type; this is even higher for former sex offenders (Holzer, 1996). Tara's husband had a very difficult time finding employment:

> A lot of the applications now will ask for permission to do a background check. And he has to check that box that they are permitted to do a background check, and that's when they find it. [He hasn't worked for] 7 years. At this point he's just given up. He's just given up.

Pamela's husband experienced similar difficulties, even at the temporary employment agencies:

> [He has been unemployed] about a year-and-a-half this time and when you go to work for a job they tell you right up front, even at the temp agency, if you're a sex offender, don't even apply. And how are you supposed to live? You wanna work but no one will give you a job? Not even as a gravedigger. I mean digging graves!

Employer discrimination was an issue for Jessica and her husband and at one point, Jessica was her husband's potential employer! When Jessica was asked if she would reconsider her relationship with her husband had she known in advance the many ramifications of the registry, she said:

> That's an interesting question, I'd like to say no, but I think if someone had really explained fully the ramifications to me, you know, oh he's on the registry, big deal, but it is a big deal! It's a huge deal! And right now the biggest deal is him not working. Putting a company on the internet means he's unemployable. I mean for the longest time he was working, but when the economy changed, he can't get a job. And I have a construction company, but I won't hire him because I can't have my company associated with him on the registry on the internet. I won't hire my own husband because I can't have my company associated with the sex offender registry. I just can't! And I know how that sounds....

170 Collateral Consequences for Partners

Jessica's husband accepted a plea at the suggestion of his public defender to the molestation of his daughter prior to meeting and marrying Jessica. His sentence was ten years on probation and six months in jail. He will serve ten years on the sex offense registry.

As well, restrictions imposed on an RSO may limit where he seeks employment. For example: restrictions on being with minors, a restriction on accessing the internet, or restrictions regarding being within a specified distance of a school (or other locations) are going to limit where an individual can seek employment. If an RSO has an offense against a minor, state and federal laws prohibit him from employment where children are present (e.g., schools, libraries, recreational activity areas, swimming pools, carnivals, etc.). Add to that, several states have regulations on types of employment for RSOs. Tara and her husband experienced such restrictions after his plea to acceptance of child pornography. After being fired from three previous jobs, her husband decided to pursue a line of work he always dreamed of:

> He decided that he would do something that he really wanted to do, so he became an EMT. He went back to school. So, he was an EMT, he got a job, and then he went for his paramedic license. And I guess somebody did a background check on him, and they relieved him from duty, and took away his license to do the EMT work, and he's been out of work ever since.

EMT is one area of employment that bans sex offenders in many states because it may involve working with minors. Tara's husband had been unemployed for more than seven years at the time of the interview. Other states also have restrictions on types of employment: in Virginia, an RSO cannot be employed driving a tow truck (VA Code §46.2–116); and in Georgia, an RSO cannot be employed as a real estate appraiser (GA Code §43–39A-14).

Sometimes an employer will hire an RSO and then later fire him due to the stigma his sex offender status brings to the place of employment. Shannon talked about her husband being fired after his job learned he was an RSO. Her husband pled guilty to sexual misconduct of a minor and spent 18 months in prison and 5 years on supervised probation. Shannon said:

> He [works] now. See, what happened was after he got out of jail, he found a job, he's in construction, a project manager, and they did not do a background check. He was there 6-and-a-half years and one of his colleagues who apparently doesn't get along with anybody, those two had a blow-up in a meeting and the following week, this man, somehow he knew that my husband was on the registry, I don't know if he went looking for it, or if he knew somebody who told him or what, but he told the boss about it and my husband got fired. Six-and-a-half years, model employee, went in every day and did his job and they fired him.

Sherry's husband experienced similar difficulties in maintaining employment:

> The problem with his employment is that they run background checks on him, everything comes out fine, there's no problem until a customer does a search on the internet and then they find out they've got a sex offender. They notify his employer that he's required to register as a sex offender. The first time he lost his job, somebody went out and put a copy of his listing, taped it to the door of the restaurant. About 2 years later he was working for another restaurant, same sort of scenario happened and he lost his job, but this time when he lost his job a person called into the corporate office and said, "Do you know you have a sex offender?" Right now he's got a job and I'm hoping and praying that it works out. He's working as a manager at a bar, so I'm hoping that people won't decide to call his employer and say, "You've got a sex offender that works there." Because what do you do? He's got to make a living, he's gotta live, and we're trying to get our lives back together ... dealing with everything that he goes through and having to be the sole supporter sometimes is difficult. You know, I'm trying to be supportive and make sure that I can keep it together for us, but it's hard and it's a lot of pressure on me.

Sherry's husband pled guilty to sexual assault and was sentenced to one-year imprisonment and will serve 15 years on the registry. Rhonda's family has dealt with a series of unstable jobs due to her husband's registry status:

> Finding a job [has been the biggest stressor], because I'm the sole provider for a family of five and I've had to work three jobs before just to maintain our bills, just to get by. Because of him being on the list a lot of places see it as a liability, so a lot of places won't hire him. You know he can't even get a simple delivery job because he may have to be near a daycare. And even though he's not considered high-risk, he's still on the list. And they don't want that, and the employer would have to be placed on the list with him and that's basically been the main issue. He hasn't been able to get a job and be able to support the family. So that's a big thing for me because I have to figure out how I'm gonna get by and support a family of five. And that's not been easy for him. He has not worked in years. He used to work at a local supermarket and that didn't work out because they didn't want their name on the list. And he has a master's degree and a bachelor's degree, it's not like he's not educated. But a lot of companies don't want their name to be associated with him. [He's been unemployed for] oh gosh, um, 6 years. He had a good job before, but after he went to court one of his co-workers found him on the internet and told the HR dept and they fired him.

He's been working odd jobs, but nothing stable. He hasn't had a stable job in 6 years.

Rhonda and her husband have been together for 13 years. He accepted a plea to statutory rape; Rhonda was the "victim." They later married and had a family. Her husband spent six months in jail, four years on probation, did 120 hours of community service, and will spend his life on the sex offense registry. As a family, they will spend the rest of their lives dealing with the collateral consequences of the relationship they had when she was young. Danielle's husband also took a plea to a charge of statutory rape. He served 18 months in prison and one year on probation prior to their marriage. He will be on the registry for ten years. Danielle talked about the stress of her husband's continued unemployment on their marriage:

> There has recently been more stress on our relationship due to him losing his job. He was the main provider. So, that's put a lot of stress on us. Also I think, "If my husband lost his job and I have to get up and go to work every day, at least he can get [our son] up and to school so that's one less thing on my list." But, it's not. What it is, is he's sitting at home waiting for us. No matter what the traffic or if I get off late … it's just … it's just me … he can't take our son to school or to the park or anywhere kids are allowed.

Other women spoke about the stress of their husband's registry status on their own lives at their places of employment.

Tracy, whose husband accepted a probationary plea to sexual misconduct of a minor said: "I lost my career over this. I had a female manager who, once [my husband] took the plea deal and was on the registry, she made my life a living nightmare. So, I just quit." Sherry said:

> I get scared at times that his situation could impact me at work. Still, to this day, I don't list our address that we live at together as my work address because I just don't want anyone knowing because I could end up losing my job myself. I don't think that would happen, but you just don't know in this day and age. So, I just don't tell anybody.

Colleen discussed the importance of keeping her work and personal life separate:

> Nobody at work knows because work is work and home life is home life. I did lose one job while I was going through the court martial proceedings because they found out. [My job] found out what my husband was being court martialed for and they thought my personal life would

make their company look bad and therefore they no longer needed my services.

Colleen's husband was found guilty at trial of molestation of his daughter and receipt of child pornography and was sentenced to 15 years in prison. At the time of the interview, he was incarcerated. For some women in the study, however, the offense happened years ago, and they are still dealing with the collateral consequences. Jessica's place of employment found out about her husband's plea to molestation of his daughter that occurred prior to their marriage and she was dealing with the fallout many years later:

> It's just really hard, I walked into work and everybody at work knew and I was just, like, uh blindsided. And nobody would talk to me and it was like I had leprosy all of a sudden. And my boss brought me in to talk to me and I was like, what's this have to do with my job? Is my husband coming up here and playing with your kids? Is he going to their house? I was like, we don't even socialize with any of you people. I didn't get fired, but they made it hell for me. [They] just kind of ignored me, shunned me, like the person in the office nobody likes. You know, and I didn't feel like I owed any of them an explanation and I tried to get them to understand this didn't just happen…this was 15 years ago! I couldn't deal … when the opportunity came up for me to move and I took it in a second.

Elizabeth was employed at a school, and remained intensely private at work about her home life:

> Absolutely not, absolutely not, I cannot tell anybody at work, I can't, no one can know. The discrimination is so intense, I would never have gotten my job at a school if they knew that I was married to a sex offender, never mind that I'm not a sex offender, they would never have hired me if they knew I was married to one. Can't tell anybody. Ever.

Elizabeth expressed fear about her school employer finding out about her husband's offense. Her husband was found guilty at a jury trial for rape and other felonies prior to their marriage. However, his case was quite complicated as his public defender was later disbarred. At the time of the interview, Elizabeth's husband was incarcerated on a sentence in excess of 200 years, but he was working with The Innocence Project to overturn his conviction.

This fear about what may happen if an employer finds out about a relationship with a sex offender is real. Prior research revealed that 82 percent of sex offender family members were unable to secure employment, while 53 percent experienced a job loss after their place of employment discovered they had a family member on the sex offense registry (Tewksbury & Levenson, 2009). Disenfranchisement

174 Collateral Consequences for Partners

from employment, despite no criminal record, merely the association with a sex offender, has real ramifications. There are changes that can be made to minimize the collateral consequences of unemployment and underemployment for registered sex offenders. First, removal of the employer's name and address from the sex offense registry would be a major step forward. While employers are disinclined to hire those with a criminal record generally, this association of their place of employment with a sex offender is a significant negative stigma that overwhelmingly employers do not want. The state government could offer tax incentives to employers that hire former offenders. This incentive would provide financial security against potential loss (Rodriguez & Avery, 2016). Employers could adhere to "Ban the Box" policies which at the initial point of application do not inquire about an individual's conviction history, and instead pushes the background check to a later point in the hiring process. As of 2019, 35 states have Ban the Box policies, and 13 states require private employers to adopt these policies (Avery, 2019).

Brief Legal History of Residency Restrictions and Legal Challenges

In addition to registration and community notification laws, many states have Sex Offender Residency Restrictions (SORRs) that define where a sex offender may reside, work, or visit. These laws, combined with the unwillingness of landlords to rent to SOs, further hinders community integration as offenders are pushed into less-desirable, potentially high-crime neighborhoods away from supportive family members. These laws have been expanded and refined over the years, making a brief legal history of SORR useful, as well as an analysis of significant legal challenges to these policies.

Like registration and community notification laws, residency restrictions are premised on the misconception of high recidivism rates of sex offenders, and on the belief that if the behavior of SOs is constrained, their recidivism can be lowered. Criminological theory, such as Routine Activities Theory, advances the notion that offenders commit crime in familiar communities and against suitable targets, when deterrent factors are absent (Cohen & Felson, 1979; Rengert & Wasilchick, 2000). Implicit in the theory behind residency restrictions is the notion that when sex offenders are left unmonitored near potential victims, the rate of sexual assault will increase.

> Indeed, lawmakers have argued that when RSOs reside near a school or other place where children commonly congregate, opportunities for contact with children are plentiful. Furthermore, it is believed that if sex offenders are able to easily view children playing from their homes, their sexually deviant preferences may be reinforced, thereby encouraging or facilitating child sexual abuse.
>
> *(Nobles, Levenon, &Youstin, 2012: 493)*

Employment, Housing, and Parenting **175**

If these ideas are accurate, residency restrictions make sense: remove potential offenders from the communities in which potentially suitable targets exist. Yet Sex Offender Residency Restrictions have come under serious criticism: "[T]hese policies have been implemented in response to political motivations, perceived public outcry, and misinformation about the true threats posed by sex offenders with little to no thought to their unintended consequences" (Burchfield, 2011: 411). Research on these policies repeatedly fails to indicate their effectiveness.

TABLE 6.1 Residency Restrictions as of 2018 by State[1]

State	Offender	Restrictions as of 2018
Alabama	All adult SOs	2,000 ft of schools, childcare facilities, or resident camps
Alaska		NONE
Arizona	Adult Tier 3 RSOs convicted of a dangerous crime against children	1,000 ft of schools and childcare facilities
Arkansas	Level 3 or 4 SOs	2,000 ft of schools, public parks, youth centers, or daycare facilities. Level 4 SOs may not reside within 2,000 ft. of a church or place of worship
California	Parolees required to register as SOs	2,000 ft of schools or parks where children regularly gather
	High-risk SOs	1/2 mile of schools, 2,000 ft of parks where children regularly gather
Colorado		NONE
Connecticut		NONE
Delaware	All SOs	500 ft of schools
Florida	Any SO with victim under 16-years-old	1,000 ft. of schools, childcare facilities, parks or playgrounds
Georgia	RSOs	1,000 ft. of childcare facilities, churches, schools, or anywhere minors congregate (specifically: parks, recreation facilities, playgrounds, skating rinks, neighborhood centers, gym, school bus stops, public libraries, community swimming pools)
Hawaii		NONE
Idaho	Adult SOs	500 ft of schools
Illinois	SOs with child victim	500 ft. of schools, playgrounds, childcare facilities, daycare, or any facility providing programs exclusively directed to those under 18-years-of-age

Continued

176 Collateral Consequences for Partners

TABLE 6.1 continued

State	Offender	Restrictions as of 2018
Indiana	SOs with child victim	1,000 ft of a school, youth program center, public park
Iowa	Adult SO convicted of aggravated offense against a minor	2,000 ft of a school or childcare facility
Kansas		NONE
Kentucky	RSO	1,000 ft of a school, preschool, publicly owned playground or daycare facility
Louisiana	SOs with a victim under age 13	1,000 ft of schools, childcare facilities, public parks or recreational facilities
	SOs with a victim under age 13, convicted of an aggravated offense	1,000 ft of schools, childcare facilities, public parks or recreational facilities, group homes, residential homes, playgrounds, youth centers, public swimming pools, or free-standing video arcades
Maine		Allows municipalities to prohibit residence by SOs up to maximum distance of 750 ft from schools
Maryland		NONE
Massachusetts		NONE
Michigan	RSOs	1,000 ft of school property "student safety zone"
Missouri	All SOs	1,000 ft of schools or childcare facilities
Minnesota		NONE
Mississippi	Any RSO, including those acquitted by reason of insanity	3,000 ft of schools, childcare facilities, children's group homes, playgrounds, ballparks, or other recreational facilities used by those under the age of 18
Montana	High-risk SOs	300 ft of schools, daycare centers, playgrounds, developed/improved parks, athletic fields or facilities that primarily serve minors
	Level 3 SOs	Judge will impose conditions of probation/parole restricting residency in proximity to schools, preschools, daycare centers, churches, or public parks
Nebraska		Allows political subdivisions to prohibit residence by "sexual predators" up to a maximum of 500 ft. from schools or childcare facilities
Nevada		NONE
New Hampshire		A Bill to ban municipalities from adopting residence restrictions is under study in the Senate
New Jersey		NONE – State Supreme Court ruling struck down local residency restrictions

Employment, Housing, and Parenting **177**

State	Offender	Restrictions as of 2018
New Mexico		NONE
New York	Parolees and probationers	At the discretion of parole/probation department, offender may be restricted from living within 1,000 ft of a school or other facility caring for children
North Carolina	RSOs	1,000 ft. of schools or daycare centers
North Dakota	High-risk SOs	500 ft. of schools or preschools
Ohio	SOs with a child victim	1,000 ft of schools or daycare centers
Oklahoma	RSOs	2,000 ft. from schools and "educational institutions," or a property for the primary purpose of working with children, playgrounds, or parks
Oregon	Parolees and probationers	The law provides a general prohibition to the State Board of Parole and Post-Prison supervision against allowing an SO to reside near locations where children are the primary occupants/users
Pennsylvania		NONE
Rhode Island	RSO (not Level 3)	300 ft of schools
	Level 3 SOs	1,000 ft of schools
South Carolina	SOs with a child victim	1,000 ft of schools, daycare centers, children's recreational facilities, parks or public playgrounds
South Dakota	RSOs	500 ft from schools, public parks, public playgrounds, or public pools
Tennessee	Adult SOs, more than 3 years older than the victim, convicted of rape, forcible sodomy on a child older than 13, or object sexual penetration on child older than 13	500 ft of schools or daycares
Texas	SO probationers and parolees with a child victim	Subject to a case-by-case analysis. May include "child safety zone" (premises where children usually gather - schools, daycares, playgrounds, youth centers, public swimming pools, or video arcade facilities)
Utah		NONE
Vermont		NONE

Continued

178 Collateral Consequences for Partners

TABLE 6.1 continued

State	Offender	Restrictions as of 2018
Virginia	Adult SOs more than 3-years older than the victim	500 ft of schools and daycares
Washington	Parolees	Department of Corrections (DOC) is authorized to reject proposed residence close to schools, childcare centers, playgrounds, or other facilities where children of similar age or circumstance as the victim are present. For high-risk offenders, DOC may restrict residence to 880 ft from facilities and grounds of schools
West Virginia	Adult SOs	1,000 ft of schools or childcare facilities
Wisconsin	Violent SOs	1,500 ft of schools, daycare centers, youth centers, churches, or public parks
Wyoming	RSOs	1,000 ft of schools

Note

1. The table is based on Savage & Windsor's (2018) research and is useful in determining which states have residency restrictions. Note however that municipalities within a state may have restrictions that are even stricter (Florida is an example of this).

Restrictions on where an offender may live, work, or travel varies dramatically by state. As of 2018, 14 states had no residency restrictions; other states had restrictions for only high-risk or Tier 3 offenders, 15 states had restrictions for all RSOs; other states had restrictions only for those on parole/probation; still other states restricted only child offenders (Savage & Windsor, 2018). See Table 6.1 for an elaboration of SORRs by state as of 2018. Distance requirements also vary by state: the minimum distance is 300 feet in Montana; the maximum is 3,000 feet in Mississippi. Most state restrictions are either 500 feet, 1,000 feet, or 2,000 feet, though some leave the discretion to probation/parole officers (Savage & Windsor, 2018). These laws are state-level and permit municipalities the option of imposing SORRs that are even stricter. For example, Florida's SORRs prohibit any sex offender with a victim under 16 years of age from residing within 1,000 feet of schools, childcare facilities, parks or playgrounds. Yet there are several counties in Florida that have expanded this boundary to 2,500 feet (almost 0.5 miles) and have expanded the types of sex offenders included. In some areas, therefore, the distance of restriction is so large, that the result is *de facto* exile from a specific city or county. Restrictions were passed in many states without any empirical demonstration of lowered recidivism or an increase in public safety, and many of the laws apply to all RSOs, not just offenders with a conviction for a crime against a child. The logic of restricting the movement of RSOs whose offense was against an adult from living near

Employment, Housing, and Parenting **179**

child zones is unclear. By way of additional example, the law in California initially was inclusive of offenders with a misdemeanor sexual offense. And, SORRs may also apply to offenders with no-contact offenses, such as possession of child pornography (Zucker, 2014).

Questions have arisen as to the legality of these restrictions. What if a sex offender owns his property and a childcare facility moves within the restricted zone? This was the foundation of *Mann* v. *Georgia Department of Corrections* (2007) in which an RSO was following the SORRs when he purchased his home/business. Later he was considered in violation because a childcare facility moved into the 1,000-foot restricted zone and his probation officer demanded he remove himself or face revocation of probation and arrest. The court in its ruling stated: "it is apparent that there is no place in Georgia where a registered sex offender can live without being continually at risk of being ejected" (*Mann* v. *Georgia Department of Corrections* 2007). Following this line of thought, the California Department of Corrections passed grandfather clauses to secure the property rights of sex offenders. Many other states followed suit. However, if the sex offender's property is to be protected, their offense must have occurred *prior* to the passage of the residency restrictions. This was evidenced in the recent court decision, *Vasquez* v. *Foxx* (2018). Both sex offenders in this case committed their offenses and were released with existing residency restrictions in Illinois. They purchased property knowing there were residency restrictions in place; therefore, the court ruled they could not have possibly had any property right expectations. In *Doe* v. *Snyder* (2016), the Sixth Circuit Court in Michigan ruled that the sex offense registry and residency restrictions were to be considered *ex post facto* punishment and inhibited an individual's right to work, travel, and parent without due process or individualized risk assessment. This is a vitally important case; the ramifications of which have yet to be seen in Michigan.

Do Residency Restrictions Prevent Sex Offenses?

As with other social control policies targeting sex offenders, public support exists despite the lack of empirical research regarding efficacy (CSOM, 2010; Comartin, Kernsmith, & Kernsmith, 2009; Levenson, Brannon, Fortney, & Baker, 2007; Schiavone & Jeglic, 2009). In a study that covered much of the United States and included over 700 community corrections professionals, researchers found significant support for SORRs. Corrections professionals more likely to indicate support for these policies were women, conservatives, and those with a greater number of children. Corrections professionals less supportive of SORRs were in the correctional field for a longer period of time, more highly educated, and more likely to view community notification as an unfair policy (Payne, Tewksbury, & Mustaine, 2016). The bottom line is that "nobody really cares if sex offenders are inconvenienced, relegated to underemployment, or limited to fewer and poorer housing choices" (Casady, 2009: 18). The public is mainly concerned with what

180 Collateral Consequences for Partners

they *believe* protects children's safety, regardless of whether those policies *actually* work to increase children's safety.

Recall from Chapter 2 the reasonably low recidivism rates for sexual offenders and the incorrect media assumptions of high recidivism. As such, policies that seek to control the behaviors and movements of convicted sex offenders to prevent a further offense, given low recidivism rates, may be misguided. Also recall the foundation of Routine Activities Theory on which SORRs are based: offenders commit crime in familiar communities and against suitable targets, when deterrent factors are absent (Cohen & Felson, 1979). Yet, studies do not substantiate the effectiveness of these policies. The premises on which SORRs are based are problematic for two reasons. First, sex offense recidivism has not been demonstrated in the research to be correlated to proximity to either daycares or schools (Zandbergen, Levenson, & Hart, 2010; Minnesota Department of Corrections, 2007). Second, the majority of sex offenders arrested would not have been subjected to a residency restriction law as they had no previous sex offense history (Ackerman, Harris, Levenson, & Zgoba, 2011; Minnesota Department of Corrections, 2007; Sandler, Freeman, & Socia, 2008).

In a study of county-level data in New York state, research found no support for SORRs on sex crimes against children or adults (Socia, 2011). Another study of SORRs that included an analysis of its effectiveness in preventing crimes against adults was conducted in Jacksonville, Florida. Data included more than 8,000 sexual offenses and 2,000 offenders. Researchers concluded that an expansion in residency restrictions to 2,500 feet failed to impact the recidivism rate (Nobles et al., 2012). An examination of the locales of child sex offenses in New Jersey was conducted spanning the years 1996 through 2007. Results showed that most child sex offenses were committed by previously unknown sex offenders and offenders that the child knew. Complete data was available for 1,456 offenses and only two offenses involved a recidivist sex offender who would have been subject to SORRs (Calkins, Colombino, Matsuura, & Jeglic, 2015). The same timeframe was used in another New Jersey study which found that undetected sex offenders committed 96 percent of sexual offenses (Colombino, Mercado, & Jeglic, 2011).

Yet another study found that an increase in the concentration of registered sex offenders in a community was not associated with the likelihood of a sex crime occurring (Tewksbury, Mustaine, & Stengel, 2008). In a study of 224 sex offenders released between 1990 and 2002 from a Minnesota prison and then rearrested and incarcerated for an additional sexual offense, researchers found that none of these offenses would have been prevented by a residency restriction (Duwe, Donnay, & Tewksbury, 2008). And in an examination of the 2,000-foot SORR in Iowa, researchers examined charges of sexual assault against minors in the year preceding the law and the 24 months after the passage of the law and found no decrease in the number of charges against minor victims. This was one indication that the residency restriction was not effective (Blood, Watson, & Stageberg,

Employment, Housing, and Parenting **181**

2008). So, study after study demonstrated the ineffectiveness of residency restrictions, yet such legislation continues to have public support. These laws continue to be passed in municipalities across the nation and continue to negatively impact the families of sex offenders.

Collateral Consequences of SORRs on the Partners of Registered Sex Offenders

Collateral consequences for sex offenders include housing limitations, increased stress, community alienation, hopelessness, and increased isolation from social supports (Burchfield, 2011). Because there are so few communities that permit RSOs, select communities may become overpopulated with sex offenders and their families. Other RSOs may be left homeless, and thus unable to register an address as required by law, due to strict residency restrictions. Many offenders are forced to move multiple times due to SORRs, forced to live unreasonable distances from work and/or treatment providers, are released from jail/prison to find their previous residence is unsuitable, or released to find that much of their city/town is unsuitable due to SORRs. Multiple studies have determined that SORRs have seriously limited the availability of housing, which has a trickle-down effect on the offender's family (Grubesic, 2010; Grubesic & Mack, 2010; Grubesic, Murray, & Mack, 2008; Mustaine & Tewksbury, 2011; Socia, 2011; Suresh, Mustaine, Tewksbury, & Higgins, 2010).

The most studied consequence of SORRs is the difficulty in securing housing. Availability of housing is perhaps the first issue. Sex offender residency restrictions limit the availability of housing options, making fewer dwellings compliant. Restrictions that are large in scope or cover many locations exacerbate housing problems for sex offenders and their families and can result in a housing crisis (Levenson & Tewksbury, 2009). Look at Georgia's SORR for example, which applies to *all* registered sex offenders. RSOs are prohibited from residing within 1,000 feet of childcare facilities, churches, schools, or anywhere minors congregate with the law specifically mentioning parks, recreation facilities, playgrounds, skating rinks, neighborhood centers, gyms, school bus stops, public libraries, and community swimming pools. That leaves very few residential areas remaining for an RSO to search for housing. Orlando, Florida, is another example. Researchers noted that 99 percent of possible residential areas were located within the 2,500-foot zone prohibited by SORRs (schools, parks, daycares, or bus stops) in Orlando (Zandbergen & Hart, 2006). In Newark, New Jersey, 93 percent of residences were within 2,500 feet of schools (Chajewski & Mercado, 2009) and in several metropolitan areas in South Carolina, more than 90 percent of the residential properties were unavailable for rent and almost half of those that were available were within 1,000 feet of either a school or a daycare (Barens, Dukes, Tewksbury, & DeTroye, 2009). Housing availability depends not only on legal access, but also in a competitive housing market, on the willingness of a

182 Collateral Consequences for Partners

landlord to rent to a registered sex offender. When provided with an option, an ex-convict (especially a sex offender) is typically not the landlord's first choice (Levenson & Cotter, 2005; Socia, 2011).

Illinois proves especially problematic for some sex offenders. Those convicted of what Illinois considers a "predatory offense"[1] must remain incarcerated until they find housing outside of the residency restrictions. Also, there must be no children at the residence and no access to internet-accessible devices (no computer, smart-TVs, or smartphones). If the offender has an additional term of parole, this term of parole does not begin during his "dead time" of incarceration. It starts after the RSO is in appropriate housing ... if the offender is able to find adequate housing. Halfway houses in Illinois are prohibited from accepting sex offenders, so this is not an option. This policy is currently part of a class-action lawsuit challenging its constitutionality and alleging that it places a disproportionate burden on the poor (Green, 2017).

Such SORRs place a significant burden on offenders and their families. Jamie and her husband were separated for a time due to residency restrictions and he lived in a hotel. She said:

> Yes. As far as distances between like, daycares and schools, where kids ... I think it has to be 1,000 feet. He had to leave here and live in a hotel for a while because we were too close to a bus stop. Thankfully the bus stop was moved, but for a while he had to live in a hotel. And to find a hotel that doesn't have a swimming pool…because you can't be around where kids could play. So, no playground, no swimming pool. It was very hard to find a hotel that he could go stay at that we could afford.

For Angela, one of the biggest stressors was housing.

> I worry, the main thing that really stresses me out was housing. It was the biggest issue for us for the longest time. This year we were able to buy a house. I feel much, much better now. It's just so difficult to find housing because apartments won't rent to him. You have to call and warn each one and ask if they will rent to a sex offender. The last time we had to move in a hurry because our landlord was raising the rent to an amount we just couldn't afford. He gave us a month to move out and we must have called 50 people looking for a new place. We only got two who said that they would rent to a sex offender. Most people just quick hang up or say no so, that was very, very difficult. We have a 2,000 feet rule or something. He's not supposed to be in like parks, schools. Those are just the little ones. There's tons of other little things he's not supposed to be near, restaurants with playgrounds, even fast-food restaurants with playgrounds. You can't live anywhere near those so it was very difficult. [We have to live] 2,000 feet [away].

Employment, Housing, and Parenting **183**

Yolanda faced similar constraints in finding housing with her husband:

> Well, we're not supposed to be within 1,500 feet of a school. You can't walk by, you can't walk your dog ... this is just [our] county law which is being challenged for being unconstitutional, but you can't live within 1,500 feet of a daycare center, we're not supposed to go to the parks, we're technically not supposed to go to the beaches, we can't go camping at the lake because we're not allowed. So, those are all off-limits supposedly, but those are county laws.

In trying to find suitable housing, both Sherry and Carol employed the strategy of searching areas in which other sex offenders resided. Sherry said: "After we got the notice to vacate the first complex we were in I found this other place by searching the sex offense registry and finding where other sex offenders were actually living." Carol similarly said: "I did my research to see where other sex offenders lived, where there would be a better chance of us getting in. I know that sounds bad, but that's how I had to do it. We have so few options."

Affordability is another barrier to stable housing for most ex-offenders trying to reintegrate into a community and is magnified for sex offenders. Sex offenders that deal with residency restrictions are found to relocate multiple times compared to sex offenders without residency restrictions and increased mobility enhances stress and decreases community integration (Roman & Travis, 2004; Rydberg, Grommon, Huebner, & Bynum, 2014; Levenson & Cotter, 2005; Levenson, 2008). SORRs may be less common in wealthier communities, though given the frequent difficulty in securing employment when on the sex offense registry, that does most offenders little good (Red-Bird, 2009). And wealthier communities have the social capital to push out a sex offender once community notification policies make their presence known. So, RSOs are left to search for housing in low-income neighborhoods, where restrictions are often plentiful. Additionally,

> convicted sex offenders with a lifetime registration requirement are ... ineligible for all public housing and other federally funded housing programs. This further limits their housing options, forcing them to cluster in high-crime areas, relocate multiple times, and experience homelessness, difficulties that may trigger some offenders to relapse.
>
> *(Farkas & Miller, 2007: 90)*

For Janet: "These residency laws were causing people to be homeless and nobody cares, but they should because that's dangerous. You take away everything that somebody has to live for and then what do they have to lose?" In a study of homeless shelters in Michigan, Ohio, Kentucky, and Tennessee, researchers found all shelters except one had a criminal history policy, and almost half of the homeless shelters prohibited sex offenders but did not prohibit

184 Collateral Consequences for Partners

those with other criminal histories (Rolfe, Tewksbury, & Schroeder, 2017). Additionally, homeless shelters were "willing to make exceptions to many policies in an attempt to fulfill their intended goal of serving the homeless, but [were] overwhelmingly unwilling to make any exceptions to the RSO policy" (Rolfe et al., 2017: 1843).

Other research has demonstrated a link between the lack of affordable housing and the transience of sex offenders (Socia, Levenson, Ackerman, & Harris, 2014). Some RSOs are pushed into rural areas which typically have fewer residency restrictions, but also have fewer housing options, fewer employment opportunities, and less access to treatment resources (Socia, 2014). Alison and her husband chose a rural environment:

> We live way out in the country which, I picked the house for that reason, I did not want the city and the stigma from city people. We are both country people and my house sits in the middle, I've got 2 acres in the middle of about 15 or 20 acres.

Residency restrictions that are excessively strict can result in the problem of sex offender homelessness. In Miami-Dade County, lack of affordable rental units and SORRs combined to result in the establishment of "Bookville" or the "Julia Tuttle Causeway Sex Offender Colony." This was a shantytown created under the causeway, with generators and cardboard structures, the residents of which were primarily sex offenders, the result of severe residency restrictions (Rabin, 2014). Sixty-five percent of sex offenders in Broward County, Florida, reported difficulty locating housing due to SORRs (Levenson, 2008). Following Jessica's Law and the implementation of SORRs in California, 32 percent of SOs reported homelessness (California Sex Offender Management Board, 2011). Sharon discussed how residency restrictions in Florida have pushed her partner to the outskirts of the area:

> [Restrictions on where he can live] are 3,000 feet. It's awful, especially in Florida because there are bus stops everywhere and schools and so that's why he lives in the middle of nowhere, he lives in the middle of a sugarcane field. It takes me 45 minutes to drive from my house to his house.

Pushing sex offenders toward homelessness is a public safety concern as it increases the likelihood of absconding from registration requirements and increases their likelihood of recidivism (California Sex Offender Management Board, 2008).

Not only is compliance with the law difficult for offenders and their families, but Alicia discussed the challenges of keeping up with frequent legal changes:

> It just varies so much to keep up with some of this stuff. [We] need a whole class in sex offender laws. I mean being in the field of corrections,

> I see that a lot. We have 80 counties in [my state] and all 80 counties administer the registry differently. Again, there's just so many restrictions. We have residency restrictions: If [the offense] was from 1993 to 2007, you can't live within 1,000 feet of a school. If [the offense] was after 2007 you can't live within 1,000 feet of a school or a daycare. If your conviction was before 1993 you have no residency restrictions. I mean just keeping up! And let's face it, your average criminal isn't always the brightest guy! (Laughs!) It's very tough. Most counties have an area that's kind of like a catch-all designated sex offender slum area. We happen to have a place here that used to be a hotel, and a lot of the guys that I worked with ended up going there to live and it's just a common thing nowadays … each one of these counties has something against sex offenders. And many of them are homeless. I mean, the residency restrictions … all these laws, are pretty pointless.

Wisconsin law requires that a sexual offender be released into the county they lived when their crime was committed. In examining a case of a sex offender being released to Milwaukee County, with 19 municipalities, each municipality had different restrictions as to where he was permitted to live. Parole officers provided no information upon his release other than the reminder that any violation would result in a return to incarceration. The offender was provided no list of approved addresses, and no list of buffer zones. He had to figure it out on his own, without access to the internet, in 12 hours before his GPS lost its battery charge (Hicks, 2016). In the entire area, there were just 55 addresses that would have met the sex offender approval requirements. A search of those addresses found "not a single sex offender living in any of them … [m]ost are single family homes – not for sale and not for rent. The few multi-units don't allow felons" (Hicks, 2016: online).

Studies reveal that housing instability is strongly associated with recidivism, violation of parole and absconding in populations of both sex offenders and general offenders (Meredith, Speir, & Johnson, 2007; Schulenberg, 2007; Willis & Grace, 2008). Thus, while SORRs may sound good in theory, in practice this policy creates administrative difficulties for law enforcement in monitoring offenders and increases the likelihood of recidivism. The assumption that underlies residency restrictions, that sexual offenders commit crime in familiar communities and against suitable targets when deterrent factors are absent, lacks empirical support. Research demonstrates that sex offenders encounter children in a variety of ways: they are neighbors, acquaintances, children of the offender's partner, family members, the babysitter, or the like. Cheryl noted the irony in SORRs:

> He can spend all day at my house and could sit in the backyard and watch the kids at the daycare all day but he can't spend the night. So, when the kids are gone, he has to be gone. How does that make sense?

Alternative policies to improve community safety would involve greater supervision of youth as a means of prevention (Savage & Windsor, 2018). Additionally, while sexual recidivism does account for a small percentage of offenses that would reinforce the need for risk assessment of sex offenders at the level that is appropriate, it is important to remember that most offenses are committed by those not convicted, which should indicate the need for a reidentification of priorities (Savage & Windsor, 2018). Victoria discussed her inability to trust the system and her belief that SORRs and other sex offender laws represent nothing more than community fear:

> Trying to trust the system again, wondering why people can't see that my rights are being violated as well.... My husband went in to register this week and [our new state] passed a new law that says that if the residency restrictions are stricter in the state from which the person came, then they have to abide by the stricter regulations rather than those in [our new state]. Which just adds a lot of work for the law enforcement, and fortunately [our old state's] laws haven't changed, but if they had we would have had to abide by them. And they just opened a daycare down the street from us and it's not in the geographic database, but if they figure that out, there's still a chance that they will force us to move. Mostly, I've learned a lot about myself and how fear impacts me and how fear impacts the community. And all of these laws are just a knee-jerk reaction to fear. There's no studies showing that residency restrictions or any of this stuff has any impact or that it's making our communities safer and by causing this instability in the offender's family, it may be making our communities less safe because we don't have a shot at a normal life and reintegrating.

Without proof of effectiveness, in fact when research shows these laws do not work, communities continue to pass Sex Offender Residency Restrictions that define where a sex offender may reside, work, or visit. In combination with the unwillingness of landlords to rent to sex offenders and their families, integration of registered sex offenders is further hindered when they are pushed into less-desirable, socially disorganized neighborhoods.

Prohibition from Contact with Minors

Many sexual offenses are classified as felonies, which results in the loss of certain civil rights that accompanies a felony conviction. These rights may include the right to own or carry a firearm; access to federal assistance programs (student loan programs, housing programs, etc.); restrictions on driving privileges; loss of voting rights; or loss of parental rights. Additionally, registration as a sex offender may result in other restrictions as a result of the nature of the crime, such as restrictions regarding being in or near school zones or other places where children gather;

residency restrictions; restrictions on where one may work; and restrictions from being near the victim of the crime. If the crime involved a minor, the court may put additional restrictions on the sex offender's interactions with minors (his own children or other minors), as well as restrictions on the offender's movements. These restrictions may occur as part probation or parole, or as part of registry guidelines, depending on the state in which the offender resides. Regardless of the impetus for such restrictions, these guidelines can last decades after an offense occurred and have serious impacts on one's ability to contribute to effective parenting and rearing of children. Schools and parks are off-limits for most types of sexual offenders (regardless of their victim's age) as minors typically congregate in these locations.

Impacts on the Parenting Role

Victoria's husband will spend his life on the sex offense registry and the impacts of his restrictions were her biggest concerns for her family.

> Again, it [the restrictions] will be dependent upon what state we end up in. It's one of my big worries. I mean, my husband and I have gone the whole gamut of "How is this label going to affect our children who had nothing to do with this?" Will he be able to go pick them up at school? Will he be able to go to soccer games? I grew up in the Girl Scouts and I always thought I would have a Girl Scout troop. Can I have a Girl Scout meeting in my home? Will that be safe? Will my kids be able to have sleepovers? How is this going to impact my children and can my children, in turn, have a father that can be a part of their life? And I don't know the answers to those things. Those are part of the daily emotional struggle for me.

Tricia, whose husband will also spend his life on the sex offense registry, had some of the same fears:

> [My fears for the future are that] I worry about when my daughter goes to school. My husband can't pick her up from school, he can't take her, he can't go to a dance recital, he can't go to an open house, he can't ... or you know, talent show at school. Who suffers? Who's being kept safe? How do you explain that to a 4-year-old child?

Most of the women in the study had already experienced the consequences of these restrictions first-hand.

Perhaps the most complicating restriction, and the one with the most significant impact on parenting, was the inability of an RSO to be associated with school functions or be on school property for any reason. Susan's husband

188 Collateral Consequences for Partners

accepted a plea to molestation of his adopted daughter and will spend his life on the sex offense registry. Susan said:

> He would have to ask special permission [to go to the school] and it's a lot of paperwork and he doesn't [go] because he doesn't want to embarrass the kids. And most schools will tell you no anyway. We've been told by a police officer in town that most will just say no because they basically have to have somebody shadow you the whole time. So, basically he doesn't go to any school events. [It makes] our 9-year-old very upset. She doesn't understand, we've never ... how do you explain it, you know? We just tell her that Daddy can't do it, and if she has any questions she can ask why, but at 9 years old, she needs to keep the innocence as long as she can before she realizes the truth.

Tara and her husband are legally challenging his prohibition from being on school property. Tara's husband pled guilty to one count of accepting child pornography and will be on the registry for ten years.

> We're challenging the State Board of Education. The biggest reason is that he's not allowed to go to any of [our daughter's] functions in school, he's not allowed to meet any of her teachers, um, and the other issue is that he can't pick her up from school. Now, we are very lucky that I have a girlfriend that picks up her [child] at the same time and she voluntarily offered to pick up my daughter after school and then he goes and picks up my daughter from there. But, like, when she's sick, in order for her to come home, I have to leave work and go pick her up because he can't. And it's easier for him to pick her up because he's home, and I wouldn't have to leave work to do it.

Another woman in the study, Kara, spoke of her husband, who will also spend 10 years on the registry. She talked about the impact of such restrictions on her family:

> You know, my husband didn't get to see my son play soccer. He didn't get to take him to the movies, doesn't get to take him to school, doesn't get to go to parent–teacher meetings for either of my kids. It's really hard that he's missed out on a lot and I'm hoping that people will see that and the one's in the higher-up ranks can see that it's not doing anything for anybody to separate families. It doesn't help at all.

Dawn's husband was permitted on school grounds according to probation guidelines, but the school would not grant him access. In fact, the school denied Dawn access as well:

Employment, Housing, and Parenting **189**

Under his probation officer his papers were modified that he could be around children. Even before he was off probation. So, he was under the impression that he could go to the school. So, we go to the school for our granddaughter because she's having a program and he's told he can't go in to watch. And I was standing next to him and I said, "Well, why can't I go in? I don't have a criminal background, I'm not a sex offender, why can't he leave and I stay?" And I was told that I was not allowed because I was married to a sex offender. They made us both leave.

The inability for both parents to have access to the school means that the mother has to effectively act as a single parent: picking the child up for all doctor's appointments, going to all parent-teacher conferences, going to all plays, sporting events, and other after-school functions, and transporting the child to and from school. While she may be legally married, she is not able to access her husband as a resource to aid in everyday child-rearing. Danielle's husband will spend 10 years on the registry for statutory rape and she discussed her life, essentially as a single parent:

And for me it's like I have to be two parents because I have to take him to school and drop him off. And I don't have the option to go to happy hour after work because I have to be mom and dad. Or … um … it affects me because it affects my child. But, I will protect my son and will not allow someone to … well, first of all, I won't allow someone else to tell him before we do, but I also won't allow anybody to run around and say, "Your Daddy is a this or that." When that phone call came and turned our lives upside down, I had a son to protect. That was the only thing I have thought of since.

Cindy felt the same sense of single-parenthood:

I need a lot of flexibility. I am the only parent who can do anything. I have to take the kids to all of their doctor appointments, their dental appointments, picking them up from school, all of things. I have to do everything. I never get a break.

Carrie elaborated the emotionally detrimental impact on her family:

It's hard on [my husband] because he feels left out, it's extremely hard on me because I bear the burden of everything by myself from parent-teacher conferences to if [our child] has a fever I have to drop everything at work and go pick him up, um, even if [my husband's] home that day and the school is only a mile and a half away. And it's hard on our son. He doesn't understand why Daddy can't come to Bingo night or Daddy never comes to have lunch. He doesn't understand that. It scars our family.

190 Collateral Consequences for Partners

Some restrictions on interacting with minors for sex offenders go beyond being on school property and attending school functions.

At the time of the interview, Carolyn was preparing for the return home of her husband after more than ten years in prison for various offenses, including a conviction for rape. He will have five years of supervised probation and Carolyn discussed the restrictions of her husband's release:

> [He has to be] 1,000 feet from a school or a playground or a daycare. My daughter's house is not quite 1,000 feet away and we talked about putting a trailer there, but that's not going to happen. Parole comes to the house, he shows up yesterday, and starts talking to me about the parole conditions. They devastated us to the point where I thought, and my daughters thought, that the world had gone insane around us. My children are so devastated that it's killing me. Okay so this is the easy stuff: he has to wear GPS on his ankle for 6-and-a-half-years, till he's off the paper, he can't get his driver's license, he can't be near a school, park, all that stuff. Here's the one that kills us: he can't see or have contact with any children, including his grandchildren, not supervised. He can't have, we can't have in the house, a photograph of any children. We can't have anything that is or resembles a toy, not even a catalog that sells toys. He can't have pictures of his own children when they were children. And I was looking at a picture of myself at the beach when I was a kid and I can't take that with me when we move. It's absurd. And like, my daughter whose kids are of age, we can't visit there if there's pictures of them when they were kids there. And they're going to polygraph him to see if he's seen pictures of any kids. My youngest daughter is due with her first child in a couple months. And he's not even going to be able to see a picture of his new grandchild, he won't be able to lay eyes on her until she's 15! I can't take this, this is insane! And he doesn't even know this yet, I have to tell him when he calls me tonight. No one from parole told him. He doesn't even know. I did tell him about the license and the GPS and now he has 3 weeks to find a place to live. And if he can't find one, they'll find him an approved place to live or they'll put him up at one of three sleaze bag hotels: one's a boarding house, but the other two are like welfare hotels. All the crackheads, the stigma and he's already going to be a registered sex offender with that stigma, but to have the stigma of living in the crackhead hotels. I mean, he could probably suck it up and do it, but the rest of us? How is being around crackhead alcoholics going to help him more than being around his own family? I mean, I can understand the child restrictions, they do that with child molesters and even their own kids, and I can see if they said, "Look you can't have other kids around that aren't your grandkids, but you can see your grandkids if you're supervised." I could understand that, and we were prepared for

all of that. But this is beyond anything we ever dreamed and none of this was told to him before the Level hearing. I think that what's disheartening to me is that we can go to a diner and have lunch and there will be strange children in the diner, but we can't go to a diner and have lunch with *our* grandchildren in a public place. And that's another thing, for the last 8 years [my daughter's] been able to send photos to [my husband]. So, my daughter can send photos to the prison of her and her kids where any creep there can get a hold of them, but she can't send photos of her kids to her father when he's living in his own house. How is that not insane?

While Carolyn's husband had multiple offenses on his record, none of those offenses involved minor victims. Yet a review of his restrictions would suggest that his offenses did involve minors.

The impacts on the children of the semi-absent father, a father who cannot attend school functions or doctor's appointments, a family who is restricted from having other minors to the home as a result of the father's RSO status, and a father who is stigmatized in the community as a sex offender are varied but emotionally and psychologically scarring. Sarah discussed trying to build bridges between her son and his father:

[Our son] had a bad basketball game one night and I said, "Is the coach kicking you off the team?" He's like, "No, why?" I said, "Well, you had a bad game." "So?" "Well, you had a bad day. Is he going to kick you off the team?" He's like, "No." "So you're telling me if you make one mistake, you're not judged by that one mistake? It's based on your whole season or your whole basketball career?" He says, "Well, yeah." I said, "So what are you supposed to be doing with your father? Aren't you judging him based on one mistake?" He says, "It's not the same thing." I know he's going to think about it even though at the time he says no, it's not the same thing. When he understands, and he will think about it. It's not my relationship to repair, but I'm doing whatever I can to plant the seeds which hopefully will make it easier for the two of them to work it out. If I hand him the phone like at Christmas or his birthday, he'll talk to him, he just won't go out of his way to talk to him. He won't email him or he won't write him a letter. Because it's easier for him to avoid it than deal with it.

Cindy spoke about the negative consequences for her children as the most important collateral impact of her husband's plea to solicitation of a minor (who was an undercover officer):

Oh, absolutely the impact to my kids. Them not having friends over and living in constant fear that people at school will find out and him not

192 Collateral Consequences for Partners

> being at things, that's the worst. The rest I could live with any day of the week. I'm not concerned with the consequences on him. I'm like, "You gotta go do community service, go do community service. You gotta go to treatment, go to treatment. We gotta pay a lot of fees, pay em." All of that I'm fine with, but it just sucks for my kids. They didn't do anything and they suffer every day.

Tanya's husband served five years in prison for statutory rape and will spend the rest of his life on probation and on the sex offense registry. The negative ramifications on their family of his status have been substantial and at the time of our interview, he had just been removed from their home … again.

> Well, recently, he was just removed from the home again because he put a diaper on my 2-year-old and he's not allowed to do that. We've been separated three times because, well when he has male probation officers, it's fine, they treat him fine, when he has female probation officers, they treat him like he's a monster. So right now, he's not allowed to be at home and he's not even allowed to see his daughters or he will be arrested. That just happened because he put a diaper on our 2-year-old. He's not even allowed to see them right now. [Before that the restrictions were] no bathing and no changing diapers. Other than that, he could have unsupervised contact with them, he could stay home alone. But they're 2 and 1, obviously, they're gonna need to have diapers changed. And he could never stay home with them for long. And I volunteer 3 days a week and I had a babysitter on the way over and [our daughter's] potty training so she takes her clothes and her diapers off constantly and he decided that rather than risk probation coming over and finding a naked toddler running around, he better put a diaper on her real quickly. Yeah, they were not too fond of that decision and he had to leave. I mean, he was honest with the probation officer, he said, you know I didn't change her, there were no wiping, none of that, I just put the diaper on her. And the probation officer said, well now you're off home again and you can have no contact with the girls, you have to see a different therapist, take a polygraph.

Valerie's husband also had a charge of statutory rape and the conditions of his 10-year probation continued to negatively impact their family:

> [A stipulation of probation is that] he can't go to the doctor with our daughter. He also couldn't go to the hospital when I gave birth. If I can't take her to the doctor, then he couldn't take her because there are other children. He's not allowed to go to the hospital unless it's for himself. So, even if his grandma is dying or I'm dying of giving birth they won't let

Employment, Housing, and Parenting **193**

him go. That's a probation rule. Yeah, we actually didn't find out, this is one I'm a little emotional about … we found out when I was pregnant with our first child and they waited 6 weeks prior to her being born [to tell us] that he couldn't go to the hospital. And I don't have any family besides my sister. I don't have my parents, and he couldn't go, and [he] plays a big role in my life. So, being told 6 weeks before that he can't be part of the birth of our child was pretty devastating. And they do it on purpose because they've done it to other probationees or probationers, I don't know what you call them, but they wait until the last minute … so, we changed it and had a home birth. We never revealed that to probation because they were also telling him, and this was all 6 weeks before, that he wouldn't be able to live in the same household when she was born. That he would have to move out, that he wouldn't be able to touch her, hold her, nothing at all. So, it was all depending on this polygraph and if you know anything about polygraphs, it makes it worse with stress, and not knowing if you're going to be able to be with your child or not is pretty big stress, so that didn't make it easy, and he failed it six times. Finally, he passed it and they acted like nothing happened. We had to pay the lawyer $50,000, and then I think it was two days before, we found out that there were no rules that applied to [our daughter]. So, he would be able to hold her, live in the same house as her, so no rules applied to her. Right. And I think that's when I realized that the probation officers always want you to … they're always like, "You shouldn't be going through such a hard time with this, it's about him, it shouldn't affect you," but yet, they did things like that that were obviously going to affect me. Whether they say they want it to or not, they have to know that waiting for that moment affects the wife, you know?

Courtney knew about her husband's offense a week into dating, so she had some conception of what the future may bring for her and her children. Her husband was found guilty at trial of molestation of his step-daughter and served just over four years of a ten-year sentence. He will spend his life on the sex offense registry. Courtney said:

I've known all along that I would have to be by myself to support the kids. He would be a substantial part of my life, but we would not have a "normal" life. We had cops in our yard constantly. Cops threatening … and it just tore me to pieces. We've never done anything wrong. We've set the ground rules, like I said, I understand, we get it. He can't stay here, we get it. So, stop already. I was not anticipating this barrage of this constant feeling of being watched. Cops come over or drive down the street and slow down – hello obvious – all the time. I can just sit on my front porch and I wave at them. And you almost get this paranoia. Because the

194 Collateral Consequences for Partners

> offense was a child under the age of 12 and I have minor children. It says on there that, he cannot live with a child that is under the age of 18 if his offense happened with a child under the age of 12. My youngest is 4, and so for 14 years we're just going to live apart. Honestly, we take it day by day. I ... 14 years is a long time to do what we're doing and stay sane. So, in 5 years, I don't know how we would be, but we just take it one day at a time. But it drives me nuts.

Courtney recognized she would act as a single parent to her children, but noted dissimilarities between her current marriage and her relationship with her ex-husband:

> I am a single parent. (laughs) It's like that to some extent. But, it's not like it was with my ex-husband where I felt like I was raising three children. [My current husband] is an active part of this family when he's here. But, a lot of time, when we walk out that door to do something, it is just me. And that's fine. Like I said, I knew what I was getting myself into. I know he can't do certain things, but I never knew that people would go so far to be so unfair. And, you know, I know that people wonder sometimes why I married him. I mean, I see them looking at me, and I don't expect people to get it, and no one has ever. I mean, my daughter knows. She knows what his title is and why he has it, but you know, she doesn't understand why he can't go here or there, and at times it's frustrating. But you just move on because if you don't it will eat you alive if you let it.

At the time of the interview, Courtney and her husband had been together for three years.

Some women, recognizing the difficulties that a family with a sex offender would bring, decided against children. Shelly was engaged to a man who pled guilty to molestation of a minor and served half of a seven-year sentence, the other half was served on parole. Shelly knew about his history from their very first date and they had been together 18 months at the time of the interview. She was still struggling with whether this was what she wanted for her future:

> [I wanted a child] before I was with him. I really wanted a child and I, we're actually, giving this relationship [a couple more months] to come to a conclusion whether I'm going to stay with him and not have a child or leave. He doesn't want children. But if it was a girl ... the only way it would ever work is if it was a boy and you can't control that. So, if it was a girl, I don't actually think that there would be ... I think that he's of such strong character now, and of course is stone-cold sober, that he would remove himself from any situation, he would just remove himself

from our lives if he felt like he was becoming attracted to his daughter. But, even given that, I can't even imagine telling my daughter, that I had her with a former sex offender and put her at risk. I just couldn't deal with that.

Sherry and her boyfriend of five years have "decided that we're not going to have any [children] with everything that he has to go though."

A semi-participating father is still a parent that is able to be present in the home and active in many aspects of the parenting role. Interviews for this research were conducted prior to 2019, and therefore no women in this study were impacted by Senate Bill 425 in Tennessee. Senate Bill 425 was signed into law by the Governor and was set to take effect July 2019. The law prohibits any sex offender whose victim was under the age of 12 from living or having overnight visits with any minor, including his children; or from living or having overnight visits with his child(ren) if s/he was a minor and was the victim of the offender (regardless of age). Three single fathers filed suit against the State of Tennessee allegedly this law would effectively terminate parental rights without due process. A federal judge delayed the implementation of Bill 425 until the trial was concluded. Alabama has a similar law that aims to separate sex offenders from their families. Other states have more narrow family-separation laws that apply to registered sex offenders (Yoder, 2019). While the inability of a registered sex offender to be associated with school functions or be on school property can have a serious impact on parenting ability, it is not the only restriction that impacts families.

Traveling Restrictions

Should a registered sex offender want to travel with his family, either to vacation, to visit extended family, or for other reasons, this raises another set of collateral consequences. Requirements for registering and restrictions vary dramatically by state for non-resident sex offenders. There is considerable variation in the number of days an RSO is permitted to visit before registration is required (between two and 30 days, and these days may be consecutive or they may be cumulative in a calendar year), and depending on the state in which the visit occurs, residency restrictions may apply as well (Rolfe, 2019). Forty-six states require non-resident sex offenders to register when visiting; 30 states place the information of visiting sex offenders on the state sex offense registry, and 22 of these states do not remove that information once the RSO has left the state to return to his home state.[2] Additionally, 21 states have residency restrictions that an RSO must follow (Rolfe, 2019). The location of registration also varies by state, with most states requiring registration at the Sheriff's Department. For some states, however, registration options are limited. By way of example: Connecticut requires a visiting RSO to register within five business days and registration must occur at the

196 Collateral Consequences for Partners

State Police Headquarters in Hartford (Rolfe, 2019). Travel registration typically involves the same information as is collected in one's own state (production of identification, background check, registry forms, fingerprinting, picture-taking, address verification of where the RSO will be staying, and sometimes the collection of DNA). Twelve states require the RSO to pay for registration, with fees ranging from $10 to $100 (Rolfe, 2019).

In a recent study of traveling restrictions for RSOs, it was determined that the guidelines by state were available if searching the sex offender website (often under the *Frequently Asked Questions* section), online on the state's page for sex offender registration laws, or by calling the designated office of registration for the state in question. That said, the language of the statutes referenced was "not easily interpretable, especially for the layperson" (Rolfe, 2019: 897), which could make compliance for an offender seeking to stay in compliance, somewhat difficult. Perhaps more states could follow Arizona's example, which provides information clearly and concisely to RSO's interested in visiting. On the state's sex offense registry page there is clear information to RSO's advising that if they intend to stay within Arizona for more than ten days that registration is required and that failure to do so is a Class 4 felony. This type of information clarity and ease of accessibility would be useful from all states for registered sex offenders.

Tracy talked about not traveling anymore because the family was unable to find registration information for some states and they did not want her husband on the registry for life in other states.

> [His] family doesn't live here. We came to the conclusion last year with them that we're not going to [his mother's] anymore because we don't know if [he] has to register in [that state] on his second or his third or his fourth stay. We can't find that information anywhere and when you travel to other states, you are required to do what those states require you to do. Over the past 2 years I've learned that if we were to go to Las Vegas, which we wouldn't, but he would have to register within 24 hours in Las Vegas and give a DNA sample. So, he'd be on the Nevada registry forever. If we go to Florida for whatever reason, to go visit somebody, to go to the beach, whatever, on the third day he would have to register, and he'll be on that registry forever. And we don't know what it is in [his mom's state] and we don't want him to be on the registry with that last name knowing that his mother and his two sisters live in there. It's scary to travel.

Paula mentioned cutting family visits short as well in order to avoid lifetime registry status in another state:

> Yeah and it's even hard because when he goes to visit his grandmother, I mean technically, if he's there for more than, I think it's more than 3 days

a year, if you go to an address, you're supposed to register and then he would be registered there permanently.

Renee and her husband resided in a state which required pre-travel approval which he would have to abide by for the 25 years he will be on the sex offense registry:

> They have restrictions, travel restrictions, those are difficult, if he's gonna be out of his home residence for more than 48 hours, he has to give a week's notice and tell them everywhere he'll be staying. So basically we're not able to go on a road trip or anything because we have to tell them exactly which motel we'll be at which night. And god forbid one of our family members has a tragedy and we have to go to a funeral, we wouldn't be able to go because we wouldn't know 7 days in advance.

To avoid non-compliance, Brandi attempted to clarify travel plans with an attorney and still ended up confused:

> We don't travel. At Christmas we went out to visit my son, but we were only gone 3 days because that's the limit of time we can be gone and not have to report it. We used to travel, we used to fly, but we don't do that anymore. We used to camp. We don't do that anymore. We used to walk in the parks, we don't do that anymore. [Also], in our state he cannot go to the parks. I went to an attorney to get some clarification on [if it's state and county parks], and again, this attorney books himself as a sex offender attorney and he said, "Oh, he can go wherever he wants." And that's a friggin' lie. He can't. We used to go to amusement parks. I love amusement parks. We don't now because I don't want to deal with, in case someone recognizes his face. I don't want to be afraid all the time that when I leave someone is going to come and vandalize my home.

Travel does not necessarily just mean out-of-state travel. There are also restrictions on visiting parks.

Parks that are restricted may include state parks, municipal parks, Green Zones (as defined by the municipality), or amusement parks (including waterparks). Laurie's husband will spend his life on the sex offense registry for possession of child pornography. She said:

> There was a bill that was passed last year that he cannot go into any municipally run park. So, any state park, any forest preserve, any, nothing with the park district. Nothing upkept by the park district or the state. The waterways are run by the state conservation something or other, so he's banned from all the waterways now.

198 Collateral Consequences for Partners

Cheryl's husband will have similar lifetime restrictions for his possession of child pornography conviction:

> He can't loiter within 500 feet of a park, any free space, or green space but it could even be a public golf course. They say if the city mows it, it's considered a park, so like bike trails and things. Even without playground equipment.

Valerie's husband was advised that for life even driving past a greenspace was not permitted:

> We were told that we could drive by parks as long as they weren't the final destination. And then later, we were told you can't drive by a park, you can't even drive within 1,000 feet of a park. And now they're saying Green Zones for us are on the list also, which had never been before. But now we can't drive by anything that's green on a map ... not within 1,000 feet. Yeah, and those are things that change all the time. But, for right now, he can't drive within 1,000 feet of any park. And schools, of course, but the main thing that has affected us has been parks and Green Zones. And Green Zones, I mean, even if it like, hasn't been mowed in 25 years and nobody could walk down there, it doesn't matter, they still consider it a Green Zone.

For Tracy, the policy of Six Flags was surprising:

> Six Flags has a no sex offender policy at all of their locations and they have locations in multiple states. They have a face scan system at Six Flags and if they let you in, they will come find you and escort you out of the park. I had no idea that this was a possibility!

In 2005, Six Flags became the first chain of amusement parks to specifically indicate on the back of its tickets that sex offenders were denied entry. So, even if the plan is to avoid waterparks and parks and greenspaces and not travel to avoid registration in other states, Tracy mentioned the need to always have a back-up plan.

> I mean, these are things we have to think of. We always need a plan. What if his car breaks down or if his car gets a flat tire and he is within 1,000 feet of a school, or a daycare, or a park? He has to get out of the car, get his phone, and abandon that car while he calls AAA or me or whatever. He can't hang out at the car if he gets a flat tire because he can't spend the time to do the flat tire repair if he's in front of a school. And if there's some kid lost and he sees this kid on the side of the road, lost or injured

Employment, Housing, and Parenting **199**

or whatever, he can't stop, he has to drive on. I mean, these are things you would never think you would have to think about. I mean, he can call 911, but he has to keep driving. God forbid he breaks down in an area he doesn't know and there's a school within a 1,000-feet that he can't see ... he's screwed!

Church Restrictions

For many individuals who are having emotionally difficult times in their life or who want an additional social outlet, church becomes a positive retreat. Overwhelmingly, the women and families in this research, did not have positive church experiences. Elizabeth's husband was incarcerated at the time of the interview and she said:

> Yes, yes. I've, I have developed a much closer walk with the Lord and have done a lot of oral praying. I can't say much church attendance because it saddens me to say there's discrimination there too, I hate to say that, I stopped going to one church because they shut me down, froze me out. And that's another area that you don't tell people about, you don't tell anybody until you see what they're made of, how they'd react.

Pamela echoed similar sentiments:

> [We have tried to go to three churches] and if you're a sex offender, they don't want you. [So we don't go at all anymore]. I can be spiritual at home, but it would be nice and it'd be a nice social outlet. But it's not available to me.

Catherine also talked of praying, but of negative church experiences:

> I pray. I don't know if it helps, but I pray. [I cannot go to church], not being the wife of a sex offender. It's a very small town, I was attending church for a while but it wasn't a positive experience, it was an awful experience and I don't need it.

For many churches, the restrictions on sex offenders are rooted in restrictions on RSOs being near places where children gather, as many churches have a daycare on the premises. Brandy said,

> From the church's perspective, I understand them not wanting to risk the liability. But it kind of flies in the face of reason to not allow offenders to go to places that might be good and healthy places for them to be.

200 Collateral Consequences for Partners

So, even though the offender may not have a conviction for victimizing a minor, even though the offense may have been decades ago, even though the daycare may not be open during church hours, even though the offender may be attending service as opposed to anywhere near the daycare, even though the offender may have chaperones with him, overwhelmingly the women in this research spoke of being shunned from places of worship, or outright prohibited from attending. Amber's boyfriend served time in prison for rape prior to their marriage. She spoke of an incident with her minister:

> So, on Friday I called my minister and [my boyfriend] had been to church with me many times and the church previously didn't know about his background. But I told the minister about his history and that our family was in crisis and that we needed ministerial and church support and you know, I had been an upstanding and active member of the church and was calling in my cards now that I needed them to rally around me. Instead my minister just kept saying, "We need to talk about how we're going to restrict [your boyfriend] if he comes to church with you." I got no support when I needed it most.

Samantha was really struggling with the treatment of her family by the church. Her husband took a plea to a charge of sexual misconduct of a minor. He claimed the allegation was false and the alleged victim later recanted. He was sentenced to 15 years on probation and served five years on a drug violation. He will spend his life on the sex offense registry. Samantha was raised in the church and sought solace there. So, the treatment of her family by the church was especially difficult for her.

> I mean, we go to church, but we can't teach a Sunday School class together and for most people that's not a big deal, but I was raised in the church my whole life and I just always thought that once you got married you would spend time teaching a Sunday School class, working with the youth groups – I really wanted to be able to do that – and I can't. The church formed a committee about whether we could come to church. It turned out that a couple of people on the committee were victims of sex abuse, so it slowly started turning into a, "Well, we really want to welcome these people, but we have to protect our church from people who might do bad things." And it just spiraled and spiraled and spiraled and they had speakers come in and talk to the committee about sexual abuse, but they never asked one of us to come to the meetings or to talk at the meetings. But they would have police come out and say, "This is how sex offenders come into your church and target children." So, it turned into a witch hunt. The committee put out an eight-page set of guidelines for how sex offenders can attend church. And the rules

were so incredibly restrictive. And they didn't even tell us how they came up with the rules. One day they just mentioned, "There's pieces of paper out in the lobby which goes over our new policy." And so, we picked up the paper and it was unreal what was on there. It was like, if we continued to go to the church, he could only enter through 1 of the 14 doors that go into the church. And he could only go into the church if a church appointed chaperone was at that door. So, if no one is there, he can't go in. And I can't be his chaperone. It had to be male and it had to be church appointed. He would also have to meet this person twice a week to be accountable to this guy. Now, this guy didn't have to be accountable to him, but he had to be accountable to this guy and tell him everything he'd done for the last 2 weeks. We would have to apply to go to any activity, Sunday School class ... any activity. And there's a committee that we would have to apply to and they would go over whether we could go that activity. That committee only meets once every other month. But every week they're announcing activities and we couldn't go to any of those because we wouldn't have time to ask permission. We couldn't go to any sporting event, and we can't go to anything outside of the church that is church-sanctioned. And anybody who was going to Sunday School class wasn't allowed to come to our house for any meetings. No one in our church could bring their children to our house. We weren't allowed to bring my step-daughter to church without the committee's permission. There were only certain areas of the church where he could stand and other areas where he would have to keep moving. I mean, it was really far out; it was devastating. There was ... there were three services and they only allowed us to go to one of them. And the one that they allowed us to go to was the one that meant if we went, we couldn't go to any of the Sunday School classes with people our age because the times were the same. If [my husband] had to go to the bathroom, his chaperone would have to go with him and stand outside of his stall. So, every day it was just crazier. The way it works sometimes is that you make these committees and then you lose control of them. Church is important to me, but this was crazy!

For many women, the negative experiences at church vastly outweighed the positive ones. Jackie, however, was intent on finding a church that would accept her and her husband:

We stopped going to church because they shunned us. It was hard, church was our life down there, it was very hard. You know, church is for sinners but here it's not, it's for the sinless, they think they're sinless anyway, so I'm having a real hard time finding a church up here, but I'll keep looking. It's very important to us!

202 Collateral Consequences for Partners

Uphill battles to find and maintain stable employment, find suitable and afford-able housing, and abide by restrictions on contacts with minors take a massive toll on the families of registered sex offenders. It impacts their financial situation, psychological and emotional well-being, and sense of security as a family. Tara talked about the importance of stepping away from the stigma that comes with the sex offender label:

> The restrictions on being able to do the things that you really need to do or want to do are the things that I really have a second thought about. There are certain things that we do anyway, even though we can't afford them, just to keep some sort of happiness in our lives, we do it. Like go on vacation. We do it anyway even though we can't afford to because you need to get that break. You need that togetherness and that need to get away and not think about anything.

The temptation may exist for wives to direct their anger at their husband, and Sarah discussed the lack of productivity of that approach:

> I am mad at what he's done and there are times, there are moments where I am angry at him for the position that he's put this family in and that he's gotten us here. But overall am I mad at him? No, I'm not. And people don't understand that. I'm like, you know, I can be mad at him, he knows what he's done, he knows what devastations he's caused. What would be the benefit of me continuing to be angry at him in that he's missing all this stuff with his kids. He didn't get to teach my son how to drive, he's gonna miss his prom, he's gonna miss his high school gradua-tion, he missed my daughter getting an award for this or that he missed her first pitch in junior varsity. You know, he missed everything. Isn't that punishment enough? What would me being angry at him do anymore? It can't cause him any more damage than the damage he's already caused himself. And I know he's sorry for what he did, so to continue to be angry, I mean, I'm hurt, and I feel loss for everything that our family is going through. And yeah, like I said, there are moments, there are days where I write him this scathing letter because I'm mad with him about something, but for the most part, it's not very often. And truthfully, it would probably be the same. You could look at every married couple and there are days where you're mad at your husband one day. It's just a convenient thing to be mad at him about. I mean, I can't be mad at him because he didn't fold the laundry or that he didn't change the oil in the car. So right now that's what I can be mad at him about. But if I were to define, are you mad at him? No, I'm not. I've seen too many people – my sister has carried anger with her all her life and I see how it affects her. I don't want that. He's so sorry for what he's done and like I said,

overall, he's a good person. He is a good person. He made one mistake, he made a mistake and unfortunately because of public hype and public perception, it's politically correct right now to hate him. If he'd gone out drunk and hit somebody, and killed them, the stigma isn't the same. Sure, he'd be talked about and whispered about, but in 8 years, who cares. Would they think about it? Probably not. But this will be with him for who knows how long until they change the laws or they put everybody on a list. Before you know it, everyone will be on a list for something.

At the time of the interview, Sarah's husband was serving a five-year sentence on a plea deal for one count of possession of child pornography. The difference between sex offender laws and other laws is that they are subject to change and change retroactively. So, for Carrie and other wives of RSOs: "Every time the assembly gathers we just cringe, worried about what other parts of our lives are going to change." Families of RSOs never know what tomorrow may bring.

Notes

1. Predatory offenses are those such as juvenile pimping, exploitation of a minor, child pornography, criminal sexual assault, kidnapping, child abduction, certification as a sexually dangerous person, conviction of a second sexual offense, sexual misconduct against a person with a disability, and aggravated criminal sexual assault.
2. Rhode Island suggests RSOs contact the SORN office prior to visiting to determine if registration is required; New York, Oregon, and Pennsylvania do not require registration but the SORN office recommends visiting RSOs make contact upon visiting the state (Rolfe, 2019).

References

Ackerman, A. R., Harris, A. J., Levenson, J. S., & Zgoba, K. (2011). Who are the people in your neighborhood? A descriptive analysis of individuals on public sex offender registries. *International Journal of Law and Psychiatry, 34*, 149–159.

Avery, Beth. (2019). Ban the box: U.S. cities, counties, and states adopt fair-chance policies to advance employment opportuniti4s for people with past convictions. *National Employment Law Project.* www.nelp.org

Barnes, J. C., Dukes, T., Tewksbury, R., & DeTroye, T. (2009). Predicting the impact of a statewide residence restriction law on South Carolina sex offenders. *Criminal Justice Policy Review, 20*, 21–43.

Blood, P., Watson, L., & Stageberg, P. (2008). *State legislation monitoring report.* Des Moines, IA: Criminal and Juvenile Justice Planning.

Brewster, Mary P., DeLong, Philip A., & Moloney, Joseph T. (2012). Sex offender registries: A content analysis. *Criminal Justice Policy Review, 24*(6), 695–715.

Brown, Kevin, Spencer, Jon, & Deakin, Jo. (2007). The reintegration of sex offenders: Barriers and opportunities for employment. *The Howard Journal, 46*(1), 32–42.

Burchfield, K. (2011). Residence restrictions. *Criminology & Public Policy, 10*(2), 411–419.

California Sex Offender Management Board (2011). *Homelessness among California's registered sex offenders.* www.casomb.org

California Sex Offender Management Board. (2008). *Homelessness among registered sex offenders in California: The numbers, the risks, and the response*. Sacramento, CA: California Division of Criminal Justice.

Calkins, C., Colombino, N., Matsuura, T., & Jeglic, E. (2015). Where do sex crimes occur? How an examination of sex offense location can inform policy and prevention. *International Journal of Comparative and Applied Criminal Justice*, 39(2), 99–112.

Casady, T. (2009). A police chief's viewpoint: Geographic aspects of sex offender residency restrictions. *Criminal Justice Policy Review*, 20(1), 16–20.

Center for Sex Offender Management (CSOM). (2010). *Exploring public attitudes and opinions about sex offender management: Findings from a national opinion poll*. Washington, DC: Office of Justice programs, U.S. Department of Justice.

Chajewski, M., & Mercado, C. C. (2009). An evaluation of sex offender residency restriction functioning in town, county, and city-wide jurisdictions. *Criminal Justice Policy Review*, 20, 44–61.

Cohen, L., & Felson, M. (1979). Social change and crime rate trends: A routine activity approach. *American Sociological Review*, 44, 588–608.

Colombino, N., Mercado, C. C., & Jeglic, E. L. (2011). Preventing sexual violence: Can examination of offense location inform sex crime policy? *International Journal of Law and Psychiatry*, 34(3), 160–167.

Comartin, E. B., Kernsmith, P. D., & Kernsmith, R. M. (2009). Sanctions and sex offenders: Fear and public policy. *Journal of Offender Rehabilitation*, 48, 605–619.

Couloute, Lucius, & Kopf, Daniel. (2018). Unemployment among formerly incarcerated people. *Prison Policy Initiative*. www.prisonpolicy.org/reports

Doe v. Snyder, 834 F.3d 696 (6th Cir. 2016)

Duwe, G., Donnay, W., & Tewksbury, R. (2008). Does residential proximity matter: A geographic analysis of sex offense recidivism. *Criminal Justice and Behavior*, 35(4), 484–504.

Farkas, Mary Ann, & Miller, Gale. (2007). Reentry and reintegration: Challenges faced by the families of convicted sex offenders. *Federal Sentencing Report*, 20(2), 88–92.

Green, Max. (November 14, 2017). For Illinois sex offenders, six years can turn into life in prison. *WCBU.org*. www.peoriapublicradio.org

Grubesic, T. H. (2010). Sex offender clusters. *Applied Geography*, 30, 2–18.

Grubesic, T. H., & Mack, E. A. (2010). Sex offenders and residential location. *Environment and Planning*, 42, 1925–1942.

Grubesic, T. H., Murray, A. T., & Mack, E. A. (2008). Sex offenders, housing and spatial restriction zones. *GeoJournal*, 73, 255–269.

Hicks, Brad. (September 11, 2016). "If this is winning, I don't want it:" Convicted sex offender talks about life after being released from prison. *Fox6Now.com*. https://fox6now.com

Holzer, Harry J. (1996). *What employers want: Job prospects for less-educated workers*. New York, NY: Russell Sage.

Justice Policy Institute. (n.d.). *What will it cost states to comply with the Sex Offender Registration and Notification Act?* www.justicepolicy.org

Kruttschnitt, C., Uggen, C., & Shelton, K. (2000). Predictors of desistance among sex offenders: The interaction of formal and informal social controls. *Justice Quarterly*, 17, 62–87.

Levenson, J. (2008). Collateral consequences of sex offender residence restrictions. *Criminal Justice Studies*, 21(2), 153–166.

Levenson, Jill S., Brannon, Yolanda N., Fortney, Timothy, & Baker, Juanita. (2007). Public perceptions about sex offenders and community protection policies. *Analysis of Social Issues and Public Policy*, 7(1), 1–25.

Levenson, Jill S., & Cotter, Leo P. (2005). The impact of sex offender residence restrictions: 1,000 feet from danger or one step from absurd? *International Journal of Offender Therapy and Comparative Criminology*, 49(2), 168–178.

Levenson, J. S., & Tewksbury, R. (2009). Collateral damage: Family members of registered sex offenders. *American Journal of Criminal Justice*, 34, 54–68.

Looney, Adam, & Turner, Nicholas. (2018). *Work and opportunity before and after incarceration*. Washington, DC: The Brookings Institution.

Mann v. *Georgia Department of Corrections*, 653 S.E.2d 740 (2007)

McAlinden, Anne-Marie, Farmer, Mark, & Maruna, Shadd. (2017). Desistance from sexual offending: Do the mainstream theories apply? *Criminology & Criminal Justice*, 17(3), 266–283.

Meredith, T., Speir, J., & Johnson, S. (2007). Developing and implementing automated risk assessments in parole. *Justice Research and Policy*, 9(1), 1–21.

Minnesota Department of Corrections. (2007). *Residential proximity & sex offender recidivism in Minnesota*. St. Paul, MN: Minnesota Department of Corrections.

Mustaine, E. E., & Tewksbury, R. (2011). Residential regulation of registered sex offenders. *American Journal of Criminal Justice*, 36, 44–57.

Nally, John M., Lockwood, Susan, Ho, Taiping, & Knutson, Katie. (2014). Post-release recidivism and employment among different types of released offenders: A 5-year follow-up study in the United States. *International Journal of Criminal Justice Sciences*, 9(1), 16–34.

Nobles, M., Levenson, J., & Youstin, T. (2012). Effectiveness of residence restrictions in preventing sex offense recidivism. *Crime & Delinquency*, 58(4), 491–513.

Payne, Brian K., Tewksbury, Richard, & Mustaine, Elizabeth Erhardt. (2016). Identifying the sources of community corrections professionals' attitudes about sex offender residence restrictions: The impact of demographics and perceptions. *Crime and Delinquency*, 62(2), 143–168.

Rabin, C. (October 23, 2014). ACLU sues over rule on where sex offenders can live in MiamiDade. *Miami Herald*. Retrieved from www.miamiherald.com

Red-Bird, B. (2009). *Assessing housing availability under Ohio's sex offender residency restrictions*. Columbus: The Ohio State University.

Rengert, G. F., & Wasilchick, J. (2000). *Suburban burglary: A tale of two suburbs*. Springfield, IL: Charles C. Thomas.

Rodriguez, Michelle Natividad, & Avery, Beth. (2016). Unlicensed & untapped: Removing barriers to state occupational licenses for people with records. *National Employment Law Project*. www.nelp.org/

Rolfe, Shawn M. (2019). When a sex offender comes to visit: A national assessment of travel restrictions. *Criminal Justice Policy Review*, 30(6), 885–905.

Rolfe, Shawn M., Tewksbury, Richard., & Schroeder, Ryan D. (2017). Homeless shelters' policies on sex offenders: Is this another collateral consequence? *International Journal of Offender Therapy and Comparative Criminology*, 61(16), 1833–1849.

Roman, C. G., & Travis, J. (2004). *Taking stock: Housing, homelessness, and prisoner reentry*. Washington, DC: Urban Institute, Justice Policy Center.

Rydberg, J., Grommon, E., Huebner, B., & Bynum, T. (2014). The effect of statewide residency restrictions on sex offender post-release housing mobility. *Justice Quarterly*, 31(2), 421–444.

Sandler, J. C., Freeman, N. J., & Socia, K. M. (2008). Does a watched pot boil? A time-series analysis of New York state's sex offender registration and notification law. *Psychology, Public Policy, and Law*, 14, 284–302.

Savage, Joanne, & Windsor, Casey. (2018). Sex offender residence restrictions and sex crimes against children: A comprehensive review. *Aggression and Violence Behavior*, 43, 13–25.

Schiavone, S. K., & Jeglic, E. L. (2009). Public perceptions of sex offender social policies and the impact on sex offenders. *International Journal of Offender Therapy and Comparative Criminology*, 53, 679–695.

Schulenberg, J. L. (2007). Predicting noncompliant behavior: Disparities in the social locations of male and female probationers. *Justice Research and Policy*, 9(1), 25–57.

Socia, Kelly M. (2014). Residence restrictions are ineffective, inefficient, and inadequate: So now what? *Criminology and Public Policy*, 13, 179–188.

Socia, K. M. (2011). The policy implications of residence restrictions on sex offender housing in upstate NY. *Criminology & Public Policy*, 10, 351–389.

Socia, Kelly M., Levenson, Jill S., Ackerman, Alissa R., & Harris, Andrew J. (2014). "Brothers under the bridge": Transience of registered sex offenders in Florida. *Sexual Abuse: A Journal of Research and Treatment*, 27(6), 559–586.

Suresh, G., Mustaine, E. E., Tewksbury, R., & Higgins, G. E. (2010). Social disorganization and registered sex offenders. *Southwest Journal of Criminal Justice*, 7, 180–213.

Tewksbury, R., & Levenson, J. (2009). Stress experiences of family members of registered sex offenders. *Behavioral Sciences and the Law*, 27, 611–626.

Tewksbury, R., Mustaine, E. E., & Stengel, K. M. (2008). Examining rates of sexual offenses from a routine activities perspective. *Victims & Offenders*, 3, 75–85.

van den Berg, Chantal, Bijleveld, Catrien, Hendriks, Jan, & Mooi-Reci, Irma. (2013). The juvenile sex offender: The effect of employment on offending. *Journal of Criminal Justice*, 42, 145–152.

Vasquez v. *Foxx, 895 F.3d 515 §7.01* (7th Cir. 2018)

Visher, Christy, Debus, Sara, & Yahner, Jennifer. (2008). *Employment after prison: A longitudinal study of releasees in three states*. Urban Institute: Justice Policy Center.

Willis, G. M., & Grace, R. C. (2008). The quality of community reintegration planning for child molesters: Effects on sexual recidivism. *Sexual Abuse: A Journal of Research and Treatment*, 20, 218–240.

Yoder, Steven. (June 28, 2019). New law forces dozens on Tennessee's sex offender registry from their homes. *The Appeal*. https://theappeal.org

Zandbergen, P. A., & Hart, T. C. (2006). Reducing housing options for convicted sex offenders: Investigating the impact of residency restriction laws using GIS. *Justice Research and Policy*, 8(2), 1–24.

Zandbergen, P. A., Levenson, J. S., & Hart, T. C. (2010). Residential proximity to schools and daycares: An empirical analysis of sex offense recidivism. *Criminal Justice and Behavior*, 37, 482–502.

Zucker, B. (2014). Jessica's law residency restrictions in California: The current state of the law. *Golden Gate University Law Review*, 44, 101–115.

PART IV
Moving Forward

7

COPING STRATEGIES AND (RE)INTEGRATION

The formal and informal social controls on sex offenders that have been detailed throughout this work have significant psychological and emotional impacts on the partners of offenders. These formal and informal social controls include registration and community notification; negative attitudes and behaviors from friends and family, the public, law enforcement and treatment professionals; unexpected reclassification of tier assignment; stigma, fear and harassment from community members; employment challenges and instability; residency restrictions; prohibition on contact with minors; travel restrictions; and church restrictions. Each of these poses an obstacle to not only the sex offender, but to his significant partner as well.

Other studies of sex offender's families have revealed families experienced isolation, loneliness, social stigma, intense stress, frustration, social marginalization, anger and resentment. Partners reported feeling overwhelmed and demoralized, many minimized external social relationships, and some sought the assistance of a counselor, or solace from religion or a support group (Farkas & Miller, 2007). With a sex offense conviction, dimensions of family functioning are dramatically altered. The family structure, financial arrangements, systems of emotional support, living arrangements, parental arrangements, and intimate relationships; the family dynamic as it was known and structured changes. A once private life becomes public and this takes a significant emotional toll on the partner of an offender.

Emotional Impacts on the Offender's Partner

Research on the female partners of sex offenders has been extraordinarily limited and sporadic. In 1975, qualitative interviews with 11 wives of rapists and seven

210 Moving Forward

wives of incest offenders being held in a maximum-security hospital were conducted. The wives were committed to supporting their husbands and asserted the marriage was stronger post-offense (Garrett & Wright, 1975). More recently, in interviews with 25 sex offender couples, researchers found a reasonable degree of relationship stability. Most couples reported an emotionally supportive male partner, and a female partner who helped keep her husband from reoffending (Iffland, Berner, Dekker, & Briken, 2016).

The 94 women involved with sex offenders in this research most frequently discussed emotional and psychological stress surrounding questions of blame, inadequacies about her own sexuality, feelings of loneliness and isolation, and worry about the public's perception that her partner would reoffend. Maria's husband was found guilty at a jury trial of sexual misconduct with a minor who was a friend of the family. He served eight years in prison and six years on parole of a sentence that could have extended to 25 years. He will be on the sex offense registry for life. Maria sometimes blamed herself for not knowing.

> I thought you know, how naïve or how stupid or how blind I was to not see something. I definitely had thoughts, not of suicide, but hiding under my bed. I didn't do it, but just you know, hitting my head against the wall because I didn't see it. Just those kind of thoughts, I didn't use the word die because the pain was just too much, sometimes, but I did go to counseling and talking to close friends, but you just had to go through it, there was no easy way.

Other women saw their partner's behavior as part of a larger addiction. Julie's husband accepted a plea to one count of possession of child pornography and was sentenced to five years on probation and life on the sex offense registry. He served three years on revocation of probation for failing a polygraph. Julie said:

> No, I knew it didn't have anything to do with me, I've been in Al-Anon for too long. What other people do is not, I can't control it, I don't cause what other people do. You know I didn't hold a gun to his head and make him do that. I know that what he did is no reflection on me, I know that.

Cindy echoed similar sentiments regarding addictive behaviors:

> I wouldn't [blame myself] … it's an addiction.… But the piece of me that wants to be an attractive, sexual woman, I think is pretty damaged. And I don't think that's healed yet. I'm not convinced it will be. I mean, I'm leaving no stone unturned, but that was pretty yucky. I absolutely don't consider my husband a sex offender. No, absolutely not! That's what sucks. I would say that the thing that sucks about this the most,

what really pisses me off, is that, you know, most, 99 percent of his acting out was not illegal. And 99 percent of his, or our, energy has to go into the consequences of that. So, to be perfectly honest, there hasn't been much, you know resources, whether it's time, money or energy left to give to our marriage.

Cindy's husband accepted a plea to a charge of solicitation of a minor who was an undercover law enforcement officer. His sentence was five years on probation and ten years on the sex offense registry. Like Cindy, several other women discussed that their sexual identity was damaged by their husband's offense. Crystal's husband was found in possession of approximately 1,200 images of child pornography. She revealed how this impacted her intimately:

A sex crime has to do with inside things, in your own bedroom. When it's a sex crime, that affects the wife at her most intimate, core level. My sex life would not be all screwed up if [he] had committed murder or if he had embezzled. I might not have wanted to have sex with him because I didn't respect him, but my own personal, deep, inner sexuality wouldn't be affected. But it is affected because it's a sex crime. This hits on a personal level in a way that no other crime can. And there's no help for women.

Similarly, Jamie discussed how her husband's molestation of his daughter impacted her feelings about her own sexuality:

[My husband's offense made me feel very different about myself] because the way he went in there and laid with [his daughter] … is that same thing that he does with me? You know, when we go in bed, when we snuggle or whatever, the first thing he does is put his hand up my shirt. And I wouldn't let him touch me for the longest time. It brought back so many of my own issues, right after this happened. And I kept thinking, "What if I'm attracted to this man because of the things that happened to me?" Because when you look at the cycles that people go through and cycles within families, it's like, "Okay, did I just follow the same cycle by marrying this man?" You know? It was hard. It was hard trying to figure out why I am attracted to this man. What is it? Was there something there that drew me to him because it was familiar? I don't think that now, but for a while I did. And it was really, really hard for me trying to stand by him through all of this. I completely became a hermit … I just turned into a recluse.

Jamie's husband accepted a plea to a six-year probationary term and life on the sex offense registry.

212 Moving Forward

The stress of informal and formal social controls also led to feelings of isolation and loneliness among many women. Sarah was just starting to acclimate to her life as a single mother during the interview. At that time, her husband was incarcerated on a five-year term for one count of possession of child pornography. Law enforcement found 15 photographs of minors on his computer. She said:

> I imagine at some point in time it'll be scary again, scary again when it gets closer to him coming home. When he does come home, we'll be walking on eggshells again. Because you're gonna be afraid, what's gonna happen? Is someone going to say something? Or is nobody going to care at that point? Is it going to be, oh, he served 5 years in federal prison? Maybe they'll be scared of him. I don't know. You know, the stigma of federal prison, who knows, but it's gonna start all over again. Am I ready for that? I don't know … sometimes I wonder if I want to jeopardize that by having him come home. There's no definitive answer. There's no right, there's no wrong. Am I 100 percent committed to having him come home? Mmm, 98 percent, because it's still scary. I've learned a lot. I've grown as a person like you would not believe. I think I'm a better person, I think I'm a much stronger person. I'm all-around a better person. I'm less judgmental. So, in that respect, a lot of what's happened has been positive. It's positive. [My husband] is relieved. He was living two lives. There's no secrets anymore. He admitted, there's no secrets, I don't have to hide anything. Everything is out in the open, I can breathe.

Jenny mourns for the family she once had publicly:

> I can't talk about him anymore. You know, I went from a single to someone with a family and a family with children and I loved it and I realized that that's gone now. And over the weekend I was with my father and his step-family. He has two step-daughters that are in their 50's and they have children and, of course, they're talking about their children, and I used to talk about my step-children and my step-grandchildren like they were my own, and now I just sit there and don't talk. And that hurts. It really does hurt.

At the time of the interview, Jenny's husband was in prison and awaiting sentencing on a plea to a charge of molestation of a family member. Maria experienced similar feelings of loneliness:

> You feel so alone. I mean, I know tons of people who are divorced and there are tons of different divorce support groups out there. But that was one of the hardest things that I was just alone with my issue, you know. I wasn't an alcoholic, I wasn't a divorcee. I was the spouse of someone in

Coping Strategies and (Re)Integration **213**

prison and then on top of it, someone who's a sex offender. I just feel so alone, I mean, set apart and not in a good way.

Catherine expressed feelings of isolation and hurt by comments from people around her as they passed judgment on her family:

> People do say things to me and about me and it hurts, and it's not his fault that it hurts. It is [stressful], you know. I actually had one co-worker say to another co-worker, "You know she's married to a sex offender, that's the same as being one. I don't know why she doesn't have to register too." I mean, I just can't believe that. That was one of the times I could actually say something, but I didn't. I just go in the other room and cry and try to get over it.

Catherine's husband committed his offense prior to their relationship. She had been with him more than a decade and was still greatly impacted by his sex offender status. Because his victim was a minor, he will be on the sex offense registry for life. Overwhelmingly the women in this study did not express anger at their partners. Jenny said:

> You know, everything in me says I should be [angry] and for some reason I'm not. I'm just not. I don't know why he did this, I don't know where it comes from, but it's changed my life dramatically. But, angry? I have to say I rarely feel angry at him. Only, the only time I feel angry with him is when I feel like I'm getting into that hatred thing. I'm getting hooked into what society thinks, and at one point I started asking myself, "Well, who would do such a thing?" That was my question. That's what a lot of my friends asked. And I realized there's no answer. There's just no rational answer for that.

The women interviewed elected to remain with their partners despite the significant collateral consequences of both formal and informal social controls that impacted their lives. Samantha explained:

> This guy was the real deal, but to be with him I would have to give up a lot of these dreams I had for myself, and I had to never hold it against him or never punish him for what our life looks like in the future. So, that was kind of hard to work through.

Most women looked past their partner's mistake and they found a supportive man and relationship.

While 90 percent (84 women) said they do not worry about their partner reoffending, several women were stressed by the possibility of their partner being

214 Moving Forward

falsely accused of sexual misconduct. Donna was in the minority and revealed she initially had concerns about reoffending behaviors which waned after her husband's treatment:

> I guess I could say that I've worried [about my husband reoffending]. There hasn't been a concern recently. I worried about it for a long time [when he was first released], but there's definitely a change in his behavior [after therapy] so I don't worry about it that much. And I feel like if things keep progressing the way they're going, I don't think there will ever be a problem with it again.

Donna's husband served one year of a five-year sentence from a plea agreement on a charge of molestation of a minor. Victoria's views were more representative of the women in this study:

> No, I don't worry about [him reoffending] at all. What worries me more is the perception of the general public throwing him into a situation where there is a false accusation. So, no, I'm not afraid of him reoffending, I'm afraid of the general public.

Victoria's husband accepted a plea to two counts of molestation of a minor and will be on the sex offense registry for life. Overwhelmingly, the women spoke of the constant and persistent nature of stress in their lives. Tara sighed when she revealed:

> Um, I think it's the stress that changed it, not so much my feelings toward him in any way. I don't really think that, I think it's just the stress of the whole situation that's changed things because it's just constant, it's just always there. It's always something that's in my head.

Elizabeth elaborated similar notions of the offense and surrounding challenges feeling like a never-ending weight:

> [My husband always says], now remember honey, don't let it out, don't let them know. But we're both really, to always feel you have to hide that part of your life, it's a constant ball and chain you have to drag around with you your entire life. The analogy, I guess is appropriate ... it's a ball and chain. You have to hide. It's a weight, it's a sadness.

Elizabeth's husband was incarcerated when they began letter-writing. The later married. His sentence is effectively a lifetime, though he maintains his innocence and is actively working with The Innocence Project to overturn his conviction.

Previous researchers have demonstrated the significance of family support in post-release outcomes for those offenders who served time in prison. Emotional support, family acceptance and encouragement were all associated with increased success post-release (La Vigne, Visher, & Castro, 2004; Visher, La Vigne, & Travis, 2003). While family was important to the success of the offender, little research has been done assessing the support networks (either formal or informal) and the coping mechanisms used by family members to mitigate the resultant stress from their supportive role. Jill noted:

> I feel like if I keep telling myself that I don't care what other people think maybe one of these days it'll be true. Maybe one of these days I'll be like I really don't give a shit. Because right now I don't want to tell people how much it hurts.

How do female partners of sex offenders mitigate their stress? How do they cope with the consequences of being in a relationship with an offender and acting as his primary support system?

Negative Coping Mechanisms

After coming to terms with the realities of life with a sex offender, partners must deal with the significant burden of dealing with negative reactions from friends, family, and the community, helping to heal any children in the family, and coping with their own emotional and psychological needs. Relationships bring many challenges and the stigma of a relationship with an individual reintegrating into society post-conviction brings greater challenges still. Ninety-seven percent of the women in this study felt the relationship was worth attempts to navigate these additional obstacles. The "courtesy stigma" of female partners as a result of their association with a registered sex offender was well-elaborated among the women, including social marginalization, ostracization, disrespect, and judgment from family, friends, and the larger community. They provided few examples of support networks and were overwhelmingly left to fend emotionally for themselves.

There were several negative coping mechanisms that ranged from minor to much more serious. Cindy talked about unhealthy food choices, occasional overconsumption of alcohol, and love addiction.

> Oh yeah. My absolute defaults are plopping down in front of mindless TV. Real housewives of anything, when I'm not making the healthiest of food choices, you know that I'm kind of eating for comfort, not fuel. When instead of having two glasses of wine, I have three. I would say we both equally ... we both teeter with co-dependence and addiction. I mean, addiction is sitting right at my fingertips in all

of those areas. Same for him. I never had the sexual addiction. But I probably had some love addiction early on. I think I'm reformed in love addiction, and if this [relationship] doesn't work out I don't want to be with anybody ever again. I think that's another reason I stay because I knew, somewhere I knew early on that I had a role in this and had my own issues. And I would just as soon work on them in this house with this family then to move on and attract the same thing into my life.

Carolyn also discussed food addiction and issues with her health:

I'm going to be 54 and my children worry about me because, I hate to say this, but I could drop dead tomorrow. I just don't know what my life expectancy will be. And that's another way of dealing – with food. I've always had a weight problem, but food is my comfort. I don't smoke, I don't do drugs, I eat.

Carolyn's husband was incarcerated at the time of the interview on a sentence of ten years plus five years supervised probation in a plea agreement he accepted for a charge of rape with a weapon.

Other women revealed more serious negative outlets that resulted from the collateral consequences of their husband's sex offense conviction. Melissa used alcohol to numb her life:

We moved and then a couple years ago I started turning to alcohol to deal mentally with the family thing. As crazy as that is. Personally, I get upset when I say something like that. It's, the family is upsetting, and I abused alcohol to deal with it at times. I'm getting to the point where I worry that I'm just numbing the pain and not dealing with it.

Victoria discussed self-injury as a negative coping mechanism she used to deal with stress:

Yeah, that period [when he was in prison] was part of the time that I thought about leaving him. Mostly because of the impact I thought it might have on my career and everything I had worked for. But, you know, I turned to some negative coping mechanisms. I started self-injuring to deal with the emotional stress and I have very little trust in anybody. And I've had some very negative interactions through the years.

For several women, the stress of the situation resulted in serious depression and thoughts of suicide. Amber's partner was found guilty at trial of rape and served

Coping Strategies and (Re)Integration **217**

three years of a four-year sentence. This occurred prior to their dating relationship and he was honest with her in their second conversation. Her partner will spend 15 years on the sex offense registry and the consequences of that began to take its toll. Amber said:

> At one point I got really depressed and tried to commit suicide. But I got help for that and now I'm on anti-depressants and I'm in therapy myself. I do advocacy and that has really, really helped me. I'm in national groups and local groups.

Jessica also spoke of suicide attempts in her relationship: "This nearly killed both of us. He has attempted suicide once. I have attempted suicide once. But we have come through those dark days together … it nearly totally destroyed us." Robin revealed a suicide plot between her and her partner prior to his term of incarceration:

> Financially, he had lost his job, we were living on my social security disability income, which isn't a lot. So, we couldn't afford to go see a therapist. I mean, I was suicidal. I was ready to kill myself. I'll be completely honest, I was not ready, I mean, I was just like, how can I even, I mean, at one point, I had him convinced to commit suicide with me. I was like, let's just end our lives, this is because, this is so, it's like, how are we gonna be able to rise above this. I was ready and he said, "Fine, where do you want to do it? How do you want to do it?" When he said that I was like, "We can't do that." I mean, I changed my mind, but I was in a lot of pain and there are still times that I am. But, at the same time, I want to be hopeful.

At the time of the interview, Robin's partner was incarcerated on a plea agreement for almost 6.5 years for seven charges of sexual assault.

Jackie was still experiencing significant stress regarding her husband's offense and conviction. Prior to their marriage, almost 25 years earlier, her husband accepted a plea to a charge of molestation of a minor. He was sentenced to three years plus ten years on probation. Jackie knew of his history from their very first date. They relocated from a state where he was to be on the sex offense registry for life, to a state where he would be on the registry for ten years. After a decade on the registry, he successfully petitioned to be removed. This is rare and extraordinary as most offenders are never removed from the sex offense registry. Yet Jackie and her husband still lived with the collateral consequences of his long-past offense: stigma from friends, family, and the community. Jackie revealed: "When I'm not on my medication, it's like the pain is just something that's never gonna end, you know you just wanna, you know both of us at times, we just want to end it all."

Positive Coping Strategies

Many of the female partners of sex offenders had positive means of coping with the consequences of being in a relationship with an offender, including self-help groups or blogs, participation in counseling, involvement in meditation or physical fitness, personal spirituality or religion, or advocating for change in sex offender legislation.

Self-Help Groups

While support groups have existed for decades to provide a forum to share experiences and problems, there has not been much research in the area of effectiveness of support groups or self-help groups. Support groups are typically peer-led and may vary considerably in their constitution. A review of the literature on self-help groups of various kinds demonstrated strong support for their effectiveness in improving the well-being of participants. Such improvements included increased feelings of hope, greater knowledge regarding personal issues and strategies to deal with them, decreased feelings of isolation, greater social support networks, greater feelings of control, less feelings of stigma, and greater knowledge about additional helpful services (Worrall, Schweizer, Marks, Yuan, Lloyd, & Ramjan, 2018). Advantages to online self-help groups included convenience, cost-effectiveness, perpetual availability of the group, anonymity, and the ability to target a population unamenable to face-to-face support groups (Griffiths, 2017). While minimal research has assessed the effectiveness of online support groups, a handful of studies have used control groups and found efficacy in reducing depression (Griffiths, 2017; Griffiths, Mackinnon, Crisp, Christensen, Bennett, & Farrer, 2012).

Brandy was not fortunate enough to have a formal support group located near her. Her husband's offense of molestation of a family member occurred prior to their marriage and they married while he was serving the eight-year sentence that he accepted a plea to on the advice of his public defender. Her husband served four years and three years on parole. He will spend his life on the sex offense registry. She spoke of his family members as her informal support group:

> It is important to have a support group of people that understand what it's like. And that is lacking. Because sex offenders, at least here, are not allowed to have contact with other sex offenders outside of their therapy groups. So, it's unlikely that the wives would end up getting to know each other. It feels kind of like the wives are just sort of left out on their own. There's not any groups that I know of that address the needs of the family members. Thankfully his family members are super supportive and I can talk to them whenever I need help.

Coping Strategies and (Re)Integration **219**

Victoria found an outlet that worked for her when she needed to discuss the stress she experienced after her husband's plea to two counts of sexual molestation of minors. He received an eight-year sentence (seven years were suspended) and five years on probation. He will spend his life on the sex offense registry. Victoria found a hotline extremely helpful:

> You asked about ways that I cope and one of the ways is a hotline called the Samaritan, and they are based on the East Coast. They are an anonymous group and I've spent years talking on the phone to those people and they are the only place I've been able to go to not feel so isolated. They have talked me off the ledge many, many times.[1]

Courtney took the online support group one step further than most ... she started her own support group for the partners of sex offenders. Courtney knew about her partner's offense a week into dating. Her husband was found guilty at trial of molestation of a family member. He was sentenced to ten years and served just under five years. He will spend his life on the sex offense registry. Courtney said:

> Sometimes ... because I have an online support group, so sometimes I'll just read messages or post messages about what I'm going through. Sometimes I'll talk to [my husband] and tell him I'm having a hard time right now and that helps. Sometimes I just get angry and go hit a pillow or something. I go through all sort of different emotions about it and I find that it's easier for me to just talk about it. But, the only person, really is him that ... you know we just talk about it. Talking has been ... I mean, a lot of people don't know what this life is like and I think that a lot of people who know me that don't know would be very surprised. But, it really ... it's complicated and complex and hard at times, but this is the happiest I've ever been. I mean, on the face of it, I have a man that I love dearly. My children love him, and he loves them. But, on the other side, sometimes that interferes with all the other stuff, but I try to keep it all in perspective and know that it's not always going to be like this.

For some women a support group either was not a viable option or was not working, so they sought out a therapist.

Counseling

Counseling provided enormous benefits to many women in this research. For numerous women, therapy was coupled with medication for depression, and several women indicated their husbands participated in non-mandated counseling as well to deal with the continued negative impacts of their experiences. Julie had

220 Moving Forward

both an Al-Anon sponsor and a therapist to deal with issues after her husband's plea to a possession of child pornography charge.

> Well, I have a very good [Al-Anon] sponsor. And I talk to her a lot. I did find somebody else. I did find a counselor, it took me a while to find one, but I did find one. She asked me, after I told her how I'd gone to the others and I told her because all they wanted to know was what he had done and that wasn't the reason I was there, I was there for me, what he did was immaterial, I was there for me. And she laughed and said you know how long it takes me to get people to that point? (both laugh) But that's what 27 years in Al-Anon did for me.

While Julie wanted to focus on her own issues, feelings, and experiences in counseling, Martha found all of the therapy sessions centered around her husband's offense:

> Well, I have recently gone on anti-depressants and I have something that I take as needed for when I start to have anxiety attacks because I do have those. I try to talk to my family because they've always supported me and I know that they really truly care about him and they know what we've been through together and what he's been through. That's usually comforting. Um, I'm in therapy once a week and his offense is almost all that we talk about so, those are the biggest things.

Martha's husband molested a minor family member prior to their relationship. He served four years and two years on parole of a two- to six-year sentence and will be on the sex offense registry for the remainder of his life.

It is a balance for women involved with a registered sex offender to work on their own identity following the conviction of their partner and to work on their intimate relationship. Tara said:

> So, we've had some people supporting us, friends who stayed close to us. People don't agree with spending all the money on lawyers and stuff like that. They feel like he should just try to move on, but it's hard when he can't get a job. If he could get a job, I think he would just move on, but right now he can't get a job, so he's constantly dwelling on it, and constantly living it. He's had a couple of nervous breakdowns. We both see therapists. He sees a psychiatrist because he's on medication, and I go to a regular therapist every 2 weeks. Since this started I've gained 40 pounds and I cry a lot. (crying) Sorry.

Women who stayed in the relationship were caught between trying to support their husband and his struggle as a result of his registration status, and the stress that she was encumbered by as a result of her relationship with an RSO. Cindy discussed the importance of immediately finding a therapist to take care of her own needs:

> I mean initially … I think that he blamed me, that's part of his addiction and addictive thinking process. You know "I deserve this, we're not having sex enough." Those kind of things. I never got … I think that because of the way this happened, so traumatically kind of, I went to a therapist the next day. I've taken really good care of myself. I think that's one thing that's changed for both of us, we're now taking better care of ourselves on every level of our lives. You know, emotionally, spiritually, physically. I don't yet know how that's going to impact our marriage.

Crystal also discussed the significance of seeing a therapist for rebuilding her own identity:

> I do have a wonderful therapist. But in the beginning, I did think about suicide. And then later when I felt like committing suicide it was because I felt that my identity had been completely eradicated. My identity as a wife, as a student, as part of [his] family, being successful … and all the way around I felt like I was back to square one in my life. No husband, no career, no job … like I said, I have all this education, but couldn't find a job. It was ridiculous.

Overwhelmingly, the women stressed two positives that resulted from counseling: a reaffirmation in their own identity and a control of their lives; and an understanding that their husband was not his offense – the man is not his action. Cindy explained:

> For me, you have to get really okay with who you are. You either have to do that or you're going to fall apart and you're going to have a hard time getting through life. And so, I went ahead and decided to take care of myself and try to heal everything that shows up and needs to be healed.

Colleen confirmed the second positive that resulted from most of the women's encounters with therapy: "I've been learning through counseling to separate the man from the action." This separation is the first step to forgiveness.

Physical Fitness

Several women mentioned that one positive strategy for coping with stress involved physical fitness. Though perhaps untraditional, Linda's approach was effective for her:

222 Moving Forward

> When I am stressed out or feeling hurt or upset or angry or scared, I lie down on the mat in a dark room and go down into the feelings and cry and scream. I've got a wiffle bat and when I'm angry I'll swing at a pillow or hit a boxing bag.

Cindy preferred meditation and exercise for her stress reduction: "I work a recovery program, I hang out with people who get it, who are in similar situations with sex addiction. I do yoga, I have added a breathing practice to my life, and a meditation practice, and exercise." Colleen's husband was incarcerated at the time of the interview after being found guilty at a bench trial for molestation of a family member and receipt of child pornography. He received a sentence of 15 years. She had incorporated exercise and animal therapy into her routine to reduce stress:

> I have started Zumba. And I have a dog and two cats, so I firmly believe in animal therapy. And I'm trying Zumba, not too successfully. I have lost about 50 pounds in the past 3 years, so I'm doing good. Deep breathing, walking the dog a lot, it's wonderful. Walking is great exercise.

Research has demonstrated that exercise is effective in improving depression, which many of the wives in this study experienced (Blumenthal, Smith, & Hoffman, 2012). Additionally, activity with one's dog has been shown in research to have positive impacts such as stress reduction, lowered blood pressure, better mental health, and increased happiness (Epping, 2011; Griffin & Esposito, 2011).

Religion

Among the general public, many find strength in religion or spirituality. As discussed in Chapter 6, however, some areas of the country prohibit sex offenders from being in or near places of worship due to the presence of a daycare on-site. As such, many partners of sex offenders do not avail themselves of the benefits of places of worship. That said, not all places of worship have these prohibitions. Some couples in this research found comfort in church, and some women found strength either in organized religion or in spirituality, while their partner was incarcerated.

Several women spoke of themselves as spiritually connected. Maria explained that her spiritual connection with God helped significantly with stress. "Um, well I guess first and foremost, I believe in the spiritual power of God. I do a lot of praying and crying out to God to help and I believe He did help me." Stacey echoed similar themes:

> I guess, I mean, we're pretty spiritual people, we use our faith to remind us that we're not in control of everything and we kind of try

to enjoy our life. We're blessed a lot more than a lot of people in similar situations.

Alison reiterated the value of prayer for her emotional health: "Praying helps us get through, I'll be honest with ya, I don't know how people who don't have faith survive a lot of things in life."

Other women, who were not prohibited from attending organized religion services, chose to do so and found that activity beneficial for their mental health. Sarah discussed the first visit to church after her husband's plea to a charge of possession of child pornography. He was incarcerated at the time.

> I am, very much so [religious]. It's kind of funny because we've always gone to the same church within the community and we sit in the front pew. But I will admit, it was one of the hardest things I've had to do, when all this was hitting the newspapers was to walk into this church and to walk up to that front pew. Many of the people who were making the rude and nasty comments were people from my church. They actually used our church directory photo [for the news story]. Somebody had given it to the TV stations, so that was the photo they were using [of my husband]. There was a lot of issues with the church initially. Since then, however, there has been some wonderful people within the church. Somebody put it to me this way, when someone comes to grips with their own sins, they're much more forgiving of others. I have to almost believe that that may be the case.

Similarly, Donna found organized religion to be like a new beginning after her husband's imprisonment for a plea to a charge of molestation of a minor. She said:

> I really felt like church was an opportunity to essentially start over. I guess that's what I like about being Catholic is that you go to confession and you confess your sins and God forgives you and you can start anew. Even though you're going to make mistakes, because that's what we do as humans, we make mistakes, and you know, we just keep going and try to do better next time. And I felt like that's really what helped me to bring me through all of it.

Current research on the relationship between religious participation and coping with stress is lacking. Research from the 1990s linked religious participation to an increased ability to positively cope with stress and demonstrated that church groups acted as legitimate support systems (Bradley, 1995; Ellison, 1991). This research is almost 30 years old, however, and much may have changed since then. That said, for women in this research who were permitted to attend church, they realized positive benefits from religious involvement.

224 Moving Forward

Advocacy for Change

Research shows that altruistic behavior gives us a sense of purpose. Community social connections and advocating for something we believe in builds mental and emotional resilience and lowers stress levels (Karlis, 2017). Several women in this study mentioned involvement in advocacy groups as a positive coping strategy. Cheryl's partner accepted a plea to a charge of possession of child pornography prior to their relationship. She found out about his offense by reading about it in the newspaper. When she confronted him, he confessed. He received a sentence of 2.5 years on probation and will be on the sex offense registry for life. Cheryl said:

> I cry a lot. I get frustrated. But the best thing I can do is try to change the laws. Even though it's the hardest thing in the world to fight. We had 20 little baby steps of progress this year. But the best thing I can do is to try to change these laws. But it takes everything out of me.

Tricia was also involved in advocacy to help change the laws impacting her husband. She spoke about the impact on her:

> Sometimes I literally just lock myself in my room and have a good cry. But I can't afford to sit and stress about it. I have to find the solutions to it. The stress of it isn't going to get us anywhere, it's the solutions that will.

Prior to their marriage, Tricia's husband accepted a plea agreement to a charge of rape of his ex-wife. His sentence was ten months plus three years on probation; however, he served three years on a probation violation for leaving the county. Tricia knew about his offense reasonably early in their dating relationship. Tricia decided that was part of her husband's past and their future was ahead of them. Her husband will spend his life on the sex offense registry as a result of his offense.

It is widely evidenced that burnout can make activists mentally and physically exhausted. Studies have revealed, however, that the negative consequences of activism were linked to the systemic issues that demanded activism, rather than involvement in activism itself (Bell, 2018). That said, it remains necessary to balance involvement in activism with one's personal life. The women in this research participating in advocacy were doing so out of necessity. They were working to change the laws that directly and significantly impacted their partners, themselves, and their children; if they do not attempt to change the laws, who will?

Reintegration of Offenders and Their Families Into Communities

Sex offenders, like other offenders, overwhelmingly return to society and need to be reintegrated into communities and usually into families as well. Consideration of reintegration of an offender into the family can be complicated and involves the offender's supervision officials, sex offender treatment personnel, input from family regarding their preference on reunification, input from child welfare agencies, legal input that may involve issues of parental rights or restrictions on access to minors, as well as complex challenges by the non-offending parent (Center for Sex Offender Management, 2005). Yet "it is neither reasonable, realistic, nor advantageous to wholly prohibit reunification efforts. Some sex offenders may pose a relatively low degree of risk to reoffend" (CSOM, 2005: 2). The guiding principle therefore needs to be the best interests of the victim. For some families healing is enhanced by family reunification (Association for the Treatment of Sexual Abusers, 2005).

With regards to community reintegration, sociologists and criminologists have known for decades the value of social ties and social networks in reintegrating an offender into society. *Social capital* is the term used to describe the benefits of social networks. In neighborhoods without social capital,

> higher-income families have fled; neighborhood resources such as schools, churches, and stores have broken down; and joblessness and poverty have taken hold. Role models disappear, informal neighborhood supervision becomes less prevalent, and residents become less and less willing to feel pride or to take responsibility in their community.
>
> *(Burchfield & Mingusm, 2008: 357)*

Both this study and others have demonstrated the need for reasonably paying jobs that are close to affordable housing, and reintegration into social networks of family, friends, and the larger community for sex offenders to remain offense-free (Kruttschnitt, Uggen, & Shelton, 2000). Studies have illustrated a myriad of barriers to accessing social capital that inhibit successful community integration for sex offenders and their families. Multiple reasons may explain these barriers, at both the individual and structural levels.

The stigma and accompanying shame of being labeled a sex offender in American society is profound. Because of this stigma, some sex offenders attempt to conceal their offender status and label, which brings with it a voluntary withdrawal from society and social ties (Goffman, 1963). At the structural level there are informal social controls such as community watch programs, flyer distribution, denial from participation in community programs, and harassment as attempts to keep an offender and his family out of the community. Also, at the structural level are formal social controls that deny offenders and their families social capital and community integration: community notification programs, residency restrictions, and parole restrictions. The result is that sex offenders and their families may end up residing in neighborhoods with lower social capital and higher levels of social disorganization (Mustaine, Tewksbury, & Stengel, 2006).

What has occurred is that laws and policies designed to lower the rate of sex offenses and sex offense recidivism instead work to negatively impact the

226 Moving Forward

reintegration of sex offenders, which can actually increase sexual recidivism (Meloy, 2005).

> [T]he sexuality of a sex offender is widely regarded as monstrous. We do not merely hate the sin; we hate the sinner, and we want the sinner to be removed from our presence, because the sex offender crosses boundaries that secure our sense of sexual identity and order. However, if law functions in part as the expression of disgust or horror, the result may be an unjust exclusion of sex offenders from the human community, or more precisely, the community of citizens who are regarded, by the United States legal system, as capable of acting as free and responsible agents ... sex offenders function as scapegoats.
>
> *(Douard, 2007: 37)*

Without doubt, laws express a society's social morality and the resultant punishment from a broken law can express social condemnation. We live in a society wherein social beliefs inform the law and the law reciprocally informs our social beliefs.

> The voting public has demanded tougher legislation with regard to sex offenders, and their demands represent the ideological and moral interests of the social norm. Their interests have both shaped and been shaped by sex offender legislation ... Political need coupled with high public demand for stricter sex offender legislation is creating a cycle of repression likely to result in the social death of numerous [sex offenders].
>
> *(Megale, 2011: 128–129)*

To create a safe society, a balance is needed between criminal laws and societal institutions (Megale, 2011). The push in the United States, however, toward overcriminalization of sexual offenses has resulted in repressive legislation which has not served to decrease rates of sexual offending.

Elizabeth found irony in the overcriminalization of sexual offenses in the United States, given the propensity in this country for "all things sex" in entertainment.

> Uh, it just astounds me that this nation is the number one exporter of sex to the world. We export it in our movies, in our music, in our literature, in our magazines, and I'm not just talking mentioning the word sex, we export porn. We export hardcore sex, weird stuff, weird shit, that is our main export. And yet we have puritanical attitudes about the very thing that we export. We're a twisted little country when it comes to our sexual attitudes. I mean, how can we export the attitudes that we have about sex in our movies, of anything goes, and then slap the wrist of a

17, just turned 18-year-old kid and put him in prison for 25 years? It's wrong, it's twisted, and for those people that belong in prison, they are truly a sex offender, what are we doing to help them? Nothing. It's, I've used this phrase before in dealing with Department of Corrections and I've asked them, "When are you just going to be honest and change the name of what you're called to the Department of Human Warehousing?" Talk about recidivism and wanting to eliminate that yet you do nothing to rehabilitate or help those inmates who are getting ready to be released, to get ready to live out here. We do nothing!

Examples of overcriminalization can be evidenced in the prosecution of statutory offenses, the application of the sex offense registry and collateral consequences of this registry, and residency restrictions in states that apply such restrictions, to name a few. What has resulted is a system that the public largely supports, despite that empirically it does not work to protect individuals from sexual violence. Support of the existing system is rooted in media-driven hysteria, propaganda, and fear of the unknown regarding sexual offenses and sexual offenders. The public is left to ponder: if we don't use this system, what horrible things will happen? April's frustration with the system led her to the suggestion of just starting over:

I would wipe the slate clean and start over again. And I would probably, I think I would do more evidence, and research some studies. I think I would try to bring some science, at least some evidence to the table and not quite so much emotion. I mean, I wonder if some of these laws aren't based on public opinion. I'll go a step further and say that I think that the media tells people what to think. I don't know that the laws as they currently have them, I don't see them being based on the research. I don't see why the laws have gone so severe in the direction they've gone other than it's good voting material.

Despite a decrease in sexual offenses in recent years, laws are being passed like there is a crisis of sexual violence in America. And stricter laws are fueled by tightening laws in nearby regions. A politician fears an influx of offenders from a neighboring jurisdiction that recently passed a harsh sex offender law and in a panic of media hysteria, that jurisdiction passes a new law as well (Hobbes, 2019). Despite evidence that these laws do not work, jurisdictions do not voluntarily loosen restrictions on sex offenders. In fact, "no enhancement of sex offense registry laws had ever failed a floor vote in a state legislature…many pass unanimously and few earn any critical media coverage" (Hobbes, 2019: np). April continued about politicians:

Politicians everywhere have gotten on the bandwagon of running their campaigns on this sex offender thing. And it does gain votes. I completely

228 Moving Forward

understand why people would vote it in … I think that while politicians use this type of offense to further their career, I also think that
there's a lot of district attorneys who do the same thing. The people who
are doing really bad things, they need to be stopped, but let's not lump
everybody into one category and, I mean, I think I read that the young-
est person on the registry is 8 years old. How did that happen? How do
you put an 8-year-old on the sex offender registry? What's wrong with
that picture? I guess I don't know … I know I have my own biases, and
I try very diligently not to be completely biased, but on the other hand,
things like that just … I mean, there are sick people in the world. The
other side of that coin is, what if they were accused of such a sick thing
and they didn't do it? Then what? I don't get it. Until politicians, until
there's some equality or rationality brought to the table, I think it's just
going to keep spinning.

April's partner will spend his life on the sex offense registry for a plea he accepted
to what he alleged were false charges of possession of child pornography. He said
that in a bitter divorce, his ex-wife planted the images on his computer. Julie
shared similar sentiments about the roles of politicians in creating fear in the
public:

I think my own personal opinion is that the politicians need something
to stir people up and so all you have to do is say sex offender and people
go nuts and then the media gets a hold of it and stirs it up even more and
that's what gets people elected. And that really irritates me because you
know I belong to an advocacy group and of course we all look at everything that's out there in the media and a lot of people who talk about
sex offenders and sex offenses have no clue what they're talking about.
You know and it's real easy to have an opinion on something you have
no facts for and a lot of them have no facts whatsoever. The news media,
they talk about, oh you need to prepare your children for stranger danger, oh baloney. Most children out there who are molested are molested
by someone they know and trust, not by a stranger … they're a bunch of
sheep … nobody looks things up for themselves.

Leah was more optimistic about the possibility of change in the future:

I don't know. It's hard. Very, very, very hard, but I have my faith. And I do
believe, it's going to take a while, but I believe that somewhere down the
line, something's going to happen where it will prove that the laws do
no good. It's already been proven a couple of times, but I just wish that
they would not be afraid to stand up against some of this stuff because
I'm not. But I don't have any money to fight and stand up. Because,

Coping Strategies and (Re)Integration **229**

you know, I ... it's just ... I'm just tired of people being controlled and told ... and there are some sick people out there, but there are also a lot of innocent people that, you know a guy peeing in public, how many years is he going to get and get thrown on the registry for that? My nephew got a naked text picture and he was going to forward it and I told him, "No! You do not do anything, nothing!" And he didn't, but the funny thing is that they don't realize that the simplest things, the littlest things they do and they're on the registry. Not just 10 years or something but could be for life.

Yolanda did not see change forthcoming until the sex offense registry impacted the life of someone "important"[2] in society.

I said to somebody one day, "He would have been better off killing somebody. At least we would have been left alone. At least people wouldn't go by our house and point." I mean, you can see us on Google, you can look at us on the internet ... where is our life? It's just sometimes too damn hard and I have to fight some days to get out of bed. But I have to fight for me and for him and at the end of the day we have to hold our heads up high because we did the right thing. No matter what the government says, we did the right thing. [Yolanda is referring to the fact that when her husband confessed to molesting their child, he turned himself in to law enforcement and accepted a plea]. And if they can't see that, screw them. But, then again, we still have those obstacles and we have to live by those rules...the rules that ... they just keep tacking on these restrictions and it would have been better for him to run somebody over or stabbed them or shot them, gone to prison for 10 years or 15 years and even though he would have been on parole, once he was off ... I mean, there's no registry for a killer. There's no registry for a thief or a crackhead or somebody who is drug dealer. And I understand the severity of his crime, but we shouldn't have a double standard. And I think that if some Senator or some higher-up had a child that was on the registry, they might look at it and say, "Huh, we might need to change some of this." But until it happens to somebody important, it's not going to change.

It is within this environment of fear that overcriminalization of sexual crimes continues with no resultant improvement in sexual offense rates.

The more the public fears, the more far-reaching laws make sense to a populace that is not impacted by the collateral consequences of these laws. Tracy discussed her views on the difficulty of reintegrating with so many legal obstacles:

Wow! So, they keep making all these rules where they make reintegration impossible because you've got to have housing and you've got to have employment and you need family support and you need religion, and in some states they won't let you go to church if you're an offender, but then they won't let you leave. (laughs) So, you know where's the sense? Because, you know, when you read an article about offenders and you read all the comments and all the despicable things that the public writes. They all say things like, "Castrate them all and put them on a slow boat to China." You know what, if there was a slow boat to China and China had what we needed with housing and employment and we could all just kind of survive and be happy together, I'm ready for, I'd be happy to go. Because what we're doing here with the labels and all these restrictions, it's just inhumane. It's out of control.

Modern-day Scarlet-lettering of sex offenders and their families is not working. Marginalizing offenders for decades (or a lifetime) from housing, employment, communities, schools, parks ... from life ... is not working. In this war against sex offenses and offenders, the American public has willingly relinquished some constitutional protections, such as our guaranteed right against *ex post facto* punishment and due process rights (Megale, 2011). And we have applied these laws to children.

Statistics show that approximately 24,000 of the registered offenders in the United States are juveniles. Of those, about 3,900 are less than 12 years old; and about 8,000 are between 12 years old and 14 years old (Der Bedrosian, 2018). Currently, 40 states put offenders that are adjudicated as juveniles on the sex offense registry. Nineteen states have no minimum age requirement for inclusion on the sex offense registry. This means that an 8-year-old, for example, would be listed with the same guidelines as an adult. Research revealed that the focus on punishing juveniles as adults decreased the likelihood of high school graduation, increased the likelihood of recidivism and suicide attempts, and did not reduce sexual violence (Der Bedrosian, 2018). The consequences for these youth are the same as those for adults, including residency restrictions, restrictions on being with other minors (including in their own home), church and travel restrictions, community stigma, community notification, and later in life impediments in finding employment and relationships (Der Bedrosian, 2018). Crystal discussed the role of fear in the creation of sex offender legislation:

> I think they've just created so many restrictions that people can't reintegrate into normal life. And it's become such a boogeyman that we don't ... people are terrified as if sex offenders have no self-control and are just going to jump out from behind bushes and attack children. Which is another thing, it's totally oriented towards children now. There are lots of sex offenses that have nothing to do with children, but if you listen to politicians and legislators, the tagline is always "we have

to protect our children," which leads everybody to believe that all sex offenders are engaging in crimes with children.

So, where do we go from here? In the experiences of female partners of sex offenders, how do we successfully reintegrate offenders into the community?

The women in this study suggested several measures to reintegrate offenders into the community with less stigma and decreased likelihood of reoffending. These suggestions included: the ability to seek out therapeutic guidance for offenses that had not been reported to the police; increased judge's discretion and changes to the registry and punishment scheme for sex offenses; and greater support from criminal justice personnel during periods of probation and/or parole.

Angela's husband spent 5 years in prison on a plea to possession and distribution of child pornography prior to their marriage. He will spend life on the sex offense registry. Angela spoke about the importance of an offender being able to get help without fear of reprisal in order to cease offending:

> I really wish that our society would take these individuals, our husbands, our boyfriends, our brothers, our fathers, our uncles, because unfortunately, most of them are relatives or close to us, and I really wish they would send them to a place where they can get help without fear of being outcast from society and thrown in prison. I think it's a really tragic situation that we basically give them, the bulk of them, a scarlet letter. It's hard for, and no wonder so many crimes and victims never have a voice, because they're too afraid to speak up for fear of their loved ones going to jail or worse. The individuals who might be committing these crimes, a lot of them, feel guilty about it but never stop because they can't go get help. They're sent to jail and away from their family and unfortunately, in this country, it's easier to get away with murder, but if you pee in public or you have photos of children on your computer, you're basically, you're written off forever its very tragic. I would make it that you could go to a place and find help for an offense, not go to jail and be charged with a sex crime. I would take so many things off the registry like, urinating in public, being 18 and having a girlfriend who's 16, or people who had sex in their house but their window was open and some kid saw it so they got charged with a sex crime. So many laws I think shouldn't be on the books and are. I would start by removing those as sex crimes. Those are just stupid mistakes. For other people, I would like to find a place that was between prison and treatment and counseling. Where they could go and say, "I have this problem." They could enter anonymously and really get help instead of just saying, "Okay, you're in prison for this many years, now you're no longer a member of society, forever." Yes, some people definitely need to go to prison. Maybe if those people had help before they got to that point,

maybe there wouldn't have been so many hurt children or women in the world.

Jenny advocated for a similar type of program that would be socially acceptable and without a stigma:

> [Offenders] would be able to go to somewhere without any kind of stigma and get evaluated and get treatment and not fear that they were going to be put on some list that exposes them. And, you know, make it socially acceptable to do this. Because there's got to be prevention! But, being the way things are, the only way to discover that it's a problem for somebody is for there to be a victim. That's wrong!

At the time of the interview, Jenny's husband was in prison awaiting sentencing on a plea on a charge of molestation of a minor family member.

Suggestions to facilitate reintegration also revolved around allowing judges some discretion, and changes to the sex offense registry and the punishment scheme generally. Although tiered classification is suggested in SORNA, many states do not implement a tiered classification system, or have a system of classifying offenders based on the legal classification of the offense, rather than a risk assessment of the offender. What is also lacking is the judge's discretion to withhold the sex offender label and sex offense registry if the offender is not deemed a risk to society. Once on the sex offense registry, the litany of collateral consequences, for both the offender and his family, begin, all of which impede successful community reintegration.

Nicole spoke about the sex offense registry and her belief that treatment would be a better objective for society.

> So that list [the sex offender registry] isn't making anybody safe, it's just making people think that they're safe. And they're spending millions and millions of dollars. And if I were the Great Chief I would take all those millions of dollars and open centers for treatment. I would make it so easy to get treatment. If I could change things, I would shut the registry down, and I would make healing our objective. And the ones that are predators, you can lock them up forever. But that's going to be so few people.

Tracy's suggestions involved many changes to existing legislation:

> I'm going to make it so that the Romeo and Juliet's with a 4-year age difference do not get put on the registry. Sexting, again, between a girlfriend and boyfriend, whether you are a minor or not, would not put you on the registry. That depending on the scale of the offense, there would be a private registry that would just be for the authorities, that

Coping Strategies and (Re)Integration **233**

the public would not see, and that you would have a chance to get off of that registry in 5 or 10 years if you have not reoffended. Um … what else … I'm trying to think; I have a gigantic list of all the bills we've tried to pass over the years. Um, of course, you need to tell [offenders] what the laws are. If you are telling [sex offenders] that they can or cannot be here, you need to actually tell them that. In my mind, the possession of child porn should not have a mandatory minimum and should not be the severe sentence that it is. If you're producing or profiting from it, then yes, [prison] time, but not just because you downloaded two pictures or someone sent you a picture and you had no idea what it was [and you opened it]. So, that's where I would start. And, of course, that an accusation alone is not enough to convict. Yeah, so that needs to be fixed.

Most of the women interviewed spoke of the need for offenders to be handled on a case-by-case basis and they expressed feelings that sex offenders were all "lumped into one group." Stacey said:

I would definitely make it a case-by-case punishment. I feel like there's this blanket stereotype and the media does not help with this at all. Just a sex offender stamp, ugh, evil people, keep them away from society. So, I would definitely change the laws to differentiate between who's really dangerous and who just messed up.

Julie echoed similar feelings:

I'd change the punishment to fit the crime. Right now the laws in [my state] are one size fits all and pardon my French but that sucks. And if I could change anything it would be changing the way people look at sexual offenses and what is considered a sexual offense as opposed to lumping everything together and saying we don't like this so we're gonna throw the book at you.

Likely part of this sense that offenders are all lumped into one group comes from the fact that both contact offenses and non-contact offenses (child pornography) can (and often do) result in lifetime on the sex offense registry and the many collateral consequences accompanying that designation. Suzanne spoke of the need for greater judge's discretion in sentencing:

I would change the whole system. I think it's a farce and if anything it doesn't work and I don't think it's something that the state or the legislature should deal with. It should be dealt with on an individual basis by a judge. To find out they are able to go back and retroactively put people on the list or change the fact that you only had so many years and now

234 Moving Forward

it's life … they're saying that it's there to protect the community, but it's not. It's there to punish the people. You're basically punishing these people. I would rather know that there was drug dealer in my neighborhood rather than a sex offender. I mean, I've met a lot of those people on the list and they're good people. They make one mistake and then have to pay for it for the rest of their life!

Natasha also felt strongly that punishments should be individualized. Prior to meeting, her husband was sentenced on a plea agreement to 16 years for statutory rape. He served eight years and eight years on parole and will be on the sex offense registry for his entire life. Natasha spoke of this as overcriminalization:

I would probably make the laws more based on individual offenses instead of just grouping together a big bunch of people. And I understand that that could be costly, but it is a very dangerous thing to lump someone like my husband who's crime was, again it was wrong, but it was very specific and with someone he knew, which they say is a lot of the time how these things happen, but you know, he thought he was in love with her. He wasn't seeking to hurt someone. His crime wasn't malicious like the man who stalks someone and rapes her or the guy who hides behind the bush and steals little children. But, unfortunately, because of the way the system works everybody is grouped together and when somebody hears "a sex offender did this" on the news, they automatically look at all sex offenders the same. So, I would advocate a system based more on the truth and individual circumstances. And one that was based more on knowledge than ignorance. People think they're so educated when they go online and see there's a sex offender in my neighborhood, but they're not. They're just operating on ignorant knowledge I guess I would call it because they don't know what those crimes actually mean. They don't know what non-violent aggravated assault means, they don't have the details, so they just can't make informed decisions. I also don't think that lifetime registration is beneficial. I'm not convinced that posting all this information online is beneficial to society period. But, specifically lifetime registration. I think if someone could prove for a certain number of time, 10 years, 15 years, based on their crime, that maybe they kind of have earned a little bit of a break. He's done nine years. He's still doing his time out here with all these restrictions, but basically society says that there's no amount of time that you could do that would suffice for what you did. You know, what you did was so bad that we're just going to watch you forever. I just don't think that's reasonable.

Yolanda discussed the unfairness of the retroactivity of legislation; specifically that the length of time on the registry could be increased as offenses are

Coping Strategies and (Re)Integration 235

recategorized by the legislature. Her husband agreed to ten years on the sex offense registry as part of his plea to molestation of a minor. The legislature in her state reclassified offenses, including the offense committed by her husband, which would mean a longer registration period due to the retroactive application of the reclassification. Yolanda said:

> You know, you want to become involved [with changing legislation], but it's taboo and nobody is going to support you, and nobody wants to be associated with you because it's not politically correct to do. And I know that it's the way our country is. They react. You know, a child gets hurt and people are outraged. But it's just gotten out of hand and I don't believe that it's the way ... it's unconstitutional. You know, we pay taxes, but my husband has no rights. We can't go to the park and listen to a free concert because it's at a park. He was only supposed to be on the registry for 10 years and once it got to be 9 years the state said they were going to change it and make registered offenders 20 years, 30 years, or life. Now, how do they do that when it was what you agreed upon when you took your plea? We didn't go to trial. He agreed to that because we thought it was okay and that we could deal with it. It's so massively unfair!

Women also spoke of various instances of harassment of themselves and their partners by probation or parole officers. As well, the women discussed specifically the need for the criminal justice system to be supportive in efforts to reintegrate offenders into society. Diana's husband was fortunate to find employment, but experienced difficulty balancing employment with parole supervision.

> The parole officer and the court system, it's like they don't want him to succeed. When he was doing the year supervision, it was like "We don't like this. Or hey come down here between 8 am and 9 am for your visit because we know you have to work from 8 am to noon." And his boss is like, "Listen I know you have to do this every week, but I'm losing 3 hours, this is bullshit." They need more support for the offenders. I mean, how do you think men are going to come back into the community without helping them or giving the tools they need?

When offenders are headed back into society, the goal needs to be successful reintegration with as few disruptions as possible. Continually adding sex offender requirements makes compliance more difficult, violation more likely, makes the work of law enforcement officials more time consuming, and does not reduce sexual violence. Susan said:

> To create a safe society you have to integrate the offender back in as much as possible. If they're willing to comply and be responsible, the

236 Moving Forward

only way that you can create a safe society is by allowing them back into their family and creating a stable environment. Because just putting them on a list and punishing them for the rest of their lives, many are homeless, many are in shelters, many of them don't register because of the implications involved. And I think that another thing that needs to be dealt with is the politicians involved, you know, every year, they create another law that makes it harder for sex offenders, and easier for the politicians to get re-elected.

And there continues to be little pushback to the passage of new sex offender legislation. Sabrina sighed: "Nobody cares. Everybody thinks we're the scum of the Earth. They think our husbands are scum and they think we're scum for marrying them." And this stereotype remained true regardless of the seriousness of the sexual offense. Mary knew about her husband's plea to statutory rape on their very first date. He served a term of six years on probation and will spend his life on the sex offense registry. She elaborated the impact of his offense on their long-term relationship:

My basic story is that yes, I've been with this person 9 years. Because of the laws and the way they are right now and the impact they have on families, we have not gotten married. I would say that, um, definitely, I would imagine that for all sex offenders, that the public would want for them to form a stable relationship with an adult female, or male, I don't know if that really matters. That what the public would really want is for that person to be rehabilitated and for that person to be in a stable, healthy relationship with an adult and you know, move on with their life. Because I think that would probably make them less likely to be out, you know, having some deviant sexual behaviors. I mean, I think that's what the public would want. But the way the laws are now it definitely discourages that. I think that I am a very unusual person, I can deal with a lot. But I think a lot of people would have been gone a very long time ago, because of the stress and the isolation, I think a lot of people would have cracked and given up this relationship a long time ago and you know, that's what these laws are causing, they're making it harder for these people to have a stable relationship because really, there aren't a whole lot of people who'd be willing to stay in one like this.

Sarah reiterated the importance of being present for her husband upon his release from prison for a possession of child pornography charge. At the time of the interview Sarah's husband was incarcerated for five years after accepting a plea agreement.

He's a good man. He was a good man before this and he's a better man after he got counseling and he'll be a great man when he comes home....

The women I talk to talk about their relationships with their husbands, are like who are these guys on the inside who say that their families have abandoned them? It's heartbreaking. Those are the guys who are going to come home and reoffend. Because there's nobody there for them.

A balance creates a safer society: a balance between criminal laws and societal institutions (Megale, 2011). In the United States, we have not struck that balance in terms of sex offender legislation: how do we move past our overcriminalization of sexual offenses and repressive legislation and try to make a legitimate attempt at decreasing rates of sexual offenses?

Policy Thoughts

In light of the #MeToo Movement, some of the women in this study felt as though sex crime legislation had become excessively harsh. Alison noted:

I think the pendulum has swung too far in the opposite direction. I can remember the time if a woman yelled rape it was always her fault, she must have did something to egg the guy on. Well, now it's gone the other direction where it's automatically the guy's fault whether he's guilty or not. I think there should be a medium ground there somewhere.

April discussed similar concerns about sexual offenses and accusations in the 21st century:

I still wonder how this happened in a modern society. And I'll go one step further and say, these people that have these memories. I have a memory 20 years ago that this happened and the next thing you know, somebody's in prison. You're like, huh? Wait a minute, what happened to evidence, what happened to a trial? I think there needs to be something substantial that says it happened, other than someone's old memory. I don't know, I just see this as being a very tough way to go in life. And then I think about schoolteachers … how do they do it? How do they go into a classroom with a bunch of kids, knowing that the mere words out of their mouth cannot only cost them their job but their freedom and their, you know … no, no, and no, I wouldn't do it. And today, the only thing I find surprising, and yet not, is that in many ways, a registered sex offender might be viewed worse than a terrorist. I mean, the point is that nobody wants to hear the story because they don't want to believe it.

How can we balance community safety and protection with reasonableness of legislation? How can we maintain a society in which one is innocent until proven guilty while safe-guarding individuals from sexual violence?

238 Moving Forward

> There are missing links between researchers, policymakers, and the law.
>
> Two key relationships are missing. First, policy makers typically do not consult with researchers prior to proposing and passing these policies. Second, policy makers do not seem to even consider the existing research when drafting and voting on these policies. As a result of these missing relationships, there are no structured feedback mechanisms with which either to stop these (ineffective) policies from being passed or to convince policy makers to repeal existing policies. Furthermore, when these policies are repealed, it has historically been a result of court rulings rather than a proactive decision by policy makers.
>
> *(Socia, 2014: 182)*

Therefore, when the public sees a policymaker move to repeal a law dealing with sex offenses, it likely has been in response to a court ruling elsewhere in the state. For example, in separate rulings in New Hampshire, local level residency restrictions were ruled unconstitutional. As a result, policymakers moved to repeal residency restrictions throughout the state. This was not a result of the significant research indicating that residency restrictions do not work. Instead it was an economic decision based on the fact that one bill repealing all SORRs would be more prudent than lawsuits that may result from attempting to enforce SORRs (Socia, 2014).

From a researcher's perspective, some suggestions moving forward involve evidence-based policymaking that is broadly criminal justice based, but clearly relevant for sex offender legislation. Research needs to be quickly and proactively disseminated to policymakers: whether this means individual researchers disseminating to policymakers their findings or writing policy briefs for organizations like the Association for the Treatment of Sexual Abusers for dissemination. While journals such as *Criminology & Public Policy* are a positive mechanism between researchers and policymakers, this still relies on active searching by policymakers. Also useful would be advisory committees that address sexual offender legislation, comprised of researchers and policymakers. These advisory committees would provide policymakers with current research regarding proposed ordinances so that decisions could be well-informed as opposed to emotionally driven. Researchers, and organizations working to counter stereotypes regarding sexual offenders, need to outreach resources to both policymakers and the public that counter the negative stigma surrounding sexual offenders. The focus needs to be on research instead of the hype that has historically driven sex legislation (Socia, 2014).

While recidivism rates vary in the research, and are influenced by a myriad of factors, what is clear is that the longer an individual remains in the community offense-free, the less likely they are to recidivate (Langan, Schmitt, & Durose, 2003). This finding should have significance for the length of time an offender is on the registry. Natasha had some thoughts about the registry and the public's sense of safety:

> How much do we really have a right to know and what gives us that right? Just because we're born in America doesn't mean we have a right to everybody's business. So, I just, I think there are a lot of flaws in the system and a lot of false security brought on by these things. People feel safe because the people who have been convicted of sexual offenses are [listed] online? That's just a false sense of security.

There should be mechanisms for removal from the registry based on participation in treatment, risk assessment, and length of time offense-free. The registry should not be a blanket lifetime punishment for an ever-widening list of crimes ranging from statutory offenses to possession of child pornography to violent rape. There needs to be a point at which the offender can move on. Brandi noted:

> When I went in front of the [sex offender panel in my state], I let them know that the one thing my mother taught me was forgiveness. And my mother was sexually molested by my grandfather. And when my grandfather was dying from leukemia, my mother went every day at lunch to help him sit up enough so he could look out the window, look outside at the beautiful world. My mother cared for him because she forgave him. I would like to see the United States show forgiveness. I would like to see where the law allows for people in our situation to say, "Look. Look at how good I am, look at how good I've done. I haven't done anything to violate these restrictions you put on me. Now let me be free of this weight around my neck, this albatross. Give my family some relief." I would like to see a government forgive. I would like to see them have a rule, a law, that honestly and truly applies to everyone. Okay? Because the law believes what you are, you always are, you're not fixing it. I would like the law to consider the children of the offenders and what they have to live with. The stress those children have to live with. It's like the families don't matter at all, basically. I want to see a law that protects the families. Really protects them.

Community notification and registration is a major obstacle in reintegration, and the longer the period of registration, the more challenging it becomes to reintegrate. Tracy explained the feelings of fear still present in her:

> We do worry. We do worry that we're going to come home one day and that the house is going to be burned down and, we have five dogs, and that they're all going to be dead. I didn't realize that that was a worry that [my husband] has until the other day when he told me, "Every time I

turn the corner on the street, first thing I do is look to see if the roofline is still there," and I asked him why, and he said, "to see if someone has set fire to the house." And I actually think about it too. All the time.

The importance of judging an individual based on more than one act in their life was conveyed by Stacey:

> You can't judge a person by a few actions in their life, you have to get to know them, I've known [my husband] for over a decade now and despite him screwing up a few times in our marriage, he's a really good person. I just tell people, you can't look at someone and judge them by something they've done, because we've all screwed up and I would hope that someone would give me the chance to make up for it when I'screwed up.

At some point, the monitoring of an offender who is no longer a risk, or very low risk, needs to end or be limited strictly to law enforcement personnel. Without an "end in sight," offenders have no goals to strive for, no reason to remain offense-free. Katherine said:

> It's surprising that there are so many people from so many walks of life with so many stories that ... once they paid their dues, supposedly, through jail time or probation or whatever, that it isn't over. It isn't over until they're in the grave.

Other factors can also reduce the likelihood of sexual recidivism: community-based treatment, intensive supervision programs, reducing transience, and for the highest risk offenders broad-based community notification (Duwe & Donnay, 2008). Releasing sexual offenders into the community after incarceration without proper reintegration skills sets them up to reoffend and provides a foundation in society for a cycle of revictimization. We need to focus on job skills and helping offenders attain gainful employment in proximity to their residence. Removal of the sex offender's place of employment from the sex offense registry would be a step in the right direction in terms of increasing the likelihood of offender employment. Reduction of transience would be assisted by the removal of residency restrictions. If policymakers and the public could rationally evaluate the evidence and move past the emotional hype and stereotypes of "stranger-danger" and "sex offenders cannot be rehabilitated," we may get to a point of passing sex offense legislation that actually reduces sexual violence and increases public safety.

The labeling of sex offenders in American society extends far beyond the offender, to his family members and significant partner. Partners were subjected to the shame and embarrassment of being tied to the stereotypical "monster." The women in this research chose to stay with their partners and were therefore

Coping Strategies and (Re)Integration **241**

implicated in the criminal justice system response and required to abide by restrictions implemented by a fear-based public. Controls were both formal and informal and persisted decades after an individual's offense. Many of the women felt victimized by the system. Andrea explained:

> We're the forgotten ones, we're the victims from what our loved ones did, from all those laws that are affecting our loved ones. I have no criminal record whatsoever. I have a retirement plan, I have excellent credit, I'm a tax-paying American and I'm suffering every day because I love somebody.

Laurie described similar feelings:

> Him being on the registry doesn't just affect him. It affects his family, it affects his friends, it affects any significant other, be that me or anyone else. It affects any future children he may have, it affects every single thing. It does.

Most of the women wished society could get to a point where an offender could find "redemption" for his misdeed. Natasha's husband pled guilty to statutory rape prior to their marriage. He served eight years and eight years of parole but will be on the sex offense registry for his lifetime. This devastated her:

> You know, sometimes you just have to hear the whole story and give people a chance and just be a little more open-minded. We pride ourselves in this country on being so open-minded and so accepting and that's really just not the case. It's not the way it really is. We're open-minded towards things that we want to be open-minded towards. If it's something that we're advocating then yeah, we're super open-minded, but if it's something that doesn't fit in our box, then we are very closed off. There are people who are incarcerated who have done things repeatedly and just can't seem to behave in society, but there are a lot of people who are incarcerated that you know, maybe they were young or maybe they were just being stupid, but that doesn't mean that there's no hope for them and that they should just be shunned and locked up forever and throw away the key.

Kelly's husband also pled guilty to a statutory rape offense. She had similar thoughts on offenders being able to re-establish themselves.

> One of the things that the laws do not consider at all are the effects of the laws on the people around sex offenders and the attitude of irredeemability. They're often not given the chance to re-establish themselves and

use their gifts toward living a full and beneficial life to their families, those around them, and society. There's an attitude of writing these people off and the sins of the father will be revisited on their friends and their wives and their children. It's an archaic way of looking at punishment and sexuality. Look at the world we're living in now, sex is so glorified, and children are seeking it out without regards to the consequences ... the laws are set up to punish them for the rest of their lives. But we're persecuting them and they're not given a chance to live their lives and put this behind them. I mean, it's ridiculous. It's out of control. It's the witch hunt of the 21st century!

The United States employs a crime control model when dealing with sexual offenders. Laws continue to be passed as though we are in an epidemic of sexual offenses, several of these laws infringing on the due process rights of offenders. Legislators and politicians continue to focus on stereotypical cases that generate fear in the public, successfully diverting attention from the structural elements in society that perpetuate sexual victimization. Education is key to solving this issue; informed by timely communication between researchers, policymakers, and legislators. Janet conveyed:

Educate the public. I mean, these things are just getting more and more out of hand. You have people that don't understand and they don't want to understand because fear is in control. And maybe it's partly because they're going to do anything to get that message out there, so how do things get changed? I don't know. I just don't know....

We need to move past media-driven stereotypes of sex offenders as "sick," "monsters," and "perverts." We need an evidence-based understanding of the circumstances that lead to offending as well as the factors that may reduce future offending. We need a realistic understanding of how legislation impacts rates of sexual offending, impacts sexual offenders and their families, and affects public safety. Legislation should not be passed merely because it serves to increase the public's feelings of safety or boost the ratings of get-tough-on-crime politicians. As April expressed: "I just think that if you're going to create laws you have to think past the emotions." We have thousands of laws that restrict the movements of registered sexual offenders and label and stigmatize RSOs and their families for what is typically a lifetime, in the name of safety. As stated by Melissa: "Everybody should be able to heal and go on, we're just not being allowed to." Community safety and the protection of the rights of women, children, and former offenders and their families can only come from balanced policies, created by working relationships between researchers, policymakers, and legislators, not based on political rhetoric and pandering, but based on current, evidence-based research.

Notes

1. The Samaritans is based in New York City and has both professional staff and more than 100 volunteers to work confidentially with callers 24 hours a day, seven days a week. Their primary mission is to provide immediate support to prevent suicide; however, they also respond "to every kind of personal, emotional or health-related problem imaginable, from a bad day or a broken heart to mood disorders and mental illness to a chronic or life-threatening disease, trauma or loss" (https://samaritansnyc.org/).
2. As with the application of other laws in the United States, a discrepancy exists regarding who is required to comply with sex offender legislation. Take the high-profile case of Jeffrey Epstein, for example. Billionaire Epstein pled guilty to solicitation of a minor prostitute in 2008, making him a Tier 3 sex offender in his home state of New York. Yet Epstein reportedly skipped court-mandated check-ins on a regular basis prior to his sex-trafficking arrest in 2019. Between 2010 and 2018,

> cops in New York state made at least 7,061 arrests for similar violations of the state's complicated sex offender registration law ... Several of those arrests include people who committed minor violations, like submitting paperwork days late, or who struggled to keep up with reporting requirements because they were living in homeless shelters or on the street.
>
> (Schulberg, 2019: np)

These numbers do not include serious crimes, but only technical violations. This is a clear example of selective criminal justice enforcement, and Epstein surely does not represent an isolated incident.

References

Association for the Treatment of Sexual Abusers (2005). *Practice standards and guidelines for the evaluation, treatment, and management of adult male sexual abusers.* Beaverton, OR: Association for the Treatment of Sexual Abusers.

Bell, Sean. (December 17, 2018). The personal is the political: Activism and mental health. *Commonspace.* www.commonspace.scot

Blumenthal, James A., Smith, Patrick J., & Hoffman, Benson M. (2012). Is exercise a viable treatment for depression? *Health and Fitness Journal,* 16(4), 14–21.

Bradley, Don E. (1995). Religious involvement and social resources: Evidence from the Americans' Changing Lives data. *Journal for the Scientific Study of Religion,* 34, 259–267.

Burchfield, K. B., & Mingus, W. (2008). Not in my neighborhood: Assessing registered sex offenders' experiences with local social capital and social control. *Criminal Justice and Behavior,* 35, 356–374.

Center for Sex Offender Management (CSOM). (2005). *Key considerations for reunifying adult sex offenders and their families.* Washington, DC: U.S. Department of Justice. www.csom.org/pubs/FamilyReunificationDec05.pdf

Der Bedrosian, Jeanette. (2018, Spring). When the abuser is a child, too. *Johns Hopkins Magazine.* https://hub.jhu.edu/magazine/

Douard, John. (2007). Loathing the sinner, medicalizing the sin: Why sexually violent predator statutes are unjust, *International Journal of Law & Psychiatry 36,* 43–44.

Duwe, Grant, & Donnay, William. (2008). The impact of Megan's Law on sex offender recidivism: The Minnesota experience. *Criminology,* 46(2), 411–446.

Ellison, Christopher G. (1991). Religious involvement and subjective well-being. *Journal of Health and Social Behavior,* 32, 80–99.

Epping, J. (2011). Physical activity recommendations and dog walking. In Johnson R., Beck A., & McCune S. (Eds.), *The health benefits of dog walking for pets and people: Evidence and case studies* (pp. 7–24). Purdue University Press.

Farkas, Mary Ann, & Miller, Gale. (2007). Reentry and reintegration: Challenges faced by the families of convicted sex offenders. *Federal Sentencing Report, 20*(2), 88–92.

Garrett, Thomas B., & Wright, Richard. (1975). Wives of rapists and incest offenders. *The Journal of Sex Research, 11*(2), 149–157.

Goffman, Erving. (1963). *Stigma: Notes on the management of spoiled identity.* New York, NY: Simon Schuster, Inc.

Griffin, J., & Esposito, L. (2011). Future directions in dog walking. In Johnson R., Beck A., & McCune S. (Eds.), *The health benefits of dog walking for pets and people: Evidence and case studies* (pp. 181–192). Purdue University Press.

Griffiths, Kathleen. (2017). Mental health Internet support groups: Just a lot of talk or a valuable intervention? *World Psychiatry, 16*(3), 247–248.

Griffiths, Kathleen M., Mackinnon, Andrew J., Crisp, Dimity A., Christensen, Helen, Bennet, Kylie, & Farrer, Louise. (2012). The effectiveness of an online support group for members of the community with depression: A randomised controlled trial. *PLoS One, 7*(12), article e53244. doi: 10.1371/journal.pone.0053244

Hobbes, Michael. (July 16, 2019). Sex offender registries don't keep kids safe, but politicians keep expending them anyway. *HuffPost.* www.huffpost.com

Iffland, J.A., Berner, W., Dekker, A., & Briken, P. (2016). What keeps them together? Insights into sex offender couples using qualitative content analyses. *Journal of Sex & Marital Therapy, 42*(6), 534–551.

Karlis, Nicole. (October 26, 2017). Why doing good is good for the do-gooder. *The New York Times.* www.nytimes.com

Kruttschnitt, C., Uggen, C., & Shelton, K. (2000). Predictors of desistance among sex offenders: The interaction of formal and informal social controls. *Justice Quarterly, 17,* 62–87.

Langan, Patrick A., Schmitt, Erica L., & Durose, Matthew R. (2003). *Recidivism of sex offenders released from prison in 1994* (NCJ 198281). Washington, DC: U.S. Department of Justice.

La Vigne, Nancy G., Visher, Christy, & Castro, Jennifer. (2004). *Chicago prisoners' experiences returning home.* Washington, DC: The Urban Institute.

Megale, Elizabeth. (2011). The invisible man: How the sex offender registry results in social death. *Journal of Law & Social Deviance, 2,* 92–157.

Meloy, Michelle L. (2005). The sex offender next door: An analysis of recidivism, risk factors, and deterrence of sex offenders on probation. *Criminal Justice Policy Review, 16,* 211–236.

Mustaine, E. E., Tewksbury, R., & Stengel, K. M. (2006). Residential location and mobility of registered sex offenders. *American Journal of Criminal Justice, 30,* 177–192.

Schulberg, Jessica. (July 22, 2019). NY cops gave Jeffrey Epstein a pass while making more than 7,000 arrests for similar offenses. *HuffPost.* www.huffpost.com

Socia, Kelly M. (2014). Residence restrictions are ineffective, inefficient, and inadequate: So now what? *Criminology and Public Policy, 13,* 179–188.

Visher, Christy, La Vigne, Nancy G., & Travis, Jeremy. (2003). *Understanding the challenges of prisoner reentry, Maryland pilot study: Findings from Baltimore.* Washington, DC: The Urban Institute.

Worrall, Hugh, Schweizer, Richard, Marks, Ellen, Yuan, Lin, Lloyd, Chris, & Ramjan, Rob. (2018). The effectiveness of support groups: A literature review. *Mental Health and Social Inclusion, 22*(2), 85–93.

APPENDIX

Partner Offenses Information

Name	Description of partner offense(s)	Sentence information	Length of time on the registry
Melissa	Molestation of a family member (step-daughter)	6 years + 18 months probation	Life
Michelle	Molestation of a family member (nephew) *claims false allegation	10 years	Life
Angela	Possession and distribution of child pornography	5 years	Life
Heather	Molestation of a family member (half-sister)	5 years suspended; violated on a DUI and sentenced to 2 years	10 years; removed as per *Wallace v. State*, 905 N.E.2d 371 (Ind. 2009)
Stephanie	Manufacture and distribution of child pornography	16 years	Currently in prison
Nicole	One count of possession child of pornography; molestation of a family member (granddaughter) *claims molestation was a false allegation	3 years +10 years probation; 15 years on a revocation for exposure on his property	Currently in prison
Jessica	Molestation of a family member (daughter) *claims false allegation	10 years probation + 6 months jail	10 years

continued

246 Appendix

APPENDIX continued

Name	Description of partner offense(s)	Sentence information	Length of time on the registry
Elizabeth	Rape, kidnapping, assault, armed robbery *claims false allegation	236 years	Currently in prison
Kelly	Two charges of statutory rape	5 years + 5 years parole	Not yet leveled
Mary	Statutory rape	6 years probation	Life
Julie	One count of possession of child pornography	5 years probation; 3-years on a revocation for failing a polygraph	Life
Sarah	One count of possession of child pornography	5 years	Currently in prison
Shannon	Sexual misconduct of a minor	18 months prison + 5 years supervised probation	Life
Christine	Molestation of a family member (step-niece)	10 years suspended + 5 year probation	Life
Tammy	Statutory rape	10 years probation	Life
Tracy	Sexual misconduct of a minor *claims false allegation	10 years probation	10 years
Karen	Statutory rape	Served 30 days; partner unsure of sentence length	Unsure
Dawn	Molestation of a family member (daughter) *claims false allegation	8 years probation	Life
Susan	Molestation of a family member (adopted daughter)	6 months + 4 years probation	Life
Andrea	Attempted rape	10 years suspended; 18 months in prison on a GPS monitoring violation	Life
Tina	Molestation of a family member (nephew)	3 years	10 years
Patricia	Statutory rape	10 years probation	Started at Level 2/Life; appealed/ reduced to Level 1/20 years
Cynthia	Molestation of a family member (step-daughter)	3 years probation	Life
April	Three counts of possession of child pornography *claims false allegation	21 months	Life

Name	Description of partner offense(s)	Sentence information	Length of time on the registry
Maria	Sexual misconduct with a minor (friend's daughter)	3–25 years; served 8 years + 6 years parole	Life
Crystal	Possession of child pornography (1200 images)	31 months	Not yet leveled
Erin	Solicitation of a minor online (sting operation)	Probation (unsure of length)	10 years
Jamie	Molestation of a family member (daughter)	6 years probation	Life
Carrie	Sexual contact with a minor	11 months + 10 years probation	Life
Tara	one count of accepting child pornography	3 years probation	10 years
Sandra	Sexual contact with a minor (offense reported more than a decade after its occurrence)	10 years; served 6 months	Life
Danielle	Statutory rape	18 months + 1 year probation	10 years
Stacey	Sexual contact with a minor (student)	6 months + 5 years probation	Life
Tanya	Statutory rape	5 years + lifetime probation	Life
Teresa	Statutory rape	8 years	Life
Pamela	Kidnapping; attempted rape	43 years; served 22 years	Life
Jill	Molestation of a family member (niece) *claims false accusation	10 years; in prison on a violation for attending a school function	Not yet leveled
Katherine	Molestation of a family member (adopted daughter) *claims false accusation	10 years probation	Life
Holly	Molestation of a family member (step-daughter) *claims false accusation	10 years + 5 years probation	Life
Erica	Molestation of a minor (foster daughter)	5 years probation; 1-year prison for a failure to participate in therapy violation	Life
Brenda	Statutory rape	7 years; served 4 years + 3-years parole	Life
Deborah	Sexual contact with a minor *claims false accusation	11 years	Life

Continued

248 Appendix

APPENDIX continued

Name	Description of partner offense(s)	Sentence information	Length of time on the registry
Sharon	Possession of child pornography	2 years + 10 years probation	Life
Donna	Molestation of a minor	5 years; served 1 year	Life
Amber	Rape *claims false allegation	4 years; served 3 years	15 years
Linda	Rape	7 to 25 years; served 11 years	10 years
Leslie	Rape and robbery (1986) Rape and abduction (2007)	First offense 33 years, served 17 years; Second offense, mandatory life without parole	Currently in prison
Kristy	Two charges of attempted rape; molestation of a minor	15 years; served 7 years + 3 years parole	Not on registry – offenses were in the 1980s
Catherine	Molestation of a family member (niece) *claims false allegation	18 weekends + 5 years probation	Life
Misty	Statutory rape	6 months + 5-years probation	Life
Heidi	Statutory rape	9 months in jail before trial; 8-years community supervision	15 years
Nancy	Rape of a family member (niece)	45 years	Currently in prison
Cheryl	Possession of child pornography	2.5 years probation	Life
Brandy	Molestation of a family member (step-son)	8 years; served 4 years + 3-year parole	Life
Robin	Seven charges of sexual assault	6 years, 4 months	Currently in prison
Alicia	Molestation of a family member (daughter)	21 years; served 19 years + 2-years parole	Life
Rhonda	Statutory rape (later married)	6 months + 4 years probation + 120-hours community service	Life
Renee	Solicitation of a minor (prostitute in Thailand); intent to distribute child pornography	2 years	25 years
Megan	Statutory rape	2 years probation	Life

Appendix 249

Name	Description of partner offense(s)	Sentence information	Length of time on the registry
Melinda	Exhibitionism, public urination; failure to register address change; residing too close to a school; history of DUIs	3 years on a failure to register violation	Currently in prison
Jackie	Molestation of a minor *claims false accusation	3 years + 10 years probation	Life in FL; Moved to TN b/c 10 years; successfully petitioned to be removed in TN
Sherry	Sexual assault *claims false accusation	1 year	15 years
Valerie	Statutory rape	10 years probation	Life
Diana	Rape and attempted rape Soliciting a prostitute (violation – resulted in unsuccessful civil commitment application)	First offense: 15 years; served 13 years + 2 years probation; On the violation: 2 years probation	Life
Paula	Molestation of a family member (step-daughters) *claims false accusation	12 weekends + 5 years probation	10-years
Margaret	Rape	14 years + 2 years probation	Life
Victoria	Two counts of molestation of a minor	8 years; 7-years suspended + 5 years probation	Life
Cindy	Solicitation of a minor (sting operation)	5 years probation	10 years
Brandi	Two counts of possession of child pornography	1 year probation	10 years
Suzanne	Sexual contact with a minor *claims false accusation	3 years probation	Life
Samantha	Sexual contact with a minor *claims false accusation	15 years probation; served 5 years in prison on a drug violation	Life
Vanessa	Two charges molestation of a family member (foster daughter) *claims false accusation	4 years + 3-years parole	Life
Deanna	Two charges molestation of a family member (step-daughter); prior armed robbery conviction	6 years + 12 years probation	Currently in prison

Continued

250 Appendix

APPENDIX continued

Name	Description of partner offense(s)	Sentence information	Length of time on the registry
Sheila	Two charges molestation of a minor	5 years probation	25 years
Carolyn	Solicitation of a prostitute; rape with a weapon; robbery	Robbery 1 year; solicitation 2 years probation; rape with a weapon 10 years + 5 years supervised probation	Currently in prison
Shelly	Molestation of a minor	7 years; served 3.5 years + 3.5 years parole	Life
Yolanda	Molestation of a family member (son)	5 years probation	10 years
Sabrina	Molestation of a family member when he was a juvenile (sister); Molestation of a family member when he was an adult (step-niece) *claims adult offense was a false accusation	First offense: 1 year + 5 years probation; violation for dating a minor; served 4 years; Second offense: 1 year + lifetime probation	Life
Laurie	Possession of child pornography	30 months	Life
Janet	Sexual contact with a minor *claims false allegation	3 years	Life
Courtney	Molestation of a family member (step-daughter)	10 years; served 4.5 years	Life
Colleen	Molestation of a family member (daughter); receipt of child pornography	15 years	Currently in prison
Carol	Sexual assault; three failure to register violations	2 years for sexual assault; 2 months for each of the first two violations; 5 years for the third violation	Currently in prison
Jenny	Molestation of a family member (granddaughter)	Not yet sentenced	Not yet leveled
Felicia	Molestation of a family member (daughter and son)	16 days served awaiting trial + 5 years probation	10 years
Alison	Sexual contact with a minor; prior conviction for malicious wounding	38 years; served 19 years	Life

Name	Description of partner offense(s)	Sentence information	Length of time on the registry
Leah	Molestation of a family member (daughter)	10 years probation	Life
Tricia	Rape (ex-wife)	10 months + 3 years probation; 3 years on a violation for leaving the county	Life
Kara	Molestation of a minor	5 years probation	10 years
Bridget	Molestation of a family member (daughter) *claims false accusation	20 years	Currently in prison
Natasha	Statutory rape	16 years; served 8 years + 8-years parole	Life
Anita	Molestation of a minor	1 year + 2 years probation	Life
Connie	Molestation of a family member (step-daughter)	8 years + 10 years probation	Life
Martha	Molestation of a family member as a juvenile (sister)	2–6 years; served 4 years and 2 years parole	Life

INDEX

Act (SORNA)
Adam Walsh Child Protection and Safety
   Act *see* Sex Offender Registration and
   Notification addiction 96–102, 210–11
adult sexual abuse 38–40
appeal to higher loyalties *see* neutralization
   theory
attitudes: partners of registrants 26; police
   25–6; prison officials 25–6; probation
   officers 25–6; public 25–7; to residency
   restrictions 179–80; to SORN laws
   136–8; students 26; teachers 26;
   treatment providers 25–6

Catoe, Theodore Roosevelt 4
changes in relationship 75–9
chemical castration 24, 27n7; *Skinner*
   v. *Oklahoma* 24
Child Abuse Prevention and
   Treatment Act 7
child pornography: characteristics of
   offenders 40–1; denial of injury 107–8;
   justification by comparison 108–11;
   pedophilia 7–8; sex crimes 8
child sexual abuse 36–8: hebephilia 37;
   pedophilia 37; prevalence 37
church: restrictions 199–201; stigma 148;
   support 199, 222–3
civil commitment 18–24, 123n2: concerns
   20; *see also* sexual psychopath laws;
   sexually violent predators
college victimization 40

Commonwealth v. *Moore* 163n7
community integration 224–6: effects
   of family 215; SORN laws impact
   138–40; suggestions for change 231–7
community notification 10, 11–12,
   27n4, 132–3: harassment 154–8;
   inconsistencies by states 134; SORN law
   impact 138–40; stigma 146–54; *see also*
   Megan's Law; Sex Offender Registration
   and Notification Act (SORNA)
Comprehensive Addiction and
   Recovery Act 7
condemnation of the condemners *see*
   neutralization theory
Connecticut Department of Public Safety
   v. *John Doe* 135
consent 105–6
coping mechanisms: addictive behaviors
   216–16; advocacy for change 224;
   counseling 219–21; depression 216–17;
   physical fitness 221–2; religion 222–3;
   self-help groups 218–19; self-injury
   216; suicide attempts 216–17
Couey, John 17
courtesy stigma 122–3, 146–54; church
   199–201; employment 172–4;
   residency restrictions 181–5; school
   prohibitions 186–95; *see also* harassment

denial of injury *see* neutralization theory
denial of responsibility *see* neutralization
   theory

Index **253**

denial of the victim *see* neutralization theory
discreditable stigma 79, 117, 127
disintegrative shaming 128
Doe v. *Harris* 135
Doe v. *Snyder* 135, 179
Dru Sjodin National Sex Offender
 Public Website 13; *see also* community
 notification; Sex Offender Registration
 and Notification Act (SORNA)

employment: challenges 168–72;
 discrimination 169–70; restrictions 170;
 unemployment 167–8, 172

failure to register 13; *see also* Sex Offender
 Registration and Notification Act
 (SORNA)
female sex offenders 43–5; as caregivers
 44; juveniles 43; prevalence 44;
 recidivism 45
Fish, Albert 4
friends: response 119–23; support 119–20

GPS monitoring 17–8; cost 18; *Grady*
 v. *North Carolina* 17

Halloween 24–5, 152–4
harassment x; by law enforcement 156–8;
 community 154–6; *Doe* v. *Poritz* x;
 employment 170–1; friends 121–2
hebephilia 37
Hendricks, Leroy 21–2
hesitations in relationship 63–7
Hoover, J. Edgar 5
housing *see* residency restrictions

incarceration 45, 59
internet offenses 40; child pornography
 40–1; internet solicitation 41
intimacy, lack of 100–1

Jacob Wetterling Act 11, 128, 138
Jessica Lunsford Act 17
justification by comparison *see*
 neutralization theory
juvenile sex offenders 42–3, 230;
 contributing factors 43; females 43; law
 application 43

Kansas v. *Crane* 22, 123n2
Kansas v. *Hendricks* 21–2, 24, 123n2
Kanka, Megan 11–13; *see also* Megan's Law
KIDS Act (Keeping the Internet Devoid
 of Predators) 14

labeling: discreditable stigma 79; of family
 members 10, 186–8; reaction to 79
labeling theory *see* social reaction theory
laws: Halloween 24–5; history
 3–10, 18; *see also* Child Abuse
 Prevention and Treatment Act; civil
 commitment; community notification;
 Comprehensive Addition and Recovery
 Act; GPS monitoring; Jessica Lunsford
 Act; KIDS Act (Keeping the Internet
 Devoid of Predators); Megan's Law;
 Romeo and Juliet law; Sex Offender
 Registration and Notification Act
 (SORNA); sexual psychopath laws;
 traveling restrictions
Lunde, Sarah 17
Lunsford, Jessica 17

Mann v. *Georgia Department of*
 Corrections 179
McGuire v. *Strange* 135
McKune v. *Lile* 47
media *see* moral panic
Megan's Law 11–13, 128; tiers; *see also*
 community notification; Sex Offender
 Registration and Notification
 Act (SORNA)
MeToo movement 9–10
moral panic 4–11; statistics 32–3, 46
motives: to start relationship 60–3; to stay
 in relationship 68–74

National Center for Missing and
 Exploited Children (NCMEC) 34, 136;
 limitations 34–6, 136
National Child Abuse and Neglect Data
 System 37
National Crime Victimization Survey
 (NCVS) 34, 38–40
National Incident Based Reporting
 System (NIBRS) 33
National Intimate Partner and Sexual
 Violence Survey 39
NCMEC *see* National Center for Missing
 and Exploited Children
NCVS *see* National Crime Victimization
 Survey
neutralization theory 94–5: appeal to
 higher loyalties 95; condemnation of
 the condemners 95, 111–12; denial of
 injury 95, 104–8; denial of responsibility
 95–104; denial of the victim 95;
 justification by comparison 95, 108–11;
 techniques of neutralization 95

254 Index

New Jersey Commission on the Habitual
Sex Offender 6
NIBRS *see* National Incident Based
Reporting System

offense reveal: involuntary 79, 81–4;
voluntary 79–82
Onstott, David 17

parenting: absent father 191–5; impact
of RSO's parents 102–4; school
prohibitions 186–95; single parenthood
189–95
pedophilia 37
People of the State of Illinois v. *Conrad
Allen Morger* 15
policy suggestions 237–42

rape *see* adult sexual abuse
rape myths 39
recidivism 46–50, 138: misrepresentation
of data 46–7; residency restrictions
180–5; SORN law impact 138–40;
treatment effect 49–50; types of
offenders 48–9
registration *see* Sex Offender Registration
and Notification Act (SORNA)
reintegrative shaming 128
relationship: changes 75–9; hesitations
63–7; motives to stay 68–74; motives to
start 60–3
religion *see* church
residency restrictions xii, 16: affordability
183–4; alternatives 186–9; criticisms
175, 178–9; homelessness 184–5;
housing instability 185; impact on
housing 16–17, 174–9, 181–3; legality
179; recidivism 180–1; schools 186–91;
by state 175–8
risk assessment 129–9, 145, 159–60
Romeo and Juliet law 33

school: prohibitions 186–95; stigma 149,
151; *see also* parenting
Sex Offender Residency Restrictions
(SORR) *see* residency restrictions
Sex Offender Registration and
Notification Act (SORNA) 13, 128–9:
attitudes toward 136–8; concerns
132–3; constitutionality 134–6;
failure to register 13, 130; fees to
register 130–1; impacts on family 141;
inconsistencies by state 131–2, 134,

163n1, 163n3; tiers 13, 128–31, 134;
parks 197–9; registration impacts 140;
removal petition 160–1; suggestions
158–62, 237–42; tier reclassification
141–5, 158; travel restrictions 195–7;
see also risk assessment; traveling
restrictions
sex offenders: definition 9, 33; females
43–5; incarceration 45, 59; juveniles
42–3; offender demographics 41–2;
recidivism 46–50
sex offenses: adult sexual abuse 38–9;
child sexual abuse 36–8; college
victimization 40; internet offenses 40–1;
overcriminalization 226–8; prevalence
34–6; reactions by partner 84–91
sexual assault *see* adult sexual abuse
sexually violent predators (SVP) 11: laws
20–4, 27n6; *see also* civil commitment;
sexual psychopath laws
sexual psychopath laws 18; concerns 20;
see also civil commitment; sexually
violent predators (SVP)
Shriner, Earl 20–1
Smith v. *Doe* 134–5
social media restrictions 14–15, 27n5
social reaction theory xi–xii, 127
SORNA *see* Sex Offender Registration
and Notification Act
Special Sex Offender Sentencing
Alternatives (SSOSA) 45
SSOSA *see* Special Sex Offender
Sentencing Alternatives
State v. *Trosclair* 135–6
stranger danger 8
stress: isolation 212–13; re-offense fear
213–14; self-blame 210–11; sexual
identity impact 211
SVP *see* sexually violent predators

techniques of neutralization *see*
neutralization theory
Thompson, Gerald 4
tier reclassification 141–5, 158; *see also* Sex
Offender Registration and Notification
Act (SORNA)
traveling restrictions 195–7, 203n2:
parks 197–9
treatment: recidivism impact 49

United States v. *Comstock* 46–7
Unknown Sex Fiend, The 6

Vasquez v. *Foxx* 179